Policing

Policing

Reinvention Strategies in a Marketing Framework

Rohit Choudhary

⑤SAGE www.sagepublications.com
Los Angeles • London • New Delhi • Singapore • Washington DC

First published in 2009 by

 SAGE Publications India Pvt Ltd
B1/I-1 Mohan Cooperative Industrial Area
Mathura Road, New Delhi 110 044, India
www.sagepub.in

SAGE Publications Inc
2455 Teller Road
Thousand Oaks,
California 91320, USAt

SAGE Publications Ltd
1 Oliver's Yard
55 City Road
London EC1Y 1SP, United Kingdom

SAGE Publications Asia-Pacific Pte Ltd
33 Pekin Street
#02-01 Far East Square
Singapore 048763

Published by Vivek Mehra for SAGE Publications India Pvt Ltd, photo-typeset in 10/12 Berkeley by Star Compugraphics Private Limited, Delhi and printed at Chaman Enterprises, New Delhi.

Library of Congress Cataloging-in-Publication Data
Choudhary, Rohit.
    Policing: reinvention strategies in a marketing framework/Rohit Choudhary.
       p. cm.
    Includes bibliographical references.
1. Police—India.   I. Title.

HV8247.C46	363.2068'8—dc22	2009	2009014955

ISBN: 978-81-7829-944-0 (PB)

The SAGE Team: Elina Majumdar, Shinjini Basu, Amrita Saha and
                    Trinankur Banerjee

Dedicated to
my children Asmi and Ishan

Contents

PART I
ASSESSMENT AND ANALYSIS

List of Tables

List of Boxes

List of Charts

Acknowledgements

I would like to express my gratitude to H. H. Sri Sri Ravi Shankar. I am grateful to the Indian Police Service, the Punjab Police, the Indian Institute of Management Bangalore and the Maxwell School, Syracuse University, NY, USA for providing me the learning platform that made the writing of this book possible.

I would also like to thank School of Leadership, The Netherlands Police, for offering me the opportunity to interact with police leaders from across the world.

*****

'Views expressed in this book are author's own views and not that of the Government.'

Introduction

For countries seeking to move ahead in the global marketplace, innovation in the public sector will be as important as it is in the private sector.

In his classic work *Capitalism, Socialism and Democracy* (1942), Joseph Schumpeter wrote that the essence of capitalism is the process of 'creative destruction', the perpetual cycle of destroying the old and less efficient product or service, and replacing it with a new and efficient one. Increasingly, the efficiencies of the free markets in the private sector are being applied to bureaucracies in the public sector.

Various states are engaged feverishly in reinventing their bureaucratic systems to present a performing government, South Korea being a classic example. For providing an environment free of problems of law and order, crime and security of property rights, many developed countries such as the USA, the UK, Australia and Canada have made impressive advances in reinventing the police. Just yesterday some of the terms like citizen focused service, performance management, balanced scorecard, strategy map, and so on, that were management mantras in the private sector, have found firm roots, quite rapidly, in the working culture of the police departments in the developed nations. New managerial practices were introduced into police organizations in applying the 'private sector solution to the public sector problem' (Dixon et al., 1998). The reforms in police administration in these nations were implemented with a view to restructure and change the internal culture of organizations and increase operational performance, efficiency and cooperation (Bayley, 1994; Cope et al., 1997; Dixon et al., 1998; Mclaughlin and Murji, 1997: 80–103).

The broader changes can be described as embodying 'new managerialism', where public sector activities are constructed as productive processes which are managed in a result-oriented manner, utilize the model of citizens-as-consumers and are subjected to regular audits (Osborne and Gaebler, 1992). This reform movement in the public sector is enhanced by the ideological triumph of market models in the private sector. Globalization and New Public Management (NPM),[1] 'one of the most striking international trends in public administration' (Hood, 1991), are undergoing profound consequences for the management of public services (Cable, 1994).

Other changes in the private sector have also taken their toll on traditional bureaucracy. Information Technology has changed the private sector so much that the experiences of citizens in the private sector and the public sector are becoming increasingly divergent (Dixon et al., 1998). This has given rise to an urgent need for departments like the police, engaged in operations and public dealing, to remodel their systems to take advantage of these advances.

We are also living in an age of niche markets where citizens demand high-quality service and have a varied choice and exposure to different cultures. They not only compare what they get to those around, but also with people of different nations. The Maastricht Treaty in Europe has set the tone for future consolidation and furthered intergovernmental cooperation in the field of justice and home affairs, including policing matters. Communities and corporations of tomorrow will demand internationally accepted principles of policing in a democratic state.[2] Today's environment necessitates that public institutions, including the police, be more flexible and adaptable in their functioning, deliver high-quality services, be sensitive to the needs of their customers, give their employees a sense of meaning, control and purpose, and empower citizens while providing them with world-class services that they have increasingly begun to expect.

Law and order remains an important function for the state to perform and is placed among minimal functions of state in addressing market failure (World Bank, 1997). The increasing flows of economic investment and business traffic between the nations bring into focus the relationship

---

[1] NPM rests on the doctrines of removing the difference between the public and the private sector, and shifting the emphasis in the public enterprise from rules and procedures to 'getting results', asserting the supremacy of market over the state. It also reflects the view that the competition between the private and the public sector makes public sector more consumer responsive.

[2] In accordance with the Internationally Accepted Principles of Policing in a Democratic State-Bonn, 25 April 1996 the essential principles of policing are:
- Police service must be oriented and operate accord with principles of democracy,
- Police conduct must be governed by professional code conduct,
- Protection of life and property is the primary function of police operations,
- Police must serve the public and are accountable to the public they serve,
- Police must conduct their activities with respect for dignity and basic human rights, and
- Police must discharge their duties in non-discriminatory manner.

between investment confidence and security and crime, the latter being important in terms of both official crime rates and the fear of crime.[3] Also, according to a study, the difference in the growth rate of the GDP between the developing economics that observe the rule of law and the economics that do not in more than 3 per cent (*Time* 2006). Realizing the need for an environment for the rule of law as an essentiality for economic growth as China opens up the country and introduces the policy of economic modernization, the Chinese government has also implemented a comprehensive legal system to shift from a system of 'rule by man' to 'rule by law'. In the general climate of establishing and perfecting socialist legality, the government stresses, in strong terms, that police administration and operation must be guided by legislative provisions, and pass numerous laws and regulations in relation to police administration and operation, thereby ushering in a new era of police development in China (Ma, 1997: 113–135).

In the developed nations, a 'new policing order' is emerging that derives its momentum not just from some government-initiated police reform document, but from the global processes of restructuring and fragmentation already apparent in many modern states and in branches of government and public bureaucracies (Leishman et al., 1996). Police reforms implemented in several nations in the 1990s also represent the dismantling of the 'old policing order', where policing was 'a regalian function of the state' (Hebenton and Thomas, 1995). In this 'new policing order' lies the trend towards greater centralization of policing with the central government increasing its influence over policing policies and 'steering' functions. This centralizing thrust is countered by increasing decentralization of operational decisions or the 'rowing' functions, privatization and internationalization of policing. If the dominance of 'public policing' in the nineteenth and twentieth centuries characterized the modern era, the emerging 'diverse totality' of policing reflects the so-called post-modern era (Reiner, 1992; Sheptycki, 1995).

The winds of change sweeping these nations will soon be touching the shores of India. The current edifice of Indian police is a legacy of the past, created during vastly different times and for different needs. Lethargic centralized bureaucracies, bound with archaic rules and regulations, and

---

[3] Citigroup Inc., an international financial services with some 200 million customers in more than 100 countries has said that the Naxalite insurgency could not only hamper India's economic growth but also restrict the Foreign Direct Investment (FDI) inflow (*Hindustan Times*, 2007a).

The Prime Minister of India, in a meeting of chief ministers on 15 April 2005, emphasized that development and security are truly mutually inter-related.

strict adherence to hierarchical chains of command, are misfits in today's ever-changing technologically advanced society.[4]

There is no denying that at times the police in different states have been able to perform extraordinarily despite all odds. There have been com-mendable individual efforts to give people the kind of service they deserve. But somewhere down the line the police have become isolated, insensitive and ineffective. The inertia of the inherent directional flaw in the philosophy of policing has been so much that the police still remain ingrained in the same old mould.

The police service is a highly visible government department that has come under mounting pressure from different stakeholders, including successive governments and also an increasingly demanding public in the recent years. Bureaucratic systems like the police are designed to be stable; but today the systems that are unable to change are doomed to failure.

It is widely recognized that there is a need for 'reinventing the police' in India.[5] Reinvention, which goes beyond introducing reforms in a public sector organization, as David Osborne and P. Plastrik wrote in *Banishing Bureaucracy* (1996), means a fundamental transformation of systems and organizations to increase their efficiency, effectiveness, adaptability and capacity to innovate. In recognizing the need for police in India to reinvent their ways of functioning, this book addresses the issue of 'marketing' the police. Although at the first instance marketing may appear to be an odd combination for policing, yet when we give a closer look an important strand emerges. Marketing framework works by keeping the customer at the centre, a requirement that may hold the key to finding solutions to the issues that the police face in current times.

Marketing concepts hold that achieving organizational goals depend upon knowing the needs and wants of target markets and delivering the desired satisfaction better than the competitor through the path of customer focus and value (Kotler and Armstrong, 2006). Policing is an activity carried out by the state to uphold the law of the land. When we say marketing the police, what kind of confluence are we trying to put

[4] Clearly, the police organization, as it stands today, is unfit to discharge its duties. How much more would it be by the turn of this century is a horrifying thought (National Police Commission,. 1977–81).

[5] The prime minister of India announced the intent of the government to set up a Police Mission in October 2006 to transform the police forces in the country into effective instruments for maintenance of internal security and facing the challenges of the next century. The Mission is charged with the responsibility of creating new vision for police, empowerment of policemen, decentralization and delegation of powers, enhancing skills and competencies at the grassroots, promoting culture of excellence in police and enhancing accountability to people.

together? It may be argued that why is marketing relevant to policing if there is nothing to sell, and that if the 'customers' have no choice of the 'product', where is the 'profitability'?

But this is not true as for the police, the community and the citizens are the customers; the police need to sell satisfaction, confidence and reassurance both to people who they come in contact with and to society at large. In this manner, the public has a choice. People can choose whether or not to contact the police, engage with them at a community level and work in partnership with them. The profitability relates to the value for taxpayers' money that the department is able to deliver by maximization of satisfaction level of customers in terms of safety, service and assurance.

However, while we discuss departments like the police which function as a compliance department with some service functions, the solutions cannot be as straightforward as in the case of enterprise management. First, it makes no sense to put the police (which is a compliance organization) in the market and let the compliers (who could be seeking undue benefits) fund the department. Then, it should also be kept in mind that a simple unimprovised private sector 'customer service' approach may not be appropriate where citizens are as concerned with more general outcomes of policing for society as they are with their own satisfaction (Davids and Hancock, 1998: 60). Some people may reject the idea that human safety can be privatized, deregulated and generally be left to individuals to secure as best they can in the market (Loader, 1999: 388). While others may feel that with an excessive focus on individual agreements, policing will omit to take account of broader societal interests (Ayling and Grabosky, 2006).

Therefore, a combination of deftly and delicately improvised private sector strategies needs to be adopted in their application to the police department. For example, in place of competition, inappropriate for a compliance organization like the police department, benchmarks for performance management can be created for managed competition in the monopoly situation wherein the emphasis is on improving performances, increasing efficiency, cost control and accountability based on indicators that can be measured.

This book is presented in the form of a marketing plan for the police using the conventional framework in marketing management. Part I covers the current situation analysis, trends in policing, Strengths, Weaknesses, Threats and Opportunities (SWOT) analysis, Segmentation, Targeting and Opportunities (STP) analysis and the reinvention strategies for the police. In Part II, the recommendations are presented in the format of 8 P's—People, Product, Price, Promotion, Pace, Process, Place and Politics—for marketing mix. It draws on some of the management principles and the recent empirical work conducted in the police service, and with appropriate improvisations, situates them within the existing literature on marketing principles. The result of this exercise is a marketing plan that delivers superior value, builds profitable customer relationship and creates customer delight. In the end, marketing orientation requires a well-developed and deeply-rooted corporate philosophy that guides every part of the police department in its activities and operations. It is not a question of floating some marketing initiatives; it has to actually reflect on everything that policemen do (Mawby, 2002).

PART I
ASSESSMENT AND ANALYSIS

Situational Analysis 1

Historical background

To understand the Indian police from a historical perspective, it is useful to organize our thoughts around (a) the pre-1861 period, (b) the period from 1861 to 1931 and (c) the period from 1931 to 1947.

Before 1861 the organization was more or less amorphous. In the earliest times, state officials and private persons were vested with the powers of policing, unlike the ubiquitous, regularly-organized and legally-controlled force of today. Big landlords maintained peace in their respective areas. In a village, the village headman was responsible and he was helped by the village watchmen, the executive police. References to the police system are found in the laws of Manu—the king. His chief duty was to restrain violence and punish the evildoers and all the subjects of the king were to assist him in this. In Kautilya's *Arthasastra*, there are fascinating details of nine kinds of spies and their specific uses under different circumstances.

Detailed accounts of the police system are available from the Mughal times, that is, the sixteenth century. The Mughals adopted a system of *subedar*, *faujdar* and *thanedar*. At the provincial level the principal officer was the governor, called *sipah salar* under Akbar and *nazim* under his successors, but popularly known as *subedar*. He looked after the maintenance of peace and dispensation of justice. The *faujdar*, the administrative head of the district, was appointed by the emperor but was under the supervision and guidance of the *subedar*. The *faujdar* acted as the local army officer besides being the chief of the police. The *thanedar* was the officer in charge of a police station under the supervision of the *faujdar*. The term *thanedar* is still in use in the Indian police. Today's *thanedar* investigates ordinary cases of crime, but in the Mughal era, ordinary crimes were settled by the local people. One Mughal official, the *kotwal*, performed duties similar to the police commissioners during the British rule in Bombay, Calcutta and Madras. The *kotwals* were not provincial officers, but were appointed by the central government in the provincial capitals and other important cities, and performed a number of executive and ministerial duties. The *kotwal*, through his assistants, kept a trustworthy person in every street, lane, bazaar and ford of the river to gather information about everything that went on, whether good or bad. The *kotwals* held a powerful position and maintained a tight grip on the goings-on in the city.

When the British took over the government of the provinces in the late eighteenth century and early nineteenth century, they adopted the system of administration that they found in each locality and made as few changes as possible. The history of the police in British India prior to 1860 was largely a series of experiments with the old system of *faujdars* and the introduction of new systems such as the appointment of a superintendent of police in 1808 in Bengal. At the initiative of Sir Charles Napier, who was appointed as the Governor of Sind (1843–47), the police in Sind was organized in the pattern of the Royal Irish Constabulary and was made a separate and self-contained organization under the supervision of its own officers. In 1847, Sir George Clerk, Governor of Bombay, on his visit to Sind, found the policing so efficient that he decided to introduce a similar pattern in the Deccan. In 1853 a superintendent of police was appointed in Bombay. A change in Madras was effected soon after in 1859. In Lucknow the force was constituted on the lines of the London police. Thus, by the time the Commission of 1860 was set up to recommend the pattern of policing in India, the stage had been set and the solution was in place in bits and pieces, for a policing system to be adopted for the entire country. The Commission's recommendations formed the basis of the Police Act of 1861 and thus began the story of the present-day police in India.

The Police Act, 1861 was modelled on the Irish police rather than the British and was a major step in streamlining police organizations and their activities. Indeed, the model of policing developed in nineteenth century Ireland—a centralized force organized and trained on military lines—became a model for colonial police forces in the British Empire (Smyth, 2002: 110–24). The key difference between the two types of policing (the British and the Irish) was that while there was a deliberate and sustained attempt to establish the legitimacy of the police in England by depoliticizing the nature of policing (Reiner, 2000: 9), the police in Ireland was faced with a population which, by and large, was hostile to the colonial rule.[1]

The Police Act, 1861 replaced the innumerable forces with organized, disciplined and supervised provincial forces. A civil police force, organized on provincial basis, headed by an inspector-general of police, was formed in every part of the country. Some of its basic principles were:

1. The police to be subject to the civil government and not the military.
2. The organization and discipline of the police to be similar to the Indian army.
3. The interior economy to be in the hands of police officers.
4. The village police to be used only for information collection and to perform no executive duties.

The Act laid out the functions of the force: prevention and detection of crime, maintenance of peace, and the escorting and guarding of prisoners and treasure. In the new scheme of things, the *darogah* was replaced by the Station House Officer. In some areas, the officers are still referred to by the name *darogah*. John Beams, in his *Memoirs of a Bengal Civilian,* described the investigative skills of the police of pre-1861 era:

> Darogah's powers of harassment were enormous; he would have a person indicted for harbouring a bad character, or failing to assist an officer in arresting a criminal. Obtaining witnesses presented no problems to the Darogah. They were splendid detectives. They were close to the people and were themselves wily and unscrupulous enough to meet the criminal on his own ground. The 'new' police by contrast after 1861, were quite inferior in detective ability. They were 'over drilled' and 'over regulated'. They failed, until they learnt to use the extralegal methods of the old police without being found out. (Beams, 1961)

The organization of policing in 1861 was a step forward, but it was not able to counter the lawlessness in the way the Metropolitan police succeeded in England. By the beginning of the twentieth century, the Indian police was in trouble. Decades of inefficient operation, poor leadership, rampant corruption and brutality, and incompetent investigation and prosecution of crime had earned the force the contempt and derision of all levels of the Indian society, and made it an embarrassment for the British administrators (Campion, 2003). The growth of communication and rail

---

[1] Also see the recommendations for Irish police reforms by Chris Patton in the document *A New Beginning: Policing in Northern Ireland,* 1999.

networks had generated new trans-provincial crimes, which the police was incapable of handling. With this there was a growing demand by the Indian newspapers, the Indian National Congress and other social groups for police reform, specifically for their greater accountability towards the provincial governments. In this paragraph if we just replace a few words, like the British with the Indian administrators, the twentieth century with the twenty-first century and rail network with increased air traffic, the situation might as well speak for today. Remarkably, how very little has changed in 100 years for the Indian police.

The young men coming into the Indian Police (IP) were of lower academic and intellectual accomplishments, compared to their civil counterparts. In 1893 the government, under the viceroyalty of Lord Lansdowne, instituted a competitive examination in England for IP candidates, modelled on the exam for the Indian Civil Service. This reform increased the quality of the probationary police officers arriving in India and was a vast improvement over the system of nominating candidates for India.[2]

In 1902, the Viceroy Lord Curzon, known for his innovativeness and an eye that scrutinized all the systems in place, convened a commission to address what he had long perceived to be a vital instrument of the British Raj—the Indian Police. In the following months, the Indian Police Commission heard testimonies from hundreds of people throughout India and from all levels of society (Indian Police Commission, 1903). The final report of the Commission told a tale of corruption, brutality and incompetence so damning that Lord Broderick, the Secretary of State for India, urged Curzon to suppress its publication for fear that it would undermine British authority and give ammunition to the increasingly vocal Indian critics of the British Raj, in the Congress and elsewhere (British Library, 1904).

In the report, the Commission had also gone into the issues of the wages and the working conditions of the policemen. The report blamed the corruption in the subordinate ranks; the Commission blamed the less-than-a-living-wage paid to the Indian constables for decades. It insisted that even the most honest and upright constable or sub-inspector with a family to support would sooner or later give in to temptation and accept the benefits of petty bribery and other forms of corruption for which he had already been assigned guilty in the public mind (Indian Police Commission, 1903: 40).

[2] Since the institution of a common civil services examination in 1977, the same quality of men join both the Indian Police Service and the Indian Administrative Service. Many of them are professionals from various fields and the quality of candidates coming into the Indian Police Service now is among the strengths of the department.

After the report of the Police Commission, a new rank of deputy superintendent of police was established. It was reserved for experienced and able Indian inspectors and qualified Indian men recruited directly from the local population. The deputy superintendents were to work alongside assistant superintendents, newly arrived from Britain and the two ranks had similar job descriptions: to assist the district superintendent of police. In practice, however, the deputies—owing to their long experience in the police and their local knowledge—served as administrative workhorses of the district police office, shouldering much of the paperwork, especially translation duties (Campion, 2003). The assistant, fresh out of college and just arrived in an alien culture, served more in a learning capacity. The assistant superintendent of police was rotated through the various duties of the superintendent, under his instruction, to develop him into an officer capable of shouldering the duties of a police chief in the districts, a practice that has continued to date.[3]

The cornerstone of the colonial police model was that it placed an enormous responsibility and authority on the shoulders of relatively young and inexperienced European officers expecting that they would successfully carry out a specific type of work that required an intuitive knowledge of the language and culture with which they were just becoming acquainted (Campion, 2003). An interesting account of the relationship between two European officers, the district magistrate and the district superintendent, is provided by J.C. Curry:

> The relation between the two officers is, in fact, typical of English arrangements with their lack of logical finish. An observer ignorant of the English character might suppose that the two could not possibly work together, and the disagreement between them must become chronic. In all but a few negligible cases they do work amicably together, and hundreds have done so consistently in the smooth times and the rough times of our story in India. Why? They are men in whom the ideal of playing the game has been ingrained since their school days. Neither tries, as a rule, to encroach on the other's sphere or to undermine his authority. They have the same ideals, the same traditions—they play cricket, hockey, polo or other games together, and they seek to achieve their ends in the same way. If they disagree they disagree honestly, and in matters of great moment their disagreement can be resolved by higher authority; in ninety-nine case out of a hundred they see eye to eye, and the hundredth case is not allowed to affect their personal relations. If this is to be so, they must be men with

---

[3] Young bright officers from varied backgrounds join the police service today and are allotted to different states in the country. Within a few years of their joining the service, they are given the most challenging and satisfying jobs of their career: heading a district police force.

balance, moderation & judgement. How such a system will work in Indian hands is a matter for speculation, as up to the present it is virtually untried; and Indians with equal balance, moderation and judgement have a different philosophy, different reactions and different traditions from our own. When the majority of district magistrates and district superintendents are Indians, they may well find it necessary to evolve new standards of relationship. (Curry, 1977)

The rising nationalism of the 1920s signalled a new relationship between the police and the people, as also between the police and the government. Riots and other confrontations were increasing in the country, the most well known being the attack on the Chauri Chaura police station in the Gorakhpur District of Uttar Pradesh in 1922. In that attack, 23 Indian policemen were burnt alive or beaten to death (Amin, 1995). On the other hand, within the government, the police became increasingly important and powerful.

With the onset of the second Civil Disobedience campaign in 1930 and 1931, the hostility between the police and the people became acute. Radical elements within the Congress and other Indian nationalist movements, like the Irish revolutionaries of the past, articulated their belief that to target the police was to strike at the heart of a government (Campion, 2003). In Uttar Pradesh, unlike in other provinces such as Punjab and Bengal, this was not limited to violent confrontation with the police (Hollins, 1954: 222). Instead, many police stations were subjected to an economic boycott. This tactic was particularly effective given the dependence of the police on the local community for the procurement of supplies.

With the emergence of movements like the Khilafat, Civil Disobedience, Home Rule Agitation and Quit India—where the police gave a good account of themselves—the government of India, sensing that the continued functioning of their existence now rested on the shoulders of an underpaid, undermanned, overworked, demoralized and publicly despised police force, took measures to raise the morale within the service. The King's Police Medal, a decoration for bravery that had been instituted in 1911 for police forces throughout the empire, was now awarded to British and Indian policemen more frequently and with greater fanfare. The medal came with a survivor's benefit, equivalent of a constable's monthly wage, to widows and children if awarded posthumously, as it often was.[4] District police football and hockey tournaments, athletic competitions, parade reviews, award ceremonies and

[4] O.I.O.C., Robins Collection, MS. Eur. R178, Robins interview, 2:1.

rallies were often held in which the provincial governor and other British officials gave speeches to the assembled policemen praising their efforts and expressing the gratitude of the state they served (Campion, 2003). However, during this time, the salaries and benefits in the force remained well below the minimum level expected by the policemen; this, and the growing unpopularity of the service among the masses, left vacancies in the ranks and led to longer duty hours and frequent cancellation of leave.

For all its flaws, policing in India during British rule saw the introduction of the armed wing of the police and the Criminal Investigation Department (CID) after the Curzon commission report, and extraordinary advances in criminology and the use of forensic science. Innovations in ballistics, photography, metallurgy, pathology and communication were exported from Britain to India, while others, like fingerprinting were invented in India, refined in Britain and then reintroduced in India and throughout the empire (Campion, 2003).

All these advances were overshadowed by the inherent weaknesses of the imperial policing model. For many in the Indian society, the police were not merely the enforcing arm of the government; they were the government and throughout this period, the police remained the most important link between the Europeans and the Indians, acting as a pivot for social exchange as well as a point of bitter conflict (Campion, 2003: 217). In the closing decades of the British rule due to the developing situation, the police in India exercised immense powers in the political structure of the country. This position was only diluted during the euphoric and development-centric phase following independence (Dhillon, 1998: 242–45).

As the Indian independence struggle gathered momentum, crushing the freedom movement became the main objective of the British rulers, for which they relied on the strength of the police force. In the process, law and order functions came to occupy centre stage among police duties, at the cost of the prevention and detection of crime.[5] At the time of independence in 1947, no restructuring and reorganization of the department could be effected, although it offered a historic opportunity to do so. Large-scale violence broke out, which became a top priority and left little time for reform. Under the scheme of the Government of India Act, 1935, the Indian leadership already had a fair experience

[5] The home minister emphasized the need to critically examine the Indian Police Act, 1861 to see whether it is meeting the requirement of the present day policing and whether there is a need for a new Police Act. The home minister said that in modern democracies, respecting human rights is as important as maintaining peace and order (PIB Press Release, 1 September 2005).

of working and leading this policing system; they continued with the same arrangement for a free nation. The only sign of change was at the top: the replacement of the British officers with the Indian officers. The officers leading the force were drawn from the army and the force followed similar regimentation. The changes that should have come with independence did not happen.

Legacy of past in the present

Unfortunately, today the discussion on the historical background of the Indian police and its evolution during the past 150 years is not merely of academic interest. The imprints of the past remain firmly etched not only on the body of the organization but also on its soul which is the culture and ethos of the police. Many of the problems of the present-day Indian Police, for example, poor relation with the public and indifference to their interests and unquestioning loyalty to the ruling establishment (Dhillon, 1998) have their roots in the organization's colonial past and can only be fully understood in relation to that legacy. The police continues to be saddled with the same age-old inherent directional flaw (Box I.1.1); this has been compounded by its inability to keep pace with the times, which have changed rapidly.

This happened not only in India, but also in other colonies, where similar repressive machinery was set up. In 1896 Kenya (a British colony in Africa) saw the first formal police structure, in Mombassa, where a force consisting of a British Assistant Superintendent, two inspectors and an Indian personnel was established. In an environment of hostility to the construction of the railway, from various African communities, the police were tied to the security of the colonial officers and the protection of their property. The police force later became the weapon of punishment and pacification of communities and carries that legacy to date there.

During the Imperial Japanese occupation from 1910 to 1945 as well as after independence in 1948 to the 1990s, the South Korean police has had a history of abusing its power for political purpose. Instead of serving and protecting the interest of the people the police have been used as a political instrument, in order to protect and maintain authoritative and illegitimate regimes. Korean police had suppressed freedom, violated civil rights, intervened election processes and served the interest of a few selected people; therefore, the Korean people have had deep hostility and suspicion toward the police until now.

Box I.1.1   **Subordination to the Executive**

The Indian Police system, as organized according to the Police Act of 1861, was specifically designed to make the police totally subordinate to the executive government in discharging its duties. No reference was made at all to the role of the police as a servant of the law as such. Thus, when on 17 August 1860, the resolution appointing the Police Commission was issued by the Governor-General-in-Council, the memorandum attached to the resolution, for the guidance of the Commission stated the following 'characteristics of a good police for India'. The first was 'that it should be entirely subject to the Civil Executive Government. It was added that this would require 'a change in the rule which, as formerly in Madras and Bombay, gave the control of the police to a judicial body—the circuit judges in Madras and the Sudder Foujdaree Adawlut in Bombay. In a non-regulation province this rule would point to the necessity of the police being under the Civil Commissioner, or other head of the executive government, rather than under the Judicial Commissioner or other substitute for a Court of Appeal'. It was further noted that 'the organization of the police must be centralised in the bands of the Executive Administration' and that 'the organization and discipline of the police should be similar to those of a military body'.

The Indian Police Act, 1861 was enacted soon after, on the model of the Madras Act, formalizing the present organizational set-up and making the police at the district level function under the control and direction of the chief executive of the district, namely, the district magistrate. The police force has since then remained an instrument in the hands of the state government.

Source: National Police Commission, 1977–81.

Functioning environment

Today operational interference by politicians in police functioning has become an accepted norm. In public estimate the police appear as an agency to implement and enforce the objectives of the government in power as distinct from enforcing law as such as an independent and impartial agency (National Police Commission, 1977–81). This perception is not without any grounds; even an agency like the Central Bureau of Investigation (CBI), which has some degree of insulation in terms of tenure assurance of the director of CBI, is not able to avoid the allegations of interference of the politicians in its affairs.[6] The state police departments are far worse off.

---

[6] (i) See *The Tribune*, 2006b. In the famous Taj Corridor case against BSP supremo Mayawati, the court expressed anguish over the manner the Central Bureau of Investigation (CBI) had dealt with the case and the growing tendency of approaching the apex court in all criminal

The top leadership in the police is from the prestigious Indian Police Service (IPS). Less than 100 officers make it to this service every year from among the lakhs of aspirants through one of the toughest competitive exams in the world today.[7] The cream of the nation's youth are thus available to serve the nation through the IPS. However, the current situation in the services makes them silent spectators, if not active collaborators, in the serving of personal interests of politicians in power, above the interests of the people. In his book *The Future of India*, Bimal Jalan has identified the tackling of moral or 'motivational issue' at the higher level of the civil services as the most critical issue. The officers exhibit perceptible decline in morale, commitment and efficiency after few years of service, give in to the politicians after a few transfers and become cynical (Jalan, 2005: 114).

Lack of functional autonomy and absence of an environment that encourages living up to ideals push the officer towards a state of apathy. At the same time, the absence of direct accountability to people has the pulling effect towards corrupt practices in the police. The orders to carry out an investigation in a particular way are routinely received from politicians and any effort to resist is not taken very kindly (National Police Commission, 1977–81: para 61.25). Those who resist are transferred to inconsequential posts. The situation is no better even for the head of the department.[8] The transfers and postings of the top leadership of the police—from the rank of deputy superintendent of police (DSP) upwards—are decided by the home department, which is controlled by a minister; the diktats of the party in power run unchecked.[9] As these

cases involving some important persons. The premier investigating agency like CBI was expected to do its duty honestly, otherwise the criminal investigation and justice delivery system would collapse like a 'heap of sand', the bench observed.

(ii) There have been allegations against the CBI, from the opposition parties, that CBI is being used by the government to target the opposition leaders. The recent example in the newspapers dated 24 February 2006 is the allegation made by Mr L. K. Advani that directions have been issued to CBI by the prime minister to act against him.

[7] For the combined civil services exams in 2006 around 400,000 candidates applied for fewer than 500 vacancies (of which 50 per cent are reserved) and around 7,500 got through the first phase and appeared in the main exam (UPSC Annual Reports). To secure a berth in the coveted IAS/IFS/IPS (in the general category) one has to secure a rank in the top 125 translating into a success rate of 0.02 per cent.

[8] See *Deccan Herald* (2006). Insubordination is also rampant as Uttar Pradesh DGP Bua Singh discovered much to his dismay that an inspector he had sent to the lines for dereliction of duty managed a plum posting for himself within hours. The inspector in question managed the feat by virtue of belonging to the same caste as the state's chief minister Mulayam Singh Yadav.

[9] According to the Bureau of Police Research and Development, 442 DSPs and 78 range DIGs were transferred in less than two years, in 2004. (*Hindustan Times*, 2007b).

conditions prevail, meeting the requirements of political masters has become the primary job of the police officers (*The Tribune*, 2007e). Also, the hierarchy of the force is threatened when lower-level officers bypass their superiors and maintain direct contact with the political bosses.[10] The superior officers remain silent spectators and at times even encourage subordinates to get the approval from the local minister, to avoid later embarrassment.[11] Middle-level police officers posted in the districts form a nexus with politicians and leaders of groups, and through this they manage to stay entrenched in their posts for a long time. This gives rise to corruption, inefficiency in the working of the police and partnership with mafias (*The Tribune*, 2006a). The nexus now extends to include the land mafia and land developers who provide the money power to work in favour of these officers.

As India surges ahead to assume the role of a major player in the world affairs and economy, the integration of the markets would demand certain international standards of policing prevalent in the country. Since the implementation of the policy of economic reform, the Chinese economy, society and legal system have undergone profound changes. To sum up the changes in the Chinese police in recent years, one has to say that the most significant aspect is that the police development now is guided by a growing number of laws and regulations, in sharp contrast to the past practice where the police administration and operation were without any legislative guidance and were done mainly at the will of party officials (Ma, 1997: 113–35). Although India today is the world's largest democracy, the police in India are still imbued with a ruler-supportive ethic—one that encourages the police to do the bidding of the political leadership rather than to stand as impartial guardians of the people's democratic rights (Dhillon, 1998).

---

[10] See (i) (*The Times of India*, 2006a).

    (ii) Political interference clips the wings of the force further. In some states, even the constables are transferred by the home department: KPS Gill, former Punjab police chief currently security advisor to the Chhattisgarh government (*The Times of India*, 2006d).

    (iii) Application under Right to Information Act revealed that in the state of Punjab from 2002 to 2006, a total of 1,313 cops were either recommended for posting or transfers of their choice. Of these 62 were made for SPs, 374 for DSPs, 91 for Inspectors, 223 for SI/ASI, 523 for head constables and 40 for promotion of constables (*The Times of India*, 2007b).

[11] 'Senior officers believe that they are only accountable to political rulers and this has fallout on functioning': Ved Marwah, former DG Police, currently with Centre for Policy Research (*The Times of India*, 2006d).

Model for policing in the UK[12] and Northern Ireland[13]

As the policing model in India is an adaptation of the Ireland model, developments in Ireland to reform the policing are of relevance to India, particularly the recommendations of the Patten report, entitled *A New Beginning: Policing in Northern Ireland*. In April 1998 what came to be known as the Belfast Agreement was accepted by the main political parties in Northern Ireland and the Republic of Ireland. A commission was duly set up under the chairmanship of Chris Patten, one-time secretary of state for Northern Ireland and the last Governor of Hong Kong. The commission consulted widely, both internally and internationally and held a large number of public meetings across Northern Ireland. The commission published its report in September 1999, making far-reaching and radical recommendations for the reform of policing. Central to the report's recommendations was a model of society where demands for security were to be met by the participation of the local community and agencies, both government and non-government, which would share the responsibility for crime and security. The focus was firmly on the problem of policing and how this problem could be addressed. As one member of the Commission commented, their terms of reference 'made it clear that policing is, and should be, more than the police' (Shearing, 2001b).

The report recommended two levels of accountability and participation: a policing board with a policing budget and extensive powers to hold the police accountable and practise oversight over their activities. The board was to negotiate the policing budget with the government and then allocate it to the chief constable. Powers were also envisaged to allow the board to monitor police performance against the allocated budget. The board would hold public meetings, make its minutes available and receive a monthly report from the chief constable at a meeting open to the public. Local accountability and responsibility were to be achieved by establishing district and community policing arrangements.

The police system which was given to India by the British is very much different than what they followed in their own country. In the UK, over a period of time, the system has further evolved and has resulted in regulatory mechanisms in the form of police authorities or boards that oversee the work of police in an independent fashion. While in older times, all the citizens were to act as policemen, the formal policing in the UK can be said to have begun from the 1285, when the Statute of

[12] See Police: Serving the Community, home office website, UK.
[13] Based on article by Smyth Jim (Smyth, 2002: 110–24).

Winchester set out some of the principles of common law which still survive, including the people's right to make a citizen's arrest. In 1361 the Justice of the Peace Act enabled the appointment of three or four Justices in each county, the original model for today's magistrates, to 'restrain offenders and rioters and to arrest, and chastise (punish) them according to the Law'[14]. Then in the year 1663, the city of London began to pay watchmen to guard the streets at night. The first paid police force was formed only in the year 1750 by Henry Fielding, who was a famous writer as well as the chief magistrate for Westminster at Bow Street. This small plain-clothed force were later called the Bow Street Runners and worked to break up criminal gangs.

A major fillip to the force organization came when in 1829 Sir Robert Peel, the home secretary, introduced legislation which enabled the recruitment of 3,000 officers into a new metropolitan police force for London. They also included Bow Street Runners, Thames river police and horse patrols. However, by 1856 over 200 police forces had come up throughout England and Wales. The London experiment reinforced the confidence in police as an agency to maintain order, as till then in many areas the army was called in to prevent crime. With the mushrooming of a variety of police forces, the Home Office in the year 1918 decided to have a national style of practice and code of conduct for all police forces. In the year 1964, in an effort to reorganize, the police forces in England and Wales were regrouped and reduced in number from 122 to 43. The first Neighbourhood Watch (also known as Home Watch) was set up in Mollington, Cheshire in 1982. The Police Service in England and Wales introduced its Quality of Service initiative in 1990.

Landmark White Paper on Police Reform (Home Office, 1993) aimed to improve both police accountability and performance by focusing on defects in police governance. The White Paper aimed to give chief constables full management responsibility for all police personnel and to enable them to direct and control local policing without unnecessary interference and to produce a satisfactory and cost-effective policing plan for their police authorities. For the police authorities it was proposed that they become free-standing corporate bodies with new statutory tasks which would make them financially more accountable and more clearly responsible for police performance. Home Secretary, was to set the broad strategic framework for policing and to appoint a significant number of members of the proposed new police authorities.

The UK police authorities were set up in their present form by the Police and Magistrates' Court Act, 1994 for each police force in England,

[14] Police.homoffice.gov.uk/publications/community-policing/police_serving_community. pdf.

Wales and Northern Ireland, except London.[15] The statutory duty of the police authority under the Act is 'to secure the maintenance of an efficient and effective police force' for its area. To enable people to decide what priorities their local police should meet, the authorities consist of local councillors, magistrates and independent members. Their role includes appointing the chief constable and other senior officers, agreeing how many police officers should be in the local force, and providing buildings and equipment. The policing arrangement is what is called the 'tripartite system' of policing—the other two elements are the Home Office and the police force itself. The authority a link between the police service and the community, as it represents the views of the public to the service and vice versa. The balance between the influences of all three is maintained so that no one of the three has the power to act as if they had a 'private' police force.

Criminal justice system in India[16]

The criminal justice system covers the entire scenario from the occurrence of crime, investigation into the facts by the enforcement agency, adjudication proceedings in court conducted by the prosecuting counsel and the defence counsel, the correctional services which help return of the delinquent person to normal behaviour and finally the administration of jails with the objective of deterring him from repeating his crime. Police, prosecutors, advocates, judges and functionaries in the correctional services and jails form the different organized wings of this system. The roles, duties, powers and responsibilities of the police in prevention and control of crime, and the maintenance of public order have to be seen in conjunction with the overall requirements for the success of the criminal justice system. With the ultimate aim of securing peace and order in society, the success of the system depends largely on a proper understanding of its objectives by all the wings and their effective and coordinated functioning to secure this objective.

The fundamental basis for criminal justice system in India is the law of the land passed by the Union Parliament and state legislatures, and

[15] The Capital's anomaly has now changes with the introduction of a new authority for the met. This was set up in July 2000 under the terms of the Greater London Authority Act. The new 1994 authorities replaced the old police committees of the county councils in most areas and were set up with a wider remit and new power. Separate, but similar, police board arrangements exist in Scotland. www.mpa.gov.uk/about/default.htm dated 16 December 2008.

[16] Source: *Report of the National Police Commission* 1977–81.

the process adopted for the evolution of law ensures a measure of public sanction for the law through consent expressed by elected representatives. Hence, the durability and credibility of the criminal justice system depends on the inherent strength or weakness of the various laws enacted and also on the availability and capability of the implementation machinery which is the police.

After laws are made by the legislative bodies, their enforcement is taken up by the various agencies set up by the government. The police is the primary law enforcement agency available to the state. Therefore the investigation by the police is the foundation of the criminal justice system. When an offence committed is brought to the notice of the police, it is their responsibility to investigate into the matter to find out the identity of the offender, ascertain the facts and circumstances relevant to the crime and collect the evidence (oral or circumstantial) which are essential to prove the case in the court. Thereafter, the matter goes for trial before the judiciary where the facts ascertained by the enforcement agency are presented by the prosecuting agency.

Criminal laws and its limitations[17]

The existing criminal law in the country itself poses a number of limitations on the working of police which need to be taken into account:

1. *Old laws and procedures*: The basic criminal law—the Indian Penal Code, the Code of Criminal Procedure and the Evidence Act have remained largely intact in their original form since the middle of the nineteenth century. This has led to the limitation of police response and can make the police appear harsh and oppressive agency, example being the provisions of cognizable and non-cognizable offences, wherein the framers took a sever view of violation of law relating to possession of property and a lenient view for offences against human body. This would mean that the police would register a case and pursue it rigorously for a petty theft, while it would leave the matter for the courts in case of assault, hurt and insult, and so on. This leads to police action contrary to public expectations and misunderstanding about police in the minds of people. Similarly, the code of criminal procedure has been so framed that the bail is provided to a person on financial security which means that the poor remains deprived of this relief

---

[17] Source: *Report of the National Police Commission* 1977–81.

and police appears to be oppressive and harsh in dealing with the poor. And it is quite common that many hardcore criminals get away with producing financial sureties and this practice does not instil in them fear for the law of the land.

2. *Large number of new legislations*: The legislators enact laws with rapid pace without involving the police in the conception stage, with the result that the implementation of these laws leaves much to be desired. Since no thought is given to the potential resources of the police to handle the fast increasing volume of law enforcement work, the situation is something like planning and executing a very large number of irrigation dams and giant reservoirs without simultaneously planning and executing an efficient canal system for orderly distribution (National Police Commission, 1977–81: para 14.4). The Central Children Act was passed in 1960 which provides that the female children should be handled only by women police, but the number of women police in India is very low. Many police stations do not have any woman police officer. Similarly, the Act seeks to provide for neglected and delinquent children whereas the available accommodation in the 'homes' is fractional compared to the requirement.

3. *Accusatorial system of criminal trials*: The system followed in India for the dispensation of criminal justice is the accusatorial system of common law inherited from the British colonial rulers. In the adversarial system, truth is supposed to emerge from the respective versions of the facts presented by the prosecution and the defence, before a neutral judge. As the accusatorial system does not impose a positive duty on the judge to discover truth he plays a passive role. The accused is presumed to be innocent and the burden is on the prosecution to prove beyond reasonable doubt that he is guilty. The system is heavily loaded in favour of the accused as we will see further. Quite often the judge acquits the accused after recording a finding that the prosecution has miserably failed to prove its case against the accused attributing the failure to defective, incompetent or dishonest investigation. (Supreme Court in AIR 1988 SC 1323 between *Kashmiri Devi vs. Delhi Administration and others*) (Malimath Committee Report, 2003).

4. *Presumption of innocence and burden of proof*: From the accusatorial system, it follows that in a criminal trial it is the prosecution side that charges the accused with a definite offence and having done so, it has the responsibility to prove it as well. Section 101 of the Indian Evidence Act, 1872 says: 'Whoever desires any court to

give judgment as to any legal right or liability dependent on the existence of facts which he asserts, must prove that those facts exist', and 'when a person is bound to prove the existence of any fact, it is said that the burden of proof lies on that person'. So the burden of proof, save in a few exceptional cases lies on the prosecution (Sarkar, 2005).[18] Professor Glanville Williams narrated the adverse affects flowing from the acquittal of the guilty persons in these words:

> The evil of acquitting a guilty person goes much beyond the simple fact that one guilty person has gone unpunished. It frustrates the arduous and costly work of the police, who, if this tendency goes too far, may either become daunted or resort to improper methods of obtaining convictions.

5. *Distrust of the police*: With proceedings pending in the courts, the police have no *locus standi* inside the court hall, except when a specified police officer is examined as a witness. Even though investigation is the foundation of the criminal justice system, it is unfortunate that it is not trusted by the laws and the courts. Our criminal law has several provisions which breathe a distrust of the police. Sections 161 and 162 of the Code provide that the statements of the witnesses examined during investigation are not admissible and that they can only be used by the defence to contradict the maker of the statement. The confession made by the accused before a police officer is also not admissible as evidence.[19] The statements recorded at the earliest stage normally have greater probative value but cannot be used as evidence. The observations of the courts in several criminal cases show that the judges are reluctant to accept the testimony of police officers.[20]

6. *Court trial rituals*: The rituals of court trials under the existing law tend to delay the proceedings in the court.[21] These delays at the

---

[18] Exceptions where the burden of proof is on the accused are the dowry death cases under sections 304B and 306 of the IPC and under the provisions of Terrorist and Disruptive Activities Act and Prevention of Terrorism Act relating to possession of unauthorized weapons in an area notified as terrorist affected.

[19] The recommendations of administrative reforms commission headed by Veerappa Moily has recommended that the police in India, like their counterparts in advanced countries, should be empowered to video record confessions. Such confessions should be admissible in evidence subjected to the condition that the accused has been informed of his right to consult a lawyer before making the statement.

[20] The evidence of police officers especially in cases of recovery of narcotics have been viewed with general mistrust, in the absence of independent witness at the time of recovery.

[21] A Delhi court will, soon begin the trial of 16 police personnel alleged to have massacred 42 Muslims from Meerut way back in 1987. It was because of such inordinate delay

stage of trial have resulted in huge pendency of criminal cases.[22] It has been established that people tend to commit crime more freely when they know that it will take several years for the law to hold them in effective custody. The ineffectiveness of court trials to produce the desired deterrence acts as a severe limitation on the success of the police in containing crime (Box I.1.2).

Box I.1.2   Convictions and Control of Crime

There is a direct relationship between the effective control of crime and the criminals being made to feel that the commission of crime almost certainly leads to conviction. The situation in the city of London before the organization of the police force under the Peel's Act, 1829 is a classic illustration. It was estimated then that there were 8,000 places where stolen goods were received and that the robberies and thefts would cost up to 2,000,000 pounds annually to the public. Within a few years of organized policing, the amount of stolen property came down to 20,000 pounds annually. This happened as the police force made it almost certain that crime would lead to conviction. Earlier it was almost certain that the criminals would get away.

Source: Curry, 1977: 342–43.

In the United Kingdom,[23] from where we inherit our system, a Royal Commission on Criminal Procedure was constituted in 1978 and its report submitted in 1981 provides a complete review of the criminal procedure. It enquires whether changes are needed in England and Wales in (a) powers and duties of police in respect of the investigation of criminal offences and the rights and duties of suspects and accused persons, including the means by which these are secured; (b) the process of and responsibility for the prosecution of criminal offences and (c) other features of the criminal procedure which relate to the mentioned features (Royal Commission on Criminal Procedure Report).

---

that the Supreme Court had shifted the case from Ghaziabad to Delhi four years ago at the instance of victims, who expected the proceedings to be fast-tracked in the Capital. The CB-CID took seven years to complete its investigation and obtain the necessary sanctions to prosecute the PAC personnel. After the chargesheet was filed in 1994, the case could not make any progress till 2000. The police failed to enforce warrants even though court issued them as many as 23 times over six years (*The Times of India*, 2006b).

[22] Sometime back the government's press department reported that the number of civil and criminal cases pending before India's courts has exceeded 30m, up from 20m in 1997 (*The Economist*, 2006).

[23] India has just 11 judges for every one million people, compared with 51 in Britain and 107 in America (*The Economist*, 2006).

Perceptions about the police

There are some important findings of surveys and commissions—both in India and abroad—that tell us the public's views on important aspects of policing. We should take note of them while developing a marketing plan for the police.

1. The police today live in a time of contradiction and confrontation that emanate from laws enacted without public consensus—laws that people do not want to be enforced or want them to be enforced under certain conditions or against certain persons; expectation of providing equal, unbiased, impersonal law enforcement with unequal, biased and emotional human beings; being criticized for supporting the 'system', while the very purpose of their existence is to support and serve established, legitimate government; functioning both civilly and militarily during civil disturbances; and peace and order versus constitutional rights (Gentel and Hanna, 1971).

2. Some critical findings of the National Police Commission of 1977 on public perception of police are that 'in the perception of the people, the egregious features of police are politically oriented partisan performance of duties, brutality, corruption and inefficiency, degrees of which vary from place to place and person to person' (National Police Commission, 1981: para 1.1).

    'Political interference is seen by the public as a major factor contributing to the poor image of the police and manifests itself in the misuse and abuse of police powers and disregard of the law by the police' (National Police Commission Report, 1981: para 15.12).

    Public perception of police performance and behaviour has been mentioned by the Report of National Police Commission of 1977 in Chapter XLI of the fifth report. The conclusions stated were:

    (i)   Police–public relations at present are in a very unsatisfactory state. While there are several reasons for it, police partiality, corruption, brutality and failure to register cognizable offences are the most important factors which contribute to this sad state of affairs.

    (ii) Police do in fact harass even those who try to help them.

    (iii) There is a certain degree of ambivalence in people's views about police efficiency; by and large they do not think the police are inefficient. A change in the style of police functioning is what they desire foremost.

(iv) Those who have interacted with the police have a slightly better opinion of it than those whose opinions are based on what they have heard.

(v)   The Indian Police Commission of 1902–03 had, after discussing police corruption 'practices of extortion and oppression', their 'unnecessary severity' harassment of people, concluded (para 26): 'What wonder is it that the people are said to dread the police, and to do all they can to avoid any connection with a police investigation'. These observations can very well apply to the conditions obtaining even today. People now may not dread the police but they certainly dread getting involved with it any capacity.

3. In the survey conducted by the Institute for Development and Communication (IDC) (Kumar, 1999), on both the police and the community, important findings were:

   (i)   The Police is viewed as the protector of the community and national security yet it is a violator of individual rights.

   (ii) While a majority of the policemen are admitted to have a negative public image, their self-image remained high as they maintained that the public was not appreciative of the conditions they worked in.

   (iii) Current predisposition—cultural acceptance of enforcement:

      (a) A majority of the policemen and community members regarded the policeman as a law enforcer rather than a person in community service.

      (b) Low rank policemen are more inclined towards the use of coercive methods.

      (c) High ranks showed their preference for democratic and participative functioning.

      (d) Lower ranks were found high on the exploitative mode with the middle ranks more dependent on the authoritarian style. As a whole, the use of democratic style was nominal.

4. Several studies conducted in different nations indicate that the community values the crime control role of police. In Australia and New Zealand, the results of four separate studies, Australian Community Research, 1992; MRL Research Group, 1993; Reark Research, 1993 and South Australia Police survey, 1993, indicated that prompt response to calls, protection of people and crime fighting or prevention functions were most important to the community. Another study of European citizens indicated that the

public wanted the police to concentrate on preventing crime, regulating traffic and peacekeeping. A more comprehensive study was conducted in the UK in 1995, with samples of citizens and police, results of which indicated that the most important police activity should be 'to respond immediately to emergencies', followed by 'detect and arrest offenders' and 'investigate crime' (Beck et al., 1999).

5. Findings from the Opal Commission in British Columbia, Canada in the 1990s did point to certain inherent attitudinal problems with the police born out of the nature of the job and the structuring of the police department, the findings also drew attention towards the emerging trends in society. This is true for India as much as it is for Canada. The report says that many citizens are dissatisfied with the distance between themselves and the police, especially on operational matters. Justice Opal finds that the public wants community policing (sometimes called *community-based policing*) which involves a closer relation with the police to solve problems of crime and disorder. As it stands now, the public sees the police as remote and uninvolved in community concerns. Few opportunities exist where the public can become engaged in a meaningful way to address community policing problems. 'The decisions and policies are typically made at the top of the police hierarchy' (Anderson, 1995).

6. Three tendencies as regards expectations could be extracted from various opinion polls conducted by the Belgian police (Bruggeman et al., 2007):

   (i) During contacts, on population's initiative: When population calls upon the police, it expects quality service dealing with the reported problem with professionalism, paying particular attention to that problem and providing information (concerning the manner in which the problem will be dealt with). Availability, accessibility and speediness are also important aspects;

   (ii) In all cases and, therefore, of course when the police take the initiative: Population expects the police to be visibly present and accessible within the neighbourhood, to make contact and to remain in contact and to adopt an active attitude towards (mainly local) problems;

   (iii) As regards the policy: in terms of policy, the expectations are generally translated into enhanced attention for the efficient solving of all problems, priority being given to local (neighbourhood) problems encountered in the immediate daily environment.

7. In a letter dated 3 August 1997, the union home minister to the state government reveals a distressing situation. The home

minister while echoing the overall popular perception that there
has been a general fall in the performance of the police and also
a deterioration in the policing system as a whole in the country
expressed that the time has come to rise above limited perceptions
to bring about some drastic changes in the shape of reforms and
restructuring of the police before the country is overtaken by
unhealthy developments.

New regulatory mechanism and National Police Mission

Taking note of the situation, the Supreme Court in Vineet Narain &
Others vs. Union of India & Anr. (1998), directed the central government
to pursue the matter of police reforms with the state governments and
ensure the setting up of a mechanism for selection/appointment, tenure
transfer and posting of not only the chief of State Police (SP), but also
all police officers of the rank of SP and above. Recommendations made
by the National Police Commission, 1977–81, the National Human
Rights Commission, the Law Commission, the Riberio Committee, the
Padmanabhaiah Committee and the Malimath Committee have culminated in the Supreme Court order No. R. 639/06 passed on 22 September
2006. The objective is to devise a supervisory mechanism without scope
of illegal, irregular interference with police functions. The important
directions are:

1. Sweeping changes in the Police Act of 1861 which would not
   only change the system of superintendence and control over the
   police but also enlarge the role of the police to make it function
   as an agency which promotes the rule of law in the country and
   renders impartial service to the community.[24]
2. Separation of the investigating wing, and the law and order wing
   in police departments. While the investigative tasks of the police
   should be beyond interference, with respect to preventive and service-oriented functions, the government should lay down broad
   policies for adoption. There should, however, be no instructions
   with regard to actual operations in the field. Policy directions

[24] The reason why the police in the UK has been able to serve and earn the respect
of the community is that the police force there is accountable to the law and not to the
government.

should be openly given and made known to the state legislatures and public.

3. A State Security Commission and Police Board should be established statutorily in each state to help the state governments discharge their superintending responsibility. The State Security Commission should: (*a*) lay down broad policy guidelines for the performance of preventive and service oriented functions by the police; (*b*) evaluate the performance of the state police every year; (*c*) function as a forum of appeal to dispose representations from officers regarding their being subjected to illegal orders and regarding their promotion and (*d*) budgeting and generally review the functioning of the state police force. Police Establishment Boards set up for transfer, postings, promotions and other service-related matters of officers of and below the rank of deputy superintendent of police.

4. The chief of the state police force should be selected from a panel of three senior most IPS officers of that state's cadre by the state government. The chief of the police and other field officers should, like the SPs and DIGs, be assured of a fixed tenure of office of minimum two years. The removal of the chief of police from his post before the expiry of the tenure should require approval of the State Security Commission.

5. Police Complaints Authority at the district level is to look into the complaints against officers up to the level DSP. Another Police Complaints Authority at the state level is to look into complaints against officers of the rank of SP and above.

6. National Security Commission for appointment of chiefs of Central Police Organizations. The commission is also to make recommendations for upgrading the effectiveness, coordination, service conditions and utilization of these forces.

The Soli Sorabjee Committee presented a draft outline of the new police act to the home minister for consideration.

Alongside, another significant development took place for the Indian police. Emphasizing that development and security are closely interlinked, in October 2005, the prime minister of India announced setting up of the National Police Mission. The Mission is different from other missions like the Rural Health Mission and the Drinking Water Mission as this is the first mission in the field of regularity and enforcement administration dealing with the sovereign functions of the state.

The Mission seeks to equip the police to think creatively and help it transform itself from a reactive to a proactive organization. The mission strives to redefine the role of the police in the context of the phenomenal changes that have taken place in the socio-economic scenario of the country and the emerging challenges of the twenty-first century. As the police is a state subject (as per the constitutional arrangement in India), the National Police Mission will strive to bring about needed police reforms and transformation in consultation with state governments.

These are significant steps towards the most important and difficult task of securing a market for professional police work in India—a public that will demand it, monitor it and stand behind it.

Police Functions and Developing Trends

2

Broad categories of police functions

The police in India perform multifarious activities, from reacting to the emergencies to the most routine activities like the guard duties. The second report of National Police Commission 1977–81 (para 14.51) has redefined the role, duties, powers and responsibilities of the police as follows:

1. Promote and preserve public order.
2. Investigate crime and, where appropriate, apprehend the offenders and participate in subsequent legal proceedings connected therewith.
3. Identify problems and situations that are likely to result in the commission of crime.
4. Reduce the opportunities for the commission of crimes through preventive patrol and other appropriate police measures.
5. Aid and cooperate with other relevant agencies in implementing other appropriate measures for the prevention of crimes.
6. Create and maintain a feeling of security in the community.
7. Aid individuals who are in danger of physical harm.
8. Facilitate the movement of the public and vehicles.
9. Counsel and resolve conflicts and promote amity.
10. Provide other appropriate services in an emergency and afford relief to people in a distress situation.

11. Collect intelligence relating to matters affecting public peace and crimes in general including social and economic offences national integrity and security and

12. Perform such other duties as may be enjoined on them by law for the time being in force.

Broadly, these duties performed by the police fall into three functions — law enforcement, order maintenance and services. However, for the officer of the Indian Police, even in the realm of public goods, from the colonial times till today, combining these incompatible functions presents the most significant dilemma. The order maintenance function of the police includes the surveillance of political leaders and religious/social leaders, the enforcement of social and censorship laws, mass arrests and the dispersal of political assemblies. The order maintenance of the police, where the police does not need or expect public co-operation and goodwill, is the one that usually leads to antagonistic relationship and bitterness between them and the community. The law enforcement and services functions of the police however involve preventing and prosecuting non-political crimes, such as murder, theft and assault and waging a constant battle against professional criminals who seek to victimize the overwhelmingly law-abiding population; these functions presuppose an amicable relationship between the police and the people (Campion, 2003). For its success they require the active and voluntary co-operation of the empowered, enthusiastic and responsible citizens cooperating with the police in the prevention and detection of crime. In this sense, the constable as a public servant enforces people's law and works in partnership with the community for the good of the common welfare (Campion, 2003).

Further, in Wilson's (1968) criteria of these three 'core' police functions, namely, law enforcement, order maintenance and services, only law enforcement remains the strongest form of a public good.[1] This is largely because it is widely viewed as economically 'impractical' to provide law enforcement through a market system. Although the police most often

---

[1] Public goods can be defined as those possessing non-exclusionary and non-divisible or non-rival characteristics. Being non-exclusionary means not being capable of excluding non-payers from using the services. Being non-rival means that one person's consumption of the services would not interfere with the consumption of the others. Public goods theories largely address the important normative questions of when and where resources should be public rather than private and who should bear the costs. They help define the positive nature of government provision and, more clearly, identify the nature and dynamics of market and state institutional arrangements.

perform order maintenance and service functions, these policing duties economically possess exclusion and divisibility properties found in market settings quite commonly, crime prevention would largely fulfil this category (Daleidan, 2006). In the services and order maintenance functions of the police, there is no market failure, which means that there can be greater participation of the private sector in these functions. This could be in the form of outsourcing and private security agencies. For instance, security patrols are collective and privately supplied according to their public and private forms. Interestingly, private security has been the fastest growing industry in the 1990s in Britain, employing around 300,000 personnel. Further expansion is projected in an increasingly voluntary surveillance society where the private sector is able to provide a range of protective functions extending from security at shopping malls to street patrols.

By considering Wilson's (1968) arrangements, clearer lines and boundaries of the police (state) and policing (market) activity are shown in Chart I.2.1. By introducing economic orientations with the politics of public goods, the contemporary institutional arrangements and political economy can be more clearly seen (Daleidan, 2006).

Chart I.2.1   Police/Policing Political Economy*

Enforcement functions
Market failure

	Private goods	Public goods
Law enforcement	Limited powers under exceptional circumstances	Seizure and search, arrest and detention, registration and investigation of cases
Order maintenance	Guard duties, crowd control, security duties	Preventive arrests, dispute resolution, crowd control, guard duties
Services	Property alarms, surveillance cameras, security patrol (private property)	Security patrol (public places), verifications, organizing public groups

Crime prevention functions
No market failure   ***Private goods***   ***Public goods***

Source: Daleidan, 2006.

Note: *Only few examples in each block are given as representatives of the category.

Constraints of the police

Police agency is an exemplar of institutionalized organization that does value work. Being an institutionalized organization, the police also face a number of environmental constraints.

Mastrofski and Uchida (1996: 213) described institutionalized organizations as:

> Here the nature of the organization's product or service and what constitutes performance are not readily specified in ways that are easy to conform empirically; the technical capacity of such organizations to produce this service is not well known or well established. However, these organizations succeed in their well-developed institutional environment to the extent that they conform to structures (procedures, programs, or policies) that are widely accepted as being right even though the relationship of these structures to actual performance is not well established.

Mastrofski and Uchida (1996) also suggested that the police operate in both technical and institutional environments. Institutional and technical environments, they offered, differed in terms of the locus of change efforts.

Institutionalized organizations operate in environments that are complex, with values. The organizations, to survive, turn their focus 'outward' to acknowledge influential constituencies and the values they represent (Meyer and Rowan, 1977). They are typically distinguished from business organizations, business organizations 'turn inward' and are focused on the efficient and competitive production of a product core. They operate as relative fixtures of constraining environments and are accompanied by taken-for-granted accounts (Jepperson and Meyer, 1991). Scott and Meyer (1983: 149), noted that:

> In institutionalized environments, organizations are rewarded for establishing correct structures and processes. This conception is often contrasted against utilitarian or instrumental concerns about ends, which are associated with product marketing in a competitive work-place.

The police are also affected by different levels of polity—state, central and local—in terms of organizational budget, policy and strategies. The fragmentation contributes to the expansion of organizational complexity (Crank, 2003).

The other constraining fact is that the police department, in its institutional environment participates with other powerful actors, called sovereigns, and receives legitimacy from these sovereigns. Sovereigns are those actors whose views are significant, that is, they are entities that have the capacity to affect the fundamental well-being of the organization (Crank and Langworthy, 1992: 342). The sovereigns tend to frame values in terms of not only public safety first, but also in terms of other values such as due process, hiring and retention, gender equity, social justice and public relations. The bottom line for police organizations is that they must display, in their organizational behaviour and design, which they care about constituents' concerns the way in which these issues are important to them (Crank, 2003).

The environmental web of complexity thus makes the job of police much more difficult and less clear cut than a business enterprise; some of the direct fallouts are:

1. The business enterprises operate within the larger systems, which are the functional markets, so the management literature focuses on changing the organization and the system is left to the economists, whereas the police department operates within fairly dysfunctional systems. The department is controlled by multiple agencies with sometimes conflicting goals and faces no direct competition or consequence for its performance. For example, there can be no policy of hire and fire, purely merit-based recruitment and promotions and need-based restructuring in the department, given constitutional obligations, political implications and government service rules. These systemic realities drive the police to act in a bureaucratic way and this is a very big handicap in building police departments as entrepreneurial organization.

2. While the police budgets are approved and sanctioned by the government, police plans are viewed with little enthusiasm, and any increase in demand is seen as an unproductive expenditure and strain on state outlay.[2] The government is generally not convinced of the requirements projected by the department (*The Economic Times*, 2007e). The constraints then become the lack of resources, resulting in compromises on the efficiency and encouragement of corrupt practices. Being viewed as a fire-fighting apparatus, there is no long-term vision for the police department and the requirements are met on an ad hoc basis from year to year.

3. Making changes in the department require far more political effort because the organization operates in the political sea. For example, the reforms and changes in present political and bureaucratic working are desired for improvement in the working of the police but they are beyond the control of the department.

---

[2] State govenments incurred an expenditure of Rs 1,49,860 per policemen per annum (Government of India, 2006).

There are strong vested interests that would not let go of the control over the powerful institution like the police to maintain their hegemony.[3]

Therefore, unless we reform the operating environment for the police improvements such as setting the internal functioning in order will not be enough. The external factors that have huge bearing on the police also should be attended to alongside. In doing this, advocacy and collaborative persuasion techniques will be of help so that the current police reforms to imulate the police from undesired influences are implemented in true spirit. Similarly, the point that has to be driven home among the policy elites is that the money spent on police goes towards setting the stage for economic activities to flourish in the state.

Characteristics of police service

There are five characteristics to a service which are applicable to the police service also and these have to be kept in mind when we think of strategies for the police.

Lack of ownership

You cannot own and store a police service like you can with a product. Services are used or hired for a period of time. For example, when there is a traffic jam, the citizens want and expect excellent service for that time.

Intangibility

You cannot hold or touch a police service unlike a product. In saying that services are intangible, the experience that citizens obtain from the service is decide by the police–citizen interaction and is a matter of personal perception.

---

[3] (i) The actual reasons for opposing reforms is that the politicians and bureaucrats in Punjab do not want to let go easily of their hold on the police. Over the years successive ruling parties in Punjab have used the police to settle scores with political opponents and enhance their electoral prospects (The Tribune, 2007b).

(ii) The unwillingness of the states to let go of its control over the police stems from the penchant of ruling parties to utilize it as a tool to settle political scores, especially in the era of coalition politics. The ultimate causality is police reforms (The Times of India, 2007e).

Inseparability

Police services cannot be separated from the service providers. A product when produced can be taken away from the producer. However, a service is produced at or near the point of purchase. For example, a complainant visits a police station to make a complaint, the waiting time, the delivery of the First Information Report (FIR) and the service provided by the police station staff are all a part of the service production process and are inseparable. The staff in the police station is a part of the process and the quality of service provided.

Perishability

Services last a specific time and cannot be stored like a product for later use. If a person is approaching the police with a particular problem, then the service lasts till the duration of the response provided. The service is developed and used almost simultaneously. Again, because of this feature of time constraint, demands on the police are more.

Heterogeneity

It is very difficult to make each service experience identical. Since the human element is involved in the service provided by the police, the police–citizen interaction will always be unique. Generally, systems and procedures (Standard Operating Procedures [SOPs]) are put into place to make sure the service provided is consistent all the time, yet, there will always be subtle differences.

Evolution of community policing

Just as many government departments are involving and empowering the citizens, in the police department too this trend has found strong manifestation in the form of community policing. In several cities across the world that have adopted community policing, residents share the responsibility with the police department and help implement crime-prevention strategies. Community policing is the need of the day and the police forces in the democracies around the world are realizing its utility and implementing community policing initiatives in varied forms.

As an innovation in the police organization and philosophy, community policing has come to centre stage (Box I.2.1). The movement is most pronounced in the USA, where a federal agency was established ('COPS', The Office of Community Oriented Policing Services) to encourage the development of community policing programmes. The turning point came in the early 1990s when life in major cities had become intolerable because of seemingly unstoppable crime. Then the new-style mayors and police chiefs, notably Guiliani and Bratton in New York as figureheads, adopted new policies which combined so-called 'zero-tolerance' with resurrected notions of community policing. The New York 'miracle' reinforced the notion that multi-agency approaches with public–private funding could lead to considerable improvement in the 'quality of life' of people in communities by reducing 'nuisance' and petty offences (Punch et al., 2002). New York provided a model that successfully linked crime fighting and crime prevention. But the movement did not remain limited only to the US, the community policing philosophy has taken root throughout the developed world. From the UK, to continental Europe, to the Far East, innovative community policing programmes have emerged over the last 10 years (Weisburd et al., 2002).

Box I.2.1   Community Policing as an Antidote

The United Nations conference on human rights in southern Europe portrayed COP as the human rights response to the treatment of Roma minorities (for example, Organization for Security and Cooperation in Europe, 2002). An otherwise highly competent report on crime and the problems of policing transitional societies (International Council on Human Rights Policy, 2003) recommends New York–style COP as the solution for countries as varied as the Ukraine and Argentina. The University of Ottawa Human Rights Centre promotes COP as the antidote to the appalling level of police and civilian death rates in Sao Paulo. At an Abu Dhabi conference (19 February 2000), experts from Arab countries, Singapore, Taiwan, France, Britain, the United States and Canada recommended the implementation of COP within Sharia and local cultural values to reduce crime. Similarly, 'Even South Africa and Brazil are amongst jurisdictions seeking Ontario Provincial Police expertise on community policing' (Community Policing Development Centre, 2001). A September 1999 seminar (Japan-Singapore Partnership Programme for the 21st century, 2001) selling Singapore-style COP was attended by police officials from South Africa, Bangladesh, Brunei, China, India, Indonesia, Laos, Malaysia, Maldives, Mongolia, Nepal, Papua New Guinea, the Philippines, the Solomon Islands, Sri Lanka and Vietnam. Across the developing nations COP has been largely introduced as an antidote to crime problems together with a fatalistic view that the history requires an inexorable path of police reform.

Source: Brogden, 2005.

What it means

Community policing is practised in various countries and is a concept that cannot be ignored by policymakers. The theory of community policing is based on normative sponsorship and critical social theory. Normative sponsorship theory proposes that most people are good and are willing to cooperate with others to satisfy their needs (Sower, 1957). In the opinion of other American authors, community policing is based on the joint effort on citizens and police towards solving neighbourhood problems which in turn satisfies the expressed needs of citizens and enhance the residents' quality of life. The role of the community police officer is equivalent to the role of the critical social scientist, the facilitator and catalyst of problems solving activities. There is also a continental concept (policing of proximity), in which community policing is a tactical strategy to increase the visibility of the police officers in specific areas (near shops, schools monuments, important streets, and so on) to prevent crime and disorder.

Therefore, it is not surprising that community policing has meant differently to various people. To Spellman and Eck (1989), it is a strategy which combines citizen interaction with imaginative problem-solving techniques which reduce the incidence of crime. To Herman Goldstein (1990), it is primarily defined in terms of the ability of the police to identify, analyse and resolve crime-related problems specific to a given community. To Skolnick and Bayley (1986), it is the enhancement of the crime-prevention strategy through the civilianization, decentralization and reorientation of the police organizational structure. To Trojanowicz and Bucqueroux (1994), it is a set of values that promises to significantly improve the police organization and its working relationship with the community it serves. To Alpert and Dunham (1988), it is the means of improving the efficiency and effectiveness of the police by adjusting policing styles to conform to specific community needs.

Popular programmes under community policing

The Fijian community police warn locals about the new green shoots of marijuana plantations. The Australian Federal Police in the Christmas and Cocos Islands include hurricane watching and a myriad of unique ancillary services under the heading of community policing. In the Solomon Islands, community policing is equated with peacekeeping as one (temporary) resolution to internal schism. In Papua New Guinea, the

Bougainvillea local constabulary is building up a system of community policing under the guidance (and financed by) the Australian and New Zealand governments. In East Timor, after the destruction left by the Indonesian-sponsored militia, community policing is being constructed under a United Nations Civilian Police (CIVPOL) mandate (Brogden, 2005). These are some extreme examples from the South Pacific that demonstrate the breadth of programmes undertaken by police under community policing today.

However, there are also many common areas where police forces practice community policing. Some of the popular programs undertaken by police forces around the world under community policing are: [4]

Schools/children programme

Special programmes are being developed by police forces and local communities all over the world in order to deal with the security problems in schools. It is important that the police make contact with children as often as possible. Developing a child's confidence in the police service will pay dividends when the child becomes an adult. Usually, it is a partnership between the school and the police (preferably with a certified officer and a member of the school). Some police forces train special teams in order to deal with school safety and how best to communicate with children. There are countries like the US where police forces provide training programmes for 'Schools Liaison Officers' (station commanders, members of safety schools teams, and so on).

Community problems/aid to the community

In some countries police forces are involved in social services. They give support to the homeless by delivering food and blankets. They also give social and health advises. They give assistance to drug addicts and alcoholics. They transport abnormal people and the handicapped to the social welfare services, and the health and medical services. They find missing children or adults and also assist refugees who have no place to live.

Police also have to act in many situations, for instance by reporting about these matters to appropriate authority for further action, these could be borderline cases of emergency situations. These are conditions of streets, street lights, buildings, equipment, electrical wiring, person taken ill in the street, fire, flooding, gas explosion, and so on.

---

[4] Adapted from the United Nations, 1999.

Domestic violence

Domestic violence is a pattern of coercive tactic which can include physical, psychological, sexual and economic abuse, perpetuated by one person against an adult partner, with the goal of establishing and maintaining power and control over the victim. Domestic violence is a problem that has significant impact on communities and society at large. In some countries, police forces are developing prevention teams/units in order to deal with domestic violence. Their mission is to give a considered response in order to help in bring domestic disputes to a satisfactory conclusion, minimizing its impact and protecting those involved and preventing a repetition.

Victim support

Some police forces are also developing Victim Support Teams working in straight collaboration with experts in these matters.

The police and the environment

While the police have a role in enforcing laws concerning littering, dumping of toxic wastes, noise pollution and similar insults to the environment, the environment is an aspect of law enforcement that has historically been overlooked or marginalized in policing. Some countries now have specialized investigative units to deal with these crimes. Such policing intervention has also been sometimes termed as 'quality of life policing'.

Community policing in India

During the Mughal administration, the *kotwal*, as per the account of Abul Fazl in *Ain-i-Akbari*, was required to engage the citizens in a pledge of reciprocal assistance and bind them to a common participation of weal and woe. As per the account of Badauni, the *kotwal* was to take cognizance of the streets and houses of the city one by one, and to require of the heads and chief persons of every street a bond that he would perform the following duties: that he would keep a close watch on every one who came in or went out, of whatever degree he might be, whether merchant, soldier or otherwise; that he would not allow troublesome and disorderly fellows or theives to take up their abode in the city; and that he would inform the chief of police of all rejoicings and feasting, and mourning and lamentations which might take place, especially marriages, births, feasts and suchlike. Later the Indian Police Act, 1861, Section 17, provided for the appointment of special police officers for the assistance of the police. However, over a period of time law and order took the centre stage and the fire fighting remained the prime preoccupation of the police in India, with the result pro active efforts remained relegated to the background.

However, as the reforms in police administration system were under consideration in the early 80's, the National Police Commission (1977) & Padmanabhaiyah Committee had made recommendation favouring community policing as an integral part of policing activities. The recommendations of the XXXIV All India Police Science Congress conceded that 'community policing' is a global standard for eliciting public cooperation and satisfaction and enhanced quality and efficiency. The Congress recommended that police organizations all over the country should strive to increase the involvement of the community of the country in local-area policing. In India, of late, efforts are underway to bring about attitudinal change in the police and to institutionalize community policing. It is being appreciated, though incrementally, that in order to give better service police cannot work in isolation from the community. Community policing is being implemented in diverse manners. Different units like women cell, child support unit, drug de-addiction programme, victim support unit, police advisory groups, neighbourhood schemes, and so on, are part of community policing efforts.

In the last two decades there have been initiatives in different states like Punjab, Delhi, Himachal Pradesh (H.P.) and Tamilnadu, while individually, in different parts of the country, many officers have put to practice various innovations for community policing. This has helped in better handling of issues relating to domestic violence, marriages, child abuse and conflicts by the policemen. In Delhi and Chennai, crime prevention through community problem solving rather than through traditional reactive policing was adopted the new solution. A police district in Tamilnadu won ITT's[5] Night Vision Community Policing Award. The Friends of Police (FOP) concept has been intitutionalized in Tamilnadu through a government order. In Gujarat the state government has accepted community policing as an important programme. In Madhya Pradesh the state government has sanctioned funds for building community halls for police–citizen interface. The British Council has organized seminars on COP for police officers in Punjab, Calcutta and Chennai. In Uttar Pradesh the state government announced that it was adopting a community policing system drawing on the practices in Singapore and

---

[5] ITT is the name of the corporation sponsoring the community policing awards in partnership with IACP (International Association of Chiefs of Police).

Japan with local adaptation. In the state of Punjab itself several initiatives were witnessed after the end of terrorism from 1994 to 2002 in
the districts of Batala, Patiala, Hoshiarpur, Ludhiana, Amritsar, Sangrur,
Faridkot and Barnala to name the few. Under these initiatives, various
activities like village games, defence committees, womens' cells at district
level and youth clubs were organized by the police chiefs to varying degree
of intensity and commitment. The above mentioned initiatives by the individual officers drew a very good response from the public and showed
the way to laying the foundation for an institutionalized effort by the policy
elites in the state of Punjab. A comprehensive plan for institutionalizing
community policing in Punjab by setting up Community Police Resource
Centres (CPRC) in all the districts was implemented in 2003.

However, there has been no central support or scheme for community policing to write about and apart from some of the initiatives
mentioned above no significant institutionalization has taken place in
India to integrate the concept in routine policing.

Fragmentation of police tasks[6]

Over the past 150 years, government bodies have been both the main
authorities controlling police tasks and the implementers of police tasks.
But today, police tasks and the police as an organization are no longer
synonymous notions. Increasing demand on police service, variety of
requirements, development of economy and rising costs have led to
adoption of various strategies over the past few decades. Public policing
today is a part of what can be termed as new security architecture which
incorporates technological measures, private participation and multi-
agency spread for security. Some of the developments that are changing
the way the police functions are:

1. Responsibilization strategies: a call on social actors to act as an
   authority and to actually perform certain police tasks; for example, stimulating neighbourhood initiatives and neighbourhood
   consultations.
2. Allowing citizen groups to defend themselves with arms, as in the
   village defence committees.
3. Transferring some tasks to private organizations (for example,
   parking management) or hiring private security firms to perform
   police tasks.

[6] See Hoogewoning, F. C., 2006: 47–51.

4. Public–Private Partnerships, for example, between government and banks or government and airlines, where private parties are allowed to perform certain controls.
5. Outsourcing: hiring private parties for such matters as property surveillance or the transportation of detainees.
6. The police hiring private experts and having civilian staff perform certain simple police tasks.

The result is that today police tasks are performed by various organizations, public and private, leading to a strong horizontal fragmentation of police functions. The ongoing horizontal fragmentation means that today, in some functions of the police, there is a choice as to who the provider will be, and there can also be benefits in terms of permanent attention for certain aspects of safety because certain domains have been assigned to different organizations. However, this also creates the problem of coordination and alignment as there is a structural multiplication of powers. Also, there is lack of clarity as to which organization is responsible in which case, meaning that administrators can shy away from their responsibilities in some respects. A further drawback is asymmetry of information, insufficient refining of information and various organizations lacking the desire to share information.

Vertical fragmentation of police tasks means that the control (authority) over police tasks on the one hand and the performance of police tasks on the other are becoming separated from each other. In a general survey, police researchers Bayley and Shearing (2001) point out how this is a global development. Because some government organizations use private parties in the public domain while there are police services also that hire the services of private parties for police tasks (outsourcing), private supervision is no longer limited to the private domain, nor is public supervision limited to the public domain. A diverse picture has arisen with many forms of a mix between public and private, where authority and control of supervision have been fragmented as well. The fact that public and private parties can act alongside each other and in various different roles (authority and/or implementing party) means that today policing can be carried out:

1. by regular police officers and by a government institution that has charged public officials with police tasks (public/public);
2. by a government institution hiring private security firms (public/private);
3. by a private security firm providing private surveillance (private/private); and
4. by a private company hiring police officers (private/public) or

This can give rise to problems in terms of responsibility, management, control and accountability.

Towards glocal policing

In the increasingly interconnected world[7] police can no longer remain locally marooned. The crimes like the drugs, illegal human trafficking, wildlife crimes, intellectual property, financial frauds and cyber crimes have largely international implications. The trend has to increase further with people bound by similar interests and ideologies coming very quickly together, cutting across the national boundaries be it a drug cartel across the nations, or the Al-Qaeda network spread across the continents. Globalization has not only increased the reach and opportunities for organized crime but has lead to coming together of their networks and resources. Policing in future will be increasingly involved in the international crimes and to a fair measure defined by it also.

Spread of air network and booming airline industry has made the transportation of humans and goods like never before with the result that no part of the world today appears out of reach.[8] These developments would also mean that the policing would in essence evolve into policing of flow and movement. Policing for extremism, terrorism, cybercrime and following the trail left by digital financial transactions of the suspects represent the emerging trend of policing flow.

A local criminal apprehended for possession of drugs may form an important link to international illegal small arms racket or to an international extremist conspiracy to carry out major terrorist strike in the capitals of different nations. This developing trend would mean that the local policing today and in the future will have to be guided by the awareness of global developments. The twin tower bombing of 11 September 2001 has proved to be landmark for the globalization of police. Further, leading to the growth of global policing market and triggering the trend of exchange of police professional and their coming together at different platforms to discuss and devise expert practices. Policing today is evolving towards more and more glocal activity where local policing is becoming increasingly intertwined with international developments.

---

[7] There are more than 1.1 billion people of the world connected online via the Internet (Global Broadband Statistics by Point Topic).

[8] Airlines worldwide offer 300 million seats in a month for the first time. Aircraft orders rise 30 per cent (Official Airline Guide 2007).

New policing order

Around the world, there have been important developments in policing in the 1990s:

1. Dismantling of the old, strict bureaucratic order in policing.
2. Bringing in more professionalism and accountability.
3. Applying private sector mentalities to the public sector to bring about result-oriented functioning, efficiency and responsiveness in police.

In its growing march towards the new police order, recently, the Belgium police have put in practice an excellence model combining the Dutch and Canadian model. The model is integration of components like community policing, intelligence-led policing and optimal management.

These developments are significant for the police in India today. The Indian police have remained isolated to these changes, even though other institutions and the economy have been rapidly integrating into the world system. The police in India will soon have no choice but to embrace the changes (Box I.2.2).

Box I.2.2   Managing Change in South Africa

By the early 1990s, the police in South Africa had acquired a reputation for brutality, corruption and ineptitude. Police organizations were militarized, hierarchical, and ill-equipped to deal with 'ordinary crime'. Street-level policing was conducted in a heavy-handed style, with bias against black citizens and little respect for rights or due process. Criminal investigations were largely reliant on confessions extracted under duress. Harsh security legislation provided, or tolerated, various forms of coercion and torture. Their policing techniques were outmoded, partly as a result of the campaign for international isolation of the apartheid government. However, despite their lack of skill in dealing with ordinary crime and criminals of the new era, the South African Police (SAP) were ruthless and notoriously effective against their political opponents.

During 1991, the main police force in South Africa, embarked on an internal reform initiative, a response to the changing political environment, the pressure of changing crime trends, and international scrutiny. The SAP's 1991 Strategic Plan highlighted five areas of change:

(Box I.2.2 continued)

(*Box I.2.2 Continued*)

1. Depoliticization of the police force;
2. Increased community accountability;
3. More visible policing;
4. Establishment of improved and effective management practices;
5. Reform of the police training system and
6. Restructuring of the police force.

The 1991 plan indicated the force's intention to 'manage change itself, in the hope of ensuring that it would not have change thrust upon it later' (Shaw, 1994).

Source: Rauch, 2000.

Reinvention Strategies in Marketing Framework 3

Setting the direction

Objective

While there are several impediments and constraints in the present situation, contrary to the general perception, it can be said that the police service in India is able to give a good account of itself in conducting general elections, in controlling communal riots or terrorism in Punjab, in tracking the criminal gangs and in anti-insurgency operations in the North-East. International comparative research into the legitimacy of government services shows that the police and the armed services are actually performing the best of all the government services.[1]

However, functioning under the constraints and handicaps of an outmoded system, the police performance has undoubtedly fallen short of the public expectation (National Police Commission, 1977–81: para 62.2). Not only society at large, but also the authorities, administrators, politicians and partners in safety have increasingly different expectations and visions as regards the desired performance of the police. Wherever the expectations and performance levels are difficult to reconcile, citizens become dissatisfied; they lose confidence in the police and the police lose their legitimacy.

The police have to aim continuously to optimize their performance and, at the same time, their public image. Undeniably, there is still a lot

---

[1] Poll conducted in the European context.

of scope for improvement in the quality and delivery of the service in the service chain. Moreover, the department does not enjoy a good public image which is not commensurate with the service it provides. It is not an exaggeration to suggest that the present-day Indian policeman is generally viewed by the public with the same loathing as were his imperial predecessors. However, the authority wielded by the policeman has diminished considerably over time. If we plot a 2X2 matrix (Chart I.3.1) of police image and performance, then presently, the department would find itself placed in Block I, *mediocre performance and low public image*, whereas, the desired situation or the objective would be to take police department to Block IV, where the department would have *high performance and high public image*. Something that can be achieved by transforming the police into an efficient and impartial law enforcement agency, fully motivated and guided by the objectives of service to the public at large, upholding constitutional rights and liberty of the people, and held in high esteem by the people and the policemen alike (National Police Commission, 1977–81: first report, para 1.1).

Chart I.3.1   2X2 Matrix of Police Image and Performance

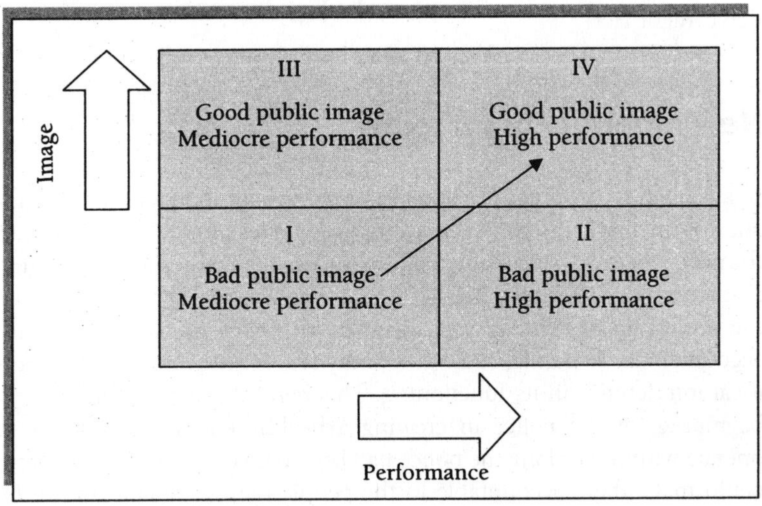

Source: Conceptualized by the author.

SWOT analysis

SWOT analysis is a powerful tool used here to make a more structured and rigorous assessment of the police department's strengths and weaknesses, which are internal to the department, as well as the threats and opportunities that the environment poses to the department. It is also used for making an objective assessment of the department's present state which is essential for appropriate strategy formulation.

All the factors affecting the police are appropriately slotted in the SWOT chart (Chart I.3.2). However, as discussed earlier in the constraints of the department, the police, being an institutionalized organization, faces a number of environmental constraints too. Thus, in the improvised SWOT chart each block has two further categories of factors: one in which the department has control of and can improve by managing its affairs better, the other that is beyond the control of the police department (see the italicized section of the list in Chart I.3.2). The developed plan for the police would be addressing the controlable weaknesses and threats to the department leveraging the strenghts and endeavouring to exploit the opportunites available to the department currently.

This assessment allows us to concentrate on the block where we can manage within the department. These are the weaknesses that can be removed or improved. Along with working on the weaknesses, the mentioned blocks of opportunities and strengths can be capitalized on to get maximum leverage while preparing for the threats that the department faces.

New managerialism route

In a general environment of liberalization, globalization and the ascendancy of the markets, that has driven police forces around the world into the new police order, the Indian police today is at the threshold of entering a new era. The 22 September 2006 Supreme Court order that has led to the setting up of regulatory mechanism for police provides for greater accountability to public, some autonomy and some insulation from political interference in its functioning. This heralds a step towards a new beginning for the police in creating a healthy environment for it to operate within. For long the police had been demanding mechanism that could make them accountable to the people they serve and not to the whims and interests of political masters in power. The new mechanism is a progression towards this, but it also places an increased responsibility on the shoulders of the police administrators towards the public.

The new environment—with regulatory bodies such as the Police Boards and State Security Commissions—accepts the principle that the police derive their power from the public and that the police must

Chart I.3.2 SWOT Analysis of the Police Department

Strengths	Weaknesses
• Wide physical and community outreach.[2] • Ability to deliver under pressure despite all odds. • Highly educated and motivated leadership.[3] • Day-to-day contact with the common man. • Huge organizing capability. • Disciplined force capable of working for long duty hours with minimal resources and support. • Uniformity of laws and procedures across the nation, facilitating co-ordination and enforcement. • *Government agency working under the law of the land.* • *Monopoly—no contestability.* • *Old organization with rich traditions and culture.* • *Resourcefulness and expertise in dealing with natural disasters.*	• Traditional bureaucratic organization—slow, insensitive, strong resistance to change, police sub-culture, police ethnocentrism.[4] • Antiquated methods of working—strict hierarchal structure, centralized decision making. • Lack of application of current management practices to the police department—individual driven, top-down approach, outdated management control systems, lack of interagency coordination, lack of motivation and commitment of policemen. • Political and bureaucratic interference in day-to-day functioning. • Shortage of manpower.[5] • Resources crunch—decremental responses. • Poor public image and unsatisfactory public dealing—colonial mindset. • Lack of role clarity—no police performance benchmarks, absence of long-term and strategic planning. • Corruption—lack of ethical framework, unethical conduct, use of extra judicial methods. • Poor training—outdated training curriculum, traditional pedagogical method and lack of organizational support. • Low police morale—culture of mistrust and negativism, autocratic leadership. • Poor performance appraisal system—traits focused approach. • Lack of transparency in selection and posting at cutting edge, rewards and punishments.

(Chart I.3.2 continued)

(Chart I.3.2 continued)

Strengths	Weaknesses
	• Poor salary structure/poor incentives.
	• Half-hearted implementation of police reforms.
	• Multiple control over the department.

	Threats
	• Political interference in recruitment, transfers and postings.
	• Increasing trend towards communalism, terrorism, Maoist and Naxalite activities.
	• Juvenile crime, white-collar crime and economic offences.
	• Large urban agglomerations throwing up organized crime and unprecedented vehicular traffic.[7]
	• Use of sophisticated gadgets and technology in crime by criminals.
	• The increase of the police product in volume, gravity and complexity, aggravated by the expanding international dimension.[8]
	• Limitations of Indian Criminal Justice System, lack of judicial reforms.
	• Rising population and aspirations of youths leading to massive unemployment.
	• The economic and political situation with social and political unrest along with tensions arising out of a rapidly changing society.
	• Growing lack of respect and fear for the institutions like police, judiciary and the legislation in the society.

Opportunities

- Technological advancements.
- New policing order—ascendancy of markets and breaking up of traditional bureaucracies, emergence of new public management.
- Community policing, resposibilization.[6]
- Nature of job—opportunities to help people in distress.
- Emerging highly developed and urbanized society.
- Increasing public awareness for the need of police reforms and change and judicial support.
- New regulatory mechanism for the police—state security commissions and police boards for transparency, autonomy and insulation from political interference in functioning.
- Booming economy, economic liberalization and globalization.
- Government support and increasing dependence of government on police.

- *Backing of enforceable laws and statutes.*
- *Easy accessibility to the political leadership.*

- *Greater acceptance of corruption in society and criminals in politics.*
- *Large floating population in cities, increased movement of people and further migration waves.*[9]
- *Misuse by politicians—accountable to the political bosses.*
- *Climatic changes.*[10]

[2] There are 12,591 police stations in the country, 65.3 per cent are in the rural areas (Government of India, 2006).

[3] The motivation level of the officers gets affected significantly in the present functioning environment as the officers progress in their careers as discussed in Chapter 1.

[4] Police ethnocentrism refers to strong tendency in police to assume that safety and security are the job of police only and looking at the world exclusively through the police lens.

[5] Twenty-five per cent of the total police stations have a strength of 11–20 personnel (Government of India, 2006).

[6] Police in India assume responsibility for safety assurance and quality of life in areas where other agencies fail to take up their responsibilities for any reasons.

[7] By 2030, Asian city dwellers will be numbering 2.6 billion. Almost all future growth will be concentrated in the cities of the developing world that are already battling with problems like poverty, scarcity of drinking water, lack of sanitation and spreading slums (UN figures) providing for a fertile breeding ground for criminals and anti-social activities. Unlike the outlaws of earlier times who took refuge in the forests, the outlaws of today and tomorrow find the vast city population an easy hiding ground.

[8] Emerging forms of crime are: denial of service attacks (in 2007 the systems of an East European country were paralyzed by one such attack); cyber stalking and new forms of international illegal trade. Emergence of social networking sites such as Facebook, Youtube and the emergence of virtual worlds like the 'Second Life' would have policing implications and pose a new challenge for the police. Another challenge is bio-terrorist attacks. According to the Stockholm International Peace Research Institute, the cost to inflict civilian casualties is USD 2000 per square kilometre with conventional weapons, USD 800 with nuclear weapons and only USD 1 with biological weapons.

[9] Mass migrations were prompted by the scarcity of water and food resulting from flooding and desertification. In the situation of shortage of supply, organized crime will exploit the opportunities.

[10] As per the Strategic Survey in 2007 by the International Institute of Strategic Studies, London, the linkage between climate change, security and policing will be unavoidable and intensified.

Source: Conceptualized by the author.

Notes: The un-italicized sentences indicate the areas where the police can improve by managing better.

The italicized sentences indicate the areas beyond control of the police department or that are not being focused on here for developing the marketing plan.

be held accountable through regulatory bodies. There are two alternative courses for the police department to pursue in its search for efficiency and image.

1. *Wait and watch*: The police department can wait and watch for the effects of the conducive external environment to percolate onto the department's functioning. As with the steps to be initiated by the Supreme Court order on setting up of security commissions, police boards, stability in tenures of field officers and complaints authorities in natural course the functioning of police would show improvement. However, the improvement would be limited to the potential of the existing structures, rules and procedures in the department.

2. *New managerialism*: The police can apply 'new managerialism' (Management Accounting: Magazine for Chartered Management Accountants, 1994) which means adoption of the managerial prin- ciples and accounting-based techniques employed in the private sector so that the resources are controlled and allocated in ways that enhance their efficiency and effectiveness. Central to such reforms has been the perceived need for public-sector organizations to be subjected to the discipline of market forces. In this model citizens are treated as consumers and the performance of the government department is subjected to regular audits. Using this emerging concept which has been applied to government departments in the developed nations around the world in the last decade, the police can review their activities, by constructing them as productive processes to be managed in a result-oriented manner. As police performance otherwise is mediocre (given the constraints), with this, the police should go in for external marketing exercise to build up a positive image for itself while improving the existing state of affairs within the department, on the matters that are within their control, as mentioned in the SWOT analysis (Chart I.3.2).

The first alternative would mean that the police is to be a silent spec- tator to the impact of the variables beyond the control of the department and on the issues related to the institutional environment in which it operates, despite the historic opportunity offered by the setting up of regulatory mechanisms to insulate the police and the National Police Mission, as discussed in the situation analysis earlier. The second alter- native aims at working on the matters well within the control of the police department with New Public Management doctrines of removing the difference between the public and the private sector and shifting the emphasis in the police department, wherever permissible, from rules and procedures to 'getting results', making the department more consumer responsive, thereby improving its image and performance. This would be a more proactive approach for the police departments to take.

The strategy for the police departments, therefore, should be to drive organizational change through strategic management—an ongoing process that seeks opportunities to enhance operational efficiencies by identifying internal issues and external influences that hinder organizational sustainability. The focus of the police department should be to create a customer-focused, high-performance new-age entrepreneurial department by working on the weaknesses and preparing for the threats, while the opportunities and strengths as mentioned in the SWOT analysis (Chart I.3.2) should be capitalized on to get maximum leverage. While referring to the private enterprise, there are terms like 'learning organization', 'high performance organization', and so on. In referring to the government organization the term 'entrepreneurial organisation' is used, which means an organization that has transformed from the industrial-era public system (Osborne and Plastrik, 1996).

Such a transformation can happen in an organization like the police in India only by its reinvention. Reinvention means fundamental transformation of systems and organizations to increase their efficiency, effectiveness, adaptability and capacity to innovate. This transformation is accomplished by changing their purpose, incentives, accountability, power structure and culture (Osborne and Plastrik, 1996) as it is not just important for the department to do better this year by comparing with the last year figures but to keep on getting better.

David Osborne and Peter Plastrik in their book, *Banishing Bureaucracy* explain:

> Reinvention is about replacing bureaucratic organizations and behavior with entrepreneurial organizations and behavior. It is about creating public organizations and systems that habitually innovate, that continually improve their quality without having to be pushed from outside. It is about creating a public sector that has a built-in drive to improve, what some call a 'self-renewing system'.

Something diametrically opposite to a stagnant department that police has remained for over a century. While applying metaphors and helpful management techniques from business, we have to guard against the business myth that the police can be improved by running it like a business enterprise. As discussed earlier there are critical differences between the police and private-sector realities that would necessitate modifications and careful selection of appropriate management principles and techniques.

Reinvention strategies[11]

Beneath the complexity of the working of government departments, including the police department, there are a few fundamental levers, according to David Osborne and Peter Plastrik,[12] that make the public institutions work as they do. Changing these levers results in cascading changes throughout the organization. For each lever there is a corresponding strategy and these strategies have been grouped by Osborne and Plastrik into five Cs. They are—core strategy, consequence strategy, customer strategy, control strategy and culture strategy. These strategies are complementary to each other and the use of one strategy would need the support of other strategies also.

The *core strategy* determines the purpose of the public system. It helps the department to obtain clarity on the purpose, role and direction that the system is taking. For example, should the department outsource its activities? The core strategy is reflected in a mission statement prepared by the department.

The *consequence strategy* determines the incentives built into the system. This can mean performance measurement as well as creating incentives and punishments for the police department.

The *customer strategy* creates some accountability to the customer. By this there is pressure on the department to improve results and not just manage. Also, the target for the department becomes customer satisfaction.

The *control strategy* determines where the decision-making power lies. Rather than responding to the situations or customer needs, the department today responds to orders from the top officials, who in turn receive their orders from the political bosses. This strategy shifts the power from outside to the department and in the department from the top to the frontline. Thereafter, taking a step further, it shifts the power from the frontline to the community through community empowerment.

---

[11] This portion has been drawn from Osborne and Plastrik, 1996.
[12] David Osborne and Peter Plastrik have been the pioneers in bringing out literature on reinventing the government. Their works on this topic have been highly acclaimed and have become reference sources.

The *culture strategy* determines the culture of the public system, including the values, norms, attitudes and expectations of the employees.

Segmentation and targeting

Segmentation

The first step in the implementation of the reinvention strategy is to define and classify the whole strata of the customers and the stakeholders, to facilitate prioritization and balancing of the needs/conflicting needs in the organization.

Citizens and community: The police department exists for the citizens and the community, and is duty bound to provide quality service. There is a need to create a positive image of the department, which has historically and inherently been dismal, and to educate people about the services provided. For this segment, the results can be achieved by the use of control strategy (community empowerment) and customer strategy (putting the citizen at the centre of policing efforts by proactive policing, customer quality assurance and creating favourably inclined customer equity making the effective use of external and interactive marketing tools).

Policemen and employees: Another extremely important segment, the internal customers, would be the policemen in the department. Police managers and employees' bodies have exhibited a traditional resistance to police organizational change (Skolnich and Bayley, 1986) and to democratize police organizations, both in terms of their internal structuring and their external public interface, leave alone implementation of private-sector mentalities and technologies aimed at increasing productivity. Bill Creech in *The Five Pillars of TQM* has given a combination of five actions for employees that make teams successful (Creech, 1994). This could be a useful template for the police department:

Trust them	after training them
Empower them	with wide latitude
Aim them	with objectives and goals
Measure them	for feedback and comparison
Support them	with backing and resources

Politicians, media and other stakeholders: In the present environment, the accountability of the police to people comes through the elected representatives, which makes them the most influencial stakeholders. The police department swims in a sea of politics and, without a map for the future, the department is like a rudderless ship left to the mercy of currents in the ocean. The department should therefore have a vision which should be internally marketed to the policemen and externally to people in general (including important stakeholders like the politicians). This vision should also be translated in terms that hold interest for them, for example, better satisfaction for people with police will result in more appreciative citizenry for the government. Additionally, it is also necessary that the police keep the politicians involved in the reform activities so that they understand and also share a part of the credit of the good work done, by allowing them to release the data.[13] Thus, a well-developed vision, working in partnership, briefing and sharing the credit can be the key to a successful relationship.

Compliers: The primary customer of the police department is the community at large, represented by the elected officials. However, those it deals with day in and day out are the 'compliers', such as the drivers, polluters, and so on, and they are also important for police. Therefore, for the compliance organization, like the police, the customer strategy will be more complex. Then there are non-compliers: people and organizations that break the law.[14] The police department has to pay attention to all these categories. The police department can use customer standards and customer voice to improve their service to the compliers as a means to improve their voluntary compliance. Many compliance organizations like the Madison Police Department have used the approach of 'winning compliance'. In this rather than concentrating on catching non-compliers, they have put more energy into encouraging voluntary compliance. As per the public strategies group, a consulting firm that pioneered this approach the steps involved are:

 (i) Involve compliers in helping make the rules.
 (ii) Educate compliers about what is expected of them.
 (iii) Provide facilities that facilitate compliance such as police helplines.

---

[13] A case worth mentioning is the 'Good Policing Competition' organized by the police in Jalandhar range in the year 2003. The chief minister's approval was taken right in the beginning for his presence in the prize distribution function and presentation, to be held at the conclusion of this competition. This resulted in an all round participation and total involvement from everyone, and in the end, the chief minister could appreciate the good work done (see Appendix 4).

[14] In the year 2006, a total of 62,07,945 people were arrested by police under IPC and SLL crimes in the country (Government of India, 2006).

(iv) Establish quality standards, guarantees, and redress for service to compliers.

(v) Give compliers feedback on their level of compliance.

(vi) Create effective incentives and consequence for compliance and non-compliance.

Targeting

The application of different reinvention strategies, in the context of the police, for different customers is mentioned in the Table I.3.1. To implement each of these strategies there are tools that can be used to get the desired transformation in the police department. Some of the useful tools are: community empowerment, customer quality assurance, breaking habits, winning minds, providing a vision, leadership, employee empowerment, training, performance related rewards and punishment, and so on.

Positioning

The police department would like to offer greater value to the customers by positioning itself as an agency in the service of the people and upholding rule of the law. It should make it clear in the customer strategy it adopts.

The customer strategy makes public organizations directly accountable to customers. (Of course, the chain of command in the organization will continue to exist, but the overall accountability will be to customers.) In the current political system, the police department functions under the control of the elected representatives, and the people in general have little say on the quality of service they receive. It is the interest groups, voters and constituencies that are cared about. The customer strategy puts the citizen in the loop and makes the customer the lever.

The basic paradigm shift required in the approach of the department would be to treat the citizen of the country as a customer.

For the police department this would mean a transformation from being a traditional militaristic bureaucracy[15] to a *new age entrepreneurial department* (Chart I.3.3).

[15] Based on the Police Act of 1861 the present police organization is not suited for the present times because an authoritarian police working under an imperialist regime cannot function well in an independent democratic country (National Police Commission, 1977–81: para 62.5).

Table I.3.1 Appropriate Strategies for Different Stakeholders in the Context of Police

Target segment	Objectives	Strategy for the segment and the metatools
Citizens and community	To provide value service, create a positive image of the department that is in conformity with the performance, to educate about the services provided.	Customer strategy—customer centric policing, create customer equity. Core strategy—identify and lead on issues that would benefit the society, strategic management, resource leverage. Culture strategy—proactive policing, challenging the current practices. Consequence strategy—customer quality assurance. Control strategy—community empowerment, Public–Private Partnerships. Effective use of external and interactive marketing tools.
Politicians, regulators, judiciary, media, pressure groups and other stakeholders	To create a friendly image, to elicit cooperation and generate atmosphere of trust.	Core strategy—strategic intent and architecture, police policy, media policy. Customer strategy—building partnerships, sharing forums, participation in activities in coordination, police media relations, cross agency processes. Control strategy—organizational empowerment, independent regulatory bodies. Effective use of external and interactive marketing tools.
Policemen, employees	To train and motivate for effective customer–policemen contact, work as a team to provide greater customer satisfaction, provide high quality customer–policemen interaction.	Consequence strategy—performance related rewards and punishment, training, motivation, SOPs. Control strategy—employee empowerment. Customer strategy—efficiency in police–public interaction. Culture strategy—breaking habits, winning minds, ethical conduct, use of appropriate technology, cooperation and horizontal linkages. Core strategy—providing a vision and leadership. Focus on both internal and interactive marketing before the external marketing.
Compliers	Use the approach of 'winning compliance'.	Customer strategy—involve compliers in helping make the rules. Consequence strategy—create effective incentives and consequence, establish quality standards, guarantees and redress for service to compliers. Culture strategy—educate compliers, helplines to facilitate compliance.

Source: Conceptualized by the author.

Chart I.3.3   Basic Paradigm Shift Required in the Approach of the Department

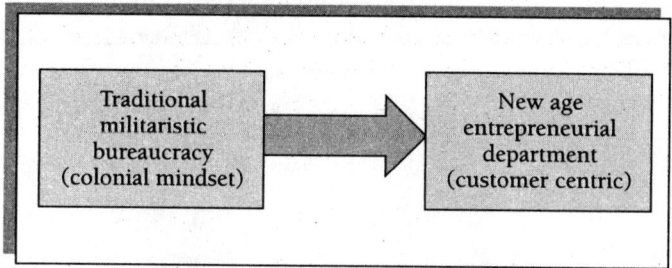

Source: Conceptualized by the author.

Managing the police service in the new-age entrepreneurial department (customer centric) would mean managing service differentiation by providing the kind of sevice that people need and require today, managing service quality by setting standards, and managing service productivity and value by providing effective service economically. These are all equally critical to the overall performance and image of the police department (Chart I.3.4).

The marketing mix

Today, the single most significant marketing doctrine is the marketing mix, which encompasses all of controllable tactical tools of the agency that it uses to influence a market segment to accomplish its objectives. This deals with the specific actionable elements of the programme used in marketing. These tactical tools are used to influence customers and in law enforcement they can help realize the police department's goal of high performance and a good image.

In choosing the appropriate tools as part of the marketing plan for the police, we must remain cognizant of the internal and external environments and uniqueness of services offered by the police department. The service marketing for the police requires more than just the traditional external marketing. As the police department's problems stem from a formidable and complex mix of weaknesses within and outside the organization, as discussed in the SWOT analysis, which cannot be addressed only by external marketing, much more will be required. Considering the complexity of the organization, two more elements—internal and interactive marketing—will be required to supplement the external marketing, in drawing a complete plan for the police department.

Chart I.3.4   Managing Service Differentiation, Quality and Productivity of the Police as New-age Entrepreneurial Department

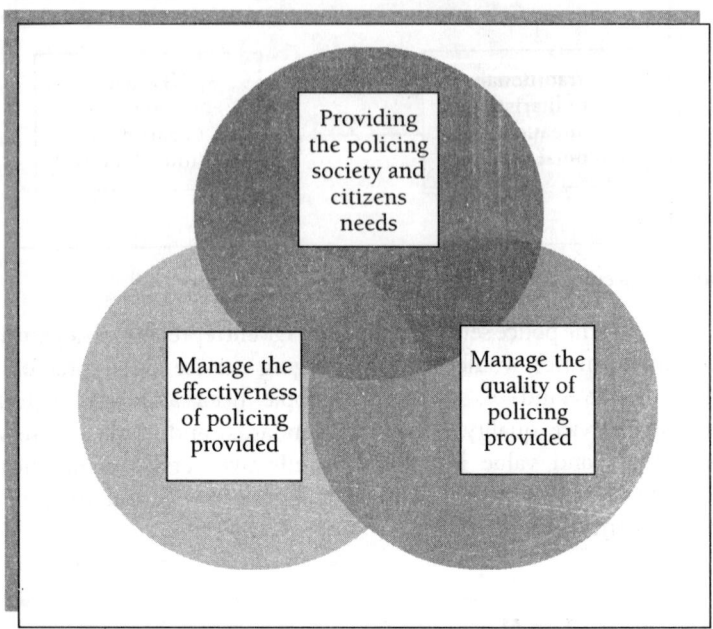

Providing the policing society and citizens needs

Manage the effectiveness of policing provided

Manage the quality of policing provided

Source: Conceptualized by the author.

Internal marketing

Police work consists of mainly routine work, in spite of the general impression about the special police operations and sensational investigations. Painstaking, unceasing and accurate work of each unit in the great machine contributes to the overall performance. The success or failure of a police organization is spelled out by the individual conduct of its members. Many times an officer is alone and must determine his course of action in a matter of seconds on the spot. The propriety of his course of action may subsequently engage the attention of a court of law and media for days, or even weeks. The other things like the media exercise, the websites, and so on, are supplementary; no doubt they are important at their own place, but it is completely outweighed by the effect of complete organization.

In order to achieve the target of customer-oriented policemen, there is a need to implant this idea first among the policemen, train them with professional skills of better customer satisfaction. This is done through internal marketing. Internal marketing is an important 'implementation' tool for an organization like the police. It aids communication and helps to overcome any resistance to change and motivates the employees. It informs and involves all the staff in new initiatives and strategies and promotes team work. The main difference is that the customers are staff and colleagues from the police department itself.

Interactive marketing

The conduct of field officers creates a lasting impression on the minds of customers. Whenever there is a sloppy job done by an officer, no amount of secondary promotion activity can help. The skills of quality police-citizen interaction are essential for policemen, as the perceived service quality depends upon the quality of this interaction. The police officer should be able to see the public as client with stress on the notion of service. The attitude and behaviour of each individual agent is crucial for the image of the whole police department. Attitude, language and body talk of the policemen are important aspects that influence interaction in different practical situations. One negative incident can annihilate all positive experiences a customer has had before. A constable on the street is not an individual but a representative of the entire force, by his conduct and appearance the image of the police department is formed in the eyes of the public. This is where the interactive marketing is very important for the police department.

In fact both these marketing, that is, the internal as well as the inter-active should preceed and prepare the ground for the external marketing. Based on this framework the total marketing plan for the police would incorporate external, internal and interactive components. Therefore, the three pronged marketing strategy for police would be consisting of internal, interactive and external components as depicted in Chart I.3.5.

The many actionable elements for marketing the police can be collected into eight groups of variables called the 8Ps: *people, product, price, promotion, pace, process, place and politics.* The 'people' refers to the personnel in the organization, 'product' would mean customer offering and address the issue of customer solution, 'price' would address cost of policing, 'place' refers to convenience and would cover the resources available to address them, 'promotion' is about communication, 'pace' is about responsiveness, 'process' about effectiveness of systems of the

Chart I.3.5   The Three Pronged Marketing Strategy for the Police

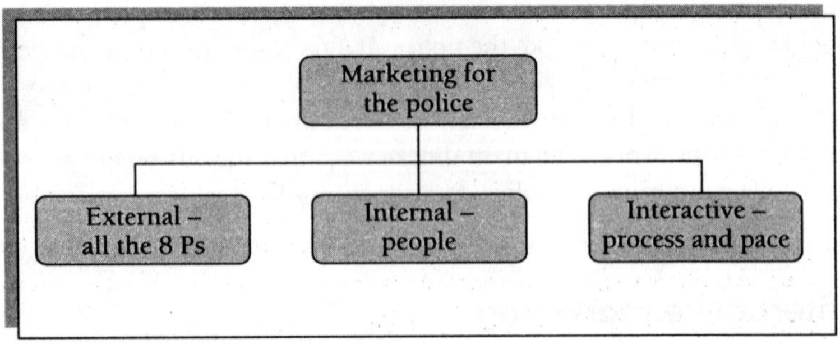

```
                    ┌──────────────────┐
                    │  Marketing for   │
                    │   the police     │
                    └──────────────────┘
            ┌─────────────┼─────────────┐
 ┌────────────────┐ ┌────────────────┐ ┌────────────────┐
 │  External –    │ │  Internal –    │ │  Interactive – │
 │  all the 8 Ps  │ │  people        │ │ process and pace│
 └────────────────┘ └────────────────┘ └────────────────┘
```

Source: Conceptualized by the author.

organization in addressing the customer concerns and 'politics' is about the interface of the organization with the political environment. All the Ps would address the aspect of external marketing, while the internal marketing would be addressed by the 'people' whereas the 'pace' and 'process' would also mainly cover the plan for interactive marketing of police department (see Chart I.3.5).

The 8Ps are discussed in Part II of this book to provide the *action plan for reinventing the police using the marketing framework*. In presenting the recommendations the 8Ps format is adopted, for categorizing different aspects that the organization needs to address today, and the reinvention strategies are applied to them.

The first P, 'people', which in the marketing framework means the policemen and the employees of the police department, would be the key and pivotal to any transformation in service delivery that is envisaged for the police department.[16] Some of the important issues that need to be addressed today in relation to the people within the department are identified in the SWOT analysis (see Chart I.3.2). The police force in India remains poorly trained, working under antiquated rules management and structures that have long outlived their utility, a demoralized insensitive lot enjoying little sense of equity and fairness within the department, prone to adopting unethical methods of working and has exhibited a strong resistance to change (National Police Commission, 1977–81: para 2.19, 62.6).

As discussed in the STP analysis (Table I.3.2), the mix of strategies adopted for the internal customer are the control strategy by employee empowerment, consequence strategy by performance related rewards/ punishment and training, culture strategy by breaking habits and

---

[16] The total strength of the Indian Police stood at about 14,10,000 policemen in the year 2006.

winning minds including the organizational culture, values and the motivational issues in police and the core strategy by providing a vision and appropriate leadership model for the department (see the following table).

Table I.3.2   Appropriate Strategies for Different Stakeholders Using STP Analysis

Control strategy	Employee empowerment (Part II, Chapter 1)
Culture strategy	Organizational culture (Part II, Chapter 2)
	Values (Part II, Chapter 3)
Consequence strategy	Measuring (Part II, Chapter 4)
	Training (Part II, Chapter 5)
Core strategy	Aiming (Part II, Chapter 6)

Source: Conceptualized by the author.

In keeping with policemen's critical role envisaged in reinvention efforts, five chapters are devoted to 'people'; each of the control, consequence, culture (two chapters) and core strategies (two chapters) are discussed in separate chapters.

The other seven Ps are discussed in Chapters 7 to 14 of Part II.

PART II
RECOMMENDATIONS

Empowerment 1

A s the most important asset of the police department is not their land and buildings, but the policemen and employees,[1] their commitment, motivation and alignment have a direct bearing on the overall performance of the organization. In the police department, undoubtedly, spectacular results can be achieved by working on the vast manpower available to the department.[2] However, Jeffery Pfeiffer in his book *The Human Equation*, discusses unfortunate findings of his extensive work, summarizing that only about half of today's organizations and their managers believe that human resources really do matter and only one-eight of today's organizations seriously work on treating human resources as capital investment to be developed and managed.

Employee empowerment

With the implementation of the Supreme Court Order of 22 September 2006, on making the police independent, the police departments in India are expected to gain greater autonomy in their functioning. However, any functional autonomy that would come to the police departments in due

[1] Singapore police force vision statement enunciates 'our people are our most valued assets'.
[2] The crux of efficient policing in our view is effective and amiable street presence of a well qualified, trained and motivated constable (National Police Commission, 1977–81: para 2.18).

course of time can translate into efficiency and effectiveness only when it is coupled with another shift of power—from the top managers in the department to the frontline officers. In the absence of this, there is a danger that greater autonomy would only result in the top police officers tightening their grip over the employees. Though the police organizations have power, authority, influence, status, prestige, privilege and personal rights distributed throughout the organization in a particular way, it is ironic that the policeman who symbolizes power and authority to the man on the street may share little of this in his own department. In the police department the rank and file members are often psychologically-deprived persons who would like to have more say in what goes on in the police department. In the event of any crisis or incidents of malpractices coming to light, typical response of the administrators in the Indian police has been to shift the decision-making power upwards and curtailing the discretion at the cutting edge. In the Indian police authoritative command structure encourages dependence and subordination, centralized management puts a premium on compliance rather than on initiative (Goldstein, 1990) and rule orientation encourages passivity and in the paramilitary model officers are expected to behave immaturely (Cizanckas and Hanna, 1977: 9). However, at a time when the police have been tasked with implementing proactive, community-oriented approaches to crime and employee empowerment may offer significant advantages over the traditional top-down police administration.[3] To empower the frontline policemen would mean to give them authority that goes with their responsibility, allow them a say in the affairs of the police department, provide an environment where they can recognize, care about and tend to citizen needs.[4]

The early police organizational structure of Japan in 1947 closely resembled the Weberian paramilitary and the Japanese police were reportedly 'oppressive and even instituted a "thought control" operation to blot out any thinking contrary to overt support of the regime in power', something like the German police during World War II (Alarid and Wang, 1997). It was the post World War II rebuilding of Japan that brought a police system which was decentralized and democratic; this was headed by the National Public Safety Commission. From 1945 to

---

[3] The constabulary should no longer be treated as a cadre meant only for duties of a mechanical character as visualized by the 1902 commission. They should be recruited and trained so that they could also be deployed on duties involving exercise of discretion and judgement, with due regard to the paramount need for securing public cooperation and understanding in any situation (National Police Commission, 1977–81: para 2.17).

[4] The Congress felt that there should be a systematic empowerment of constables by assigning them task involving responsibility such as investigation of cases, enquiry into complaints and community policing task (Resolution passed by XXXV All India Police Science [AIPS] Congress, Source www.bprd.gov.in).

1948, the US occupation policymakers[5] planted the seeds of reform and carefully cultivated the system until it became the envy of other industrialized nations. If the Japanese policing is indeed the 'best' in the world, then part of the credit belongs to an earlier form of the US police system which served as the model for the Japanese reform (Alarid and Wang, 1997). In 1954, Japan enacted a Police Law to restructure the police appropriate to cultural needs (Box II.1.1).

Box II.1.1   Japanese Police and Theory Z

The Police Law, 1954 used principles resembling Management Theory Z[6] to rejuvenate a four-level centralized bureaucracy while maintaining a community service orientation. The first level was the National Public Safety Commission which functioned as supervisor of the National Police Agency and to sustain political neutrality. The second level contained seven regional bureaus which supervised the prefectural police. As of July 1996, there were a total of 220,000 police officers and 30,000 civilian employees working for the prefectural police. The prefectural police and Metropolitan Police Department in Tokyo are further divided into district police stations which constitute the third layer. The bottom layer consists of police boxes. As of 1995 April, 1,261 district police stations supervised a total of 6,498 urban *koban* and 8,379 rural *chuzaisho* police boxes throughout the country. In the Japanese police, non-specialized career paths are directly related to achieving rank through a nine-tier promotional system.[7] Career paths within the department differ greatly between 'first-liner' and 'elite' officers.[8] Management Theory Z provides the consistency in structure and management processes which allows a national police force to be decentralized into a semi-autonomous neighbourhood-centred system of fixed posts, referred to as *koban*s in urban areas and *chuzaisho* in rural sectors. A three-shift system is working for urban police boxes. Each *koban* is headed by a police sergeant or higher ranking officer who is the single most important officer in the police box. Sergeants are directly accountable for the actions of their subordinates and middle managers frequently defer their authority to the patrol officer without losing respect over subordinates.

Source: Alarid and Wang, 1997.

---

[5] Credit goes to General MacArthur who made police reform one of his first priorities and invited two noted experts on policing to Japan. Arriving in 1946, these were Oscar G. Olander, a specialist on rural police systems and Lewis J. Valentine, former New York City police commissioner. Valentine suggested a complete overhaul of the Japanese system to see the Japanese police force patterned on that of New York City. General Robert L. Eichelberger was an important aide in this campaign.
[6] Borrowing from the management concepts of Japanese firms, Ouchi created Theory Z: consensual decisions, infrequent appraisal, slow promotion and comprehensive concern. Theory Z also included long-term employment, moderately specialized career paths and implicit/informal appraisal with explicit/formalized measures.

For the empowerment to have any real meaning in the police department this would have to be embedded by re-engineering the organizational components. Most organizations that embrace employee empowerment take different measures for smooth transfer of power. Some use total quality management and business process reengineering to let the employees redesign their work processes and some break down rigid functional silos that organizational bureaucratic design has created (Osborne and Plastrik, 1996). The police departments in India too would have to embrace these measures to varying degree. Tools that could be useful in the police department for empowering the frontline policemen are participation, delayering and decentralization in the police department.

Participatory management

The police management in India occurs within an old model of quasi-military organization that is recognized by its reliance upon direct hierarchical control and rigid superior–supervisor relationships in an ascending order from the lowest ranks to the highest, which, in contrast to the lower ranks, contains most of the decision making power. Typically, 'decision making is rarely participative or collegial across rank lines' (Bayley, 1994), whereas when officers do receive such influence upward, they seem to be more satisfied with their jobs, with their supervisors and managers, and they are more likely to express identification with their organization and feel a sense of responsibility for meeting organizational goals.[9] Essentially, all ranks require an opportunity to influence one another about their individual functions within the organization.

[7] The rank of the Japanese police are from top to bottom: superintendent general (*keishisokan*), superintendent supervisor (*keishikan*), chief superintendent (*keishicho*), senior superintendent (*keishisei*), superintendent (*keishi*), police inspector (*keibu*), assistant police inspector (*keibuho*), police sergeant (*junsabucho*), senior police officer (*junsacho*) and police officer (*junsa*).

[8] First liners are the lower ranking police officers with entry as police officer at the lowest rank in Japanese police. Most first liner officers (80 per cent of the force) work in police boxes for the duration of their career. First liners are transferred among the bottom-level positions with salary increases every six months and regular promotions based on seniority and assured of retirement at the rank of sergeant or above. The elite officers graduate from Tokyo University's law department and enter the system as an assistant inspector. Elite officers stay in the *koban* for a short stint and are quickly promoted to upper-middle positions. They are transferred among different divisions within the system.

[9] Now with greater education and mass consciousness there should be an effort to promote motivation by participation and shared goals (National Police Commission, 1977: para 62.7).

Administrators in the Indian Police need to go to greater lengths to ensure that the organization has mechanisms by which a variety of important psychological and working requirements are met in daily routine activities, not just when crisis occurs and immediate mobilization of effort required 'to put out fires' created by certain situations.

The Singapore Police Force (SPF), the premier law enforcement agency in the Republic of Singapore responsible for the safety and security of the island state, presents an exemplary model for supportive environment for learning in an organization. The SPF has a staff strength of more than 12,000 full-time officers in diverse units separable by staff and line functions. The SPF actually works effectivly on a relativly flat heirarchical structure to allow for greater ownership and faster resolution of problems (Box II.1.2).

Then, without doubt, like any work-based organization, it is crucial to bring all members of the police organization on board during processes of change or transition and this is best achieved through participatory practices (Goldstein, 1990). In the Netherlands employees are entitled to participate in the process by which strategic decision are taken by the organization for which they work. The establishment of a works council representing the personnel is laid down by the Works Councils Act. Each regional force has its own works council, which consults regularly with force management about operational management and general personnel issues. The works council has the right to be consulted about proposed reorganizations and the consent of the works council is required for decisions to alter policy in certain other fields such as training and the quality of work (Police Department of Netherlands, 2004).

Participative management techniques have reaped great benefits for industry in terms of productivity, quality and worker satisfaction, but such power-sharing arrangements seem to have found little acceptance in law enforcement circles in India. It may be somewhat self-deceptive to place a great deal of faith in authoritarian management styles which may be only required in certain crisis situations. The research suggests that participative police administration can help make employees feel more valued and supported by their organization, more committed to its objectives, can cultivate better labour-management relations, and may even promote greater productivity (Wuestewald and Steinheider, 2006) (Box II.1.3).

The experience from the BAPD experiment suggests that probably the most difficult aspect of undertaking a participative approach to management is for senior executives to accept the decisions of others. Having reached to a position of authority, in an autocratic setup after being conditioned and on the receiving end for the entire length of

---

Box II.1.2   Singapore Police Force Leadership Group

From their experience Singapore Police realized the need to empower their groung officers to act decisively in the course of their work. They equip the officers with skills in leadership competency and allow the officers to gain easy access to procedures and distilled policy positions. The Commissioner, Khoo Boon Hui, carries a dream of empowering every officer with the decision making skills of a Commissioner of Police.

At the strategic level, the SPF adopts a collective leadership model, manifested by way of the Leadership Group (LG). The SPF rejects the notion of a 'superstar' leader but instead emphasises collective wisdom. The LG comprises of leaders from various units. Though each member is a leader of a self-sufficient unit with different mandates, the LG serves as a common ground for collective thinking. It would appear that the collective leadership model is in inherent conflict with the hierarchical structure bound by rank differentiation, as with all uniformed organizations. But this is not so in the SPF. In fact, the duality compliments, not contradicts, each other. This is possible because the SPF operates a rather flat hierarchy. The duality allows for greater flexibility to deal with situations. In times of crises, where command and control is necessary for quick response, the LG is able to exercise authoritative leadership. The LG is facilitated through several platforms for the congruence of minds. At the highest and most strategic level, the SPF has the annual corporate retreat where LG members gather in an informal setting to chart directions for a new year. On a bi-weekly basis, the LG also participates in the Leadership Group Forum (LGF) where they mull over strategic issues with long-term impacts or brainstorm innovation solutions to current problems in an informal setting. The forum is normally facilitated by young officers, who are in turn exposed to strategic thinking of the LG. At more formal meetings such as Commissioner of Police's Command Conference (CPCC) and CP's Staff Conference (CPSC), issues such as command, operational and developmental issues are debated. These range from the formulation of policies, long-term strategies and short-term goals to the softer aspects such as organizational development.

Source: Singapore Police Commissioner, 2007.

their careers, they should turn around and relinquish a good portion of their power is perhaps asking too much. Yet, this is precisely what must happen if officer empowerment is to have any real meaning (Wuestewald and Steinheider, 2006).

Management delayering

The shift towards a more localized, community-oriented policing style with participatory management, which is required today, demands more

---

Box II.1.3   BAPD Leadership Team

Some police agencies have experimented with various aspects of employee participation. One such agency is the Broken Arrow, Oklahoma, Police Department (BAPD). Since 2003 the agency has had participative management in the form of a cross-functional steering committee called the 'leadership team'. The BAPD leadership team was conceived as a way of incorporating frontline personnel into the important decision making processes of the department. Comprising of 12 individuals representing the labour union (the Fraternal Order of Police or the FOP), management, and most of the divisions, units, ranks and functions in the department, the leadership team's bylaws established it as an independent body, with authority to effect change and make binding decisions on a wide range of policy issues, working conditions, and strategic matters. Sworn and non-sworn members of the team are selected by a variety of methods, including direct appointment by the department administration and open election by peers. Membership on the leadership team was never based on rank and the team's composition has become more representative of the lower echelons of the department. Notably, the chief's office is not represented on the team and all decisions are made democratically. The chief of police retains control of the team's agenda, but once an issue is referred to it, its decisions are considered final and binding on all concerned. The first two years of the BAPD Leadership Team were a whirlwind of activity, as it took on a series of difficult issues. Essentially, the team created new policy on how the agency recruits, hires, evaluates, disciplines, rewards and promotes its people, and how it uses force, drives its cars, trains its officers and protects their wellbeing. The team took on nearly every issue that typically causes problems for police agencies. Additionally, the team improved process, streamlined procedures and aided in problem resolution.

Source: Wuestewald and Steinheider, 2006.

flexible responses to community problems; police supervisors for such a working are required to promote, rather than restrict, creativity and problem-solving approaches (Birzer, 1996). Police Departments in India have 12 ranks, from the constable to the director general of police and multiple layers where no decisions are taken, some of these layers only add to delays, clashes and rigidity in functioning.[10] Management delayering eliminates such layers of middle level officers, that perform overlapping functions. Peter Drucker in his classic book *The Practice of Management* had recommended seven layers as maximum necessary for any organization, but that was in 1954. Tom Peters in his another classic

---

[10] A plethora of ranks and lateral entry at senior levels should be reduced. The Congress felt that there should be only three levels of entry in the police. The first level shall be of constables and the third the IPS. The second level should be decided by the concerned states (www.bprd.gov.in).

book *Thriving on Chaos* in 1987 recommends maximum five layers for very complex firms. Much of the problem of sluggishness comes from excessive layering and supervision. The files moves up and down through multilple layers, only adding to the delay, while the decision is taken only at the top. For example, Dowdell of Du Pont suggest that top management can go from 30 signatures to one, but it is painful, which is why most move so slow (Peters, 1987: 362).

The extra staff taken out from such delayering can be put in the field. To ensure direct accountability of the executive staff to the chief and improve performance, the Washington State Police (see Box II.12.2) eliminated the assistant chief's position, created the Management Services Bureau and civilianized two positions formerly held by captains: administrator of the Human Resources Division and director of the Budget and Fiscal Services Division (Serpas, 2004). In India, likewise, some posts can be done away with and some may be redrafted towards meeting the emerging requirements such as the requirement for strategic officer in the police department[11] and improved quality can be brought about even within the existing strength of the civil police by larger numbers at the middle levels of assistant sub-inspector/sub-inspector/inspector offset by somewhat smaller numbers at the lower levels of Constables (National Police Commission, 1977–81: para 50.38).

However, as mentioned earlier, delayering in itself is not a solution unless the power is passed on down to the field staff and there is a strong sense of self-efficacy in the field staff.

Organizational decentralization

A 2002 national survey of police departments in the US revealed that although 70 per cent of the agencies had decentralized some operations in support of community policing, only 22 per cent had reduced bureaucratic hierarchy or pushed authority and decision making down in the organization to any significant degree (Fridell, 2004). The Turkish police organizational structures have changed dramatically since their inception and it is likely that further organizational changes and restructuring in police services will take place in the near future. Currently, there is a trend slowly towards decentralization from the existing highly centralized system. However, although there is evidence of decentralization, it is likely to take long time to realize a decentralized policing system in Turkey (Ayden, 1996).

---

[11] Strategic manager for police department discussed later under *1.7 Vision*.

Such a problem is not confined to the US and Turkey, but is more pronounced within the police departments in India. Empowerment would necessitate shift of control from top-level officers to the districts and the police stations in field. Though much of work is to be done in the police stations and districts, there are many wings operating from the central police office also. Such wings need to be kept at the minimum and the work needs to be handled mostly at the district level. High priority should be given to the restructuring and the strengthening of the police station—the basic and the most important unit of all police work and policing where fulfillment of the organizational goals of the police department get tested (National Police Commission, 1977–81: para 50: 2). In restructuring the National Police Commission of 1977 (para 50.29) important recommendations were made. In the restructured hierarchy, all police stations with a crime figure of 300 cognizable IPC offences, and above and important police stations requiring sizeable manpower should be placed under inspectors. Similarly, in police stations with a crime record of over 900, no officer below the rank of deputy superintendent of police/assistant superintendent of police should be the Station House Officer. When this takes place, the officer would perform dual functions, that is, he will be the SDPO or Circle Officer plus the Station House Officer. This would imply that the next supervisory level will be the additional superintendent of police or superintendent of police. The commission felt that this will add to the general efficiency of the police stations and improve the quality of investigation.

Similarly, the policing at the district level needs to be strengthened. One way of doing this could be by raising the rank level for holding the charge particularly in the bigger districts from that of senior superintendent of police to the level of inspector general of police. For this, larger towns having population of more than 10 lakhs can be made into commissionerates, a recommendation also made by the Sorabjee police reforms committee. This will ensure that larger number of officers are available to serve the people at the district level, rather than remote controlling the districts from the headquaters, cut off from the ground realities.

In such restructuring, the headquater should have a skeletal existence playing the role of coordinator and minimum essential administrative functions.[12] The staff at the headquaters should be seek to identify and exploit opportunities for interlinkages. The out-of-touch headquater

---

[12] See *The Tribune*, 13 September 2006. Enquiries made by *The Tribune* show that the seniors at the state police headquaters have little work to do. With so many DGPs and ADGPs, little is done with regard to law and order and normalizing functioning of police stations on the ground. Coffee gossip, golf and club are the pastime of these seniors at Chandigarh.

staff should not be doing 'Ivory Tower Planning' and making the heavy-handed operations strategies for the district units but in its place there should be what has been termed by Prahalad in his book, *Competing for Future*, as enlightened 'collective strategy' formulation along with the field units. The role of the headquarter core–top officers should be limited to forming the broad policy framework, laying down key state objectives supported by the performance indicators for police, giving the direction in which the police forces in the districts should operate. The operation of the policy and the service delivery should be decentralized to local police and local authorities that may be allowed greater managerial and operational discretion within the policy framework set by the headquarter. Thus, separating the steering and rowing, the 'steering' function remains central but the 'rowing' function of the police needs to be decentralized. The same should further apply to the districts, the field staff should be given greater freedom in planning the operational aspects rather than the district headquarter.

Organizational structure for the districts/units

For the Indian Police, in the districts/units, an organizational structure which allows meaningful and constant exchanges between superiors and subordinates participatory management is part of the answer. Likert (1961) has used the term 'linking pin' function to characterize the supervisor or manager in that form of organization which gives such staff members influence upward and downward. In such an organization, each hierarchical level has its functioning 'linking pin' personnel, usually a supervisor, who is there to ensure that channels of communication between levels of the organization remain open and operating continuously. In this way, top men in the districts/units do not lose touch with the daily needs of subordinates and avenues are open for upward communication. This organizational concept is illustrated in the in Chart II.1.1.

Likert has given an important functional aspect of organizational families for this kind of organizational pattern. Each 'family' is made up of a supervisor and his subordinates; the function of the groups is to meet regularly, to talk fully and freely about work problems. The supervisor communicates ongoing problems upward to higher levels so that remedial action and adjustment can take place at the appropriate level of decision making in the organization. Decisions can than be based upon full information. Informal groups will always exist among employees, informal groups which exist among rank and file members of the police

Chart II.1.1   Linking Pin Organizational Structure

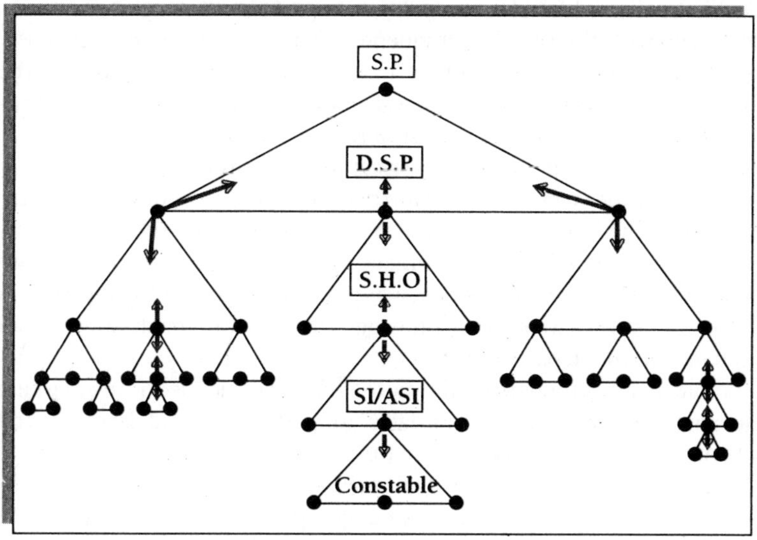

Source: Likert, 1961.

organization who are dissatisfied and unhappy may lead to criminal behaviour. Under the open system of communication, this form of behaviour is less likely to occur, and if it does tend to arise, corrective measures can be taken early before real damage is done. This is not surprising under the present strictly hierarchical form of organization; the district chief of police is often the last person to learn about important specific problems at the patrolmen's level. Just an improvement in upward and downward communication would be of considerable assistance to the police chief and to other top officers in the department and would lead to greater organization commitment and job satisfaction among the lower level police officers.

Employee suggestion and grievance programmes

In the police department, supervision is usually based upon a pattern of downward communication, from higher-ranking members to lower-ranking members, with less opportunity for lower-ranking members to communicate upward other than to acknowledge receiving an order to carry out. A spillover effect is the extension of this pattern on expression of grievances and suggestions from below and an absence of a flexible mechanism by which communication from below to higher positions can occur with the ease and frequency often needed. In another sense, grievances in such organizations can be said to exist because of the absence of appropriate informal and inadequate formal mediation procedures between superiors and subordinates. Along with this, there is also a need to give policemen a formal mechanism for sharing with top officers their ideas about how to improve functioning of the department, as some of the best ideas come from the cutting-edge employees. This would help in improving performance and in eliminating unnecessary rules and practices. However, the message should go that the top officers really want suggestions and good suggestions that are made should lead to change in the department.

Table II.1.1 summarizes the new look strategies for implementing the empowerment which translates to participation, delayering and decentralization for the police department

As summarized earlier, control strategy of employee empowerment should be combined with other strategies particularly the consequence and the culture strategies (see Table I.3.1). The empowerment should be designed to foster effectiveness and not democracy. Empowerment does not mean that the rule of consensus would prevail in the police department, orders will still come down from the top but they will be fewer. There would also be need to ensure that the lower-level officers are not hoarding power, just because the top officers wants the power to flow down does not mean that power has reached the frontline officers. Then it is very easy for the police department to revert to the old ways of functioning on any pretext. The police department has an age-old relationship with the authoritarian structure and a failure or two, even a small one, can make the department very quickly fall back into old

Table II.1.1   Implementing the Empowerment—Participation, Delayering and Decentralization in the Police

Thesis	Antithesis	Synthesis
Police headquater Centralized	Police units/districts Decentralized	Interlinkages Collective, steering
Bureaucratic	Empowered	Directed, leading not managing
Strict hierarchy	Two way communication, delegated	Linking pin structure, participatory

Source: Hamel and Prahalad, 2002: 322.

ways. Therefore, it is essential to embed empowerment into the police organizational structure and institutionalize it. In this regard an important recommendation is made by the Soli Sorabjee Committee report, of scrapping the post of the constables in civil police and replacing it with the empowered Civil Police Officer (Grade II), who will be recruited only after three-year graduation course at the training centres.

Still, there are limits to decontrol in a police organization; some controls are necessary to protect citizens rights. When citizens are to be treated identically, it makes sense to remove discretion from the policemen, for example, in the procedures to be followed for arrests and seizures. Also, the senior officers cannot abdicate the role of providing direction to the force. However, it would then mean that the top officers would have an increased responsibility to assume the role of the leaders of the force and not just the managers.

Empowering the Indian Policemen

- Embed empowerment of frontline policemen by reengineering organizational components.
- Develop mechanism, like a more flat organizational structure, by which important psychological and working requirements are met with in daily routine activities.
- Participatory practices for maintaining a constant dialogue between the superiors and subordinates and to bring all members of the police department on board in change management.
- Eliminate management layer of the middle level officers that performs overlapping functions.
- Restructure the police hierarchy.
- Headquarter to play the role of co-ordination and perform minimum essential administrative functions.
- Give the field staff greater freedom for planning the operational aspects.

Culture 2

Organizational culture

E mployee empowerment in the police department would only be successful when there is a change of the organizational culture which is as old, rigid and unique as the organization itself. In order to transform the organization, the police will have to ring out the old culture and ring in the new culture of improving quality, preventing crime, ethical conduct, fair and encouraging environment and building strong relations with the community. This would have to be developed, through the implementation of culture strategy, as a part of internal marketing, to make the scheme successful (Table I.3.1).

Police sub-culture

Organizations have distinct cultures which are the set of behavioural, emotional and psychological frameworks that are deeply internalized and shared by the department. The police department too has a very strong culture of people's habits, routines, rituals, conventions and the stories in the department. The fundamentals of politics, hierarchy, bureaucracy and monopoly give rise to the culture of the police department. Some of the dominant grains of the culture in the department are: do not take responsibility for the actions and do not innovate out of fear of making mistakes; accept mediocrity rather than reaching for excellence and strongly resist change rather than adopting it; clannishness, secrecy, insulation from others in society, the police tend to socialize together, believe that their occupation cuts them off from relationships with civilians and the police members of all ranks attach deep cultural significance to police organizations as havens of discipline, restraint and authority in a milieu of chaos.

Change management

The above account of the police sub-culture makes change management a critical yet neglected area in the police departments in India. To change the culture in the police organization would require a commitment for a long haul to bring about a change in the minds and hearts of the police officers. The leadership in the police organization not only have to want change but have to be the change. As a part of the culture strategy, concepts of change management have to be put in practice. The Federal Bureau of Investigation (FBI) in the US has made it mandatory, for its officers at the senior and middle level, to undergo the course 'Navigating Strategic Change', on change management at the North West University.

Change must make sense to those on the frontline. If this does not occur, rank-and-file police officers are likely to feel threatened by change. They should also be a part of the decision making processes with regard to change, otherwise, they may feel disillusioned, manipulated, frustrated, threatened by change and thus, would lack motivation. It would be necessary to create a sense of mission in the department giving the basic purpose of the department, build a shared vision of the future that the department is there to accomplish, articulate the department's values, beliefs and principles, use new language to replace the language of the bureaucracy and train the change agents. Shearing has argued that changes need to be incorporated in such a way that these changes are experienced 'as unremarkable as the air they breathe' (Shearing, 1992).

In the subsequent discussion, at different stages, we will be able to see how these lessons have been put to practice by some of the organizations and their leaders.

Judicious placement of officers

William Bratton was appointed the police commissioner of New York in 1994 when the department was going through one of the most difficult periods in history. The crime rate was high and out of control, officers were underpaid, promotion had no relevance to performance and the work force of 35,000 was difficult to manage. Yet, in less than two years, Bratton, without any increase in budget, turned New York into the safest large city in the US. Bratton's success was found to be special by the observers of management as he succeeded in record time, despite all the odds, that managers claim block high performance: an organization wedded to status quo, limited resources, a demotivated staff and opposition from powerful vested interests. Even Jack Welsh, the legendary ex-chief executive officer (CEO) of General Electric (GE) company, needed 10 years and tens of millions of dollars to turnaround GE. Research has lead to conclude that Bratton's success in New York (Kim and Mauborgne, 2003: 3–4) and Boston are textbook examples of what is termed as 'tipping point leadership' (Kim and Mauborgne, 2003: 6). The theory of tipping point hinges on the insight that, in any organization, once the beliefs and energies of a critical mass of people are engaged, conversion to an idea will spread like an epedemic, bringing about fundamental change very quickly (Box II.2.1). Such a movement can only be made by agents who make unforgettable and unargueable calls for change, who concentrate the resources on what really matters, who mobilize the commitment of key players in the organization and

---

Box II.2.1 Tipping Point Leadership

Leaders like Bratton use a four-step process to bring about rapid, dramatic and lasting change with limited resources. Out of the four hurdles, two— cognitive and resource—are faced by the organization in reorienting and formulating strategy. The motivational and political hurdles prevent the rapid execution of strategy. In dealing with the:

Cognitive hurdle: Bratton put police officers face-to-face with the problems and customers, for example, he asked the officers to travel by the night local trains to understand the crime problem. He found new ways to communicate through press and videos to send across the strong internal messages, instead of relying on memos.

Resource hurdle: He focused on hotspots and concentrated resources where the need and the likely payoffs were greatest, and bargained with the partner organizations.

Motivational hurdle: He put the stage lights on and framed the challenges to match the department's various levels; cops were given the target of beat and commanders were to make precinct safe. He singled out key influencers, like the commanders, and when they were hit right, it had a cascading effect.

Political hurdle: He identified and silenced internal opponents and isolated the external ones. His alliance with the mayor's office and the *New York Times* silenced the courts that were opposed to his zero-tolerance policy.

Source: Kim and Mauborgne, 2003.

who succeed in silencing the most vocal naysayers. All these things were done by Bartton in all his turnarounds (Kim and Mauborgne, 2003: 4). A similar message comes across from Punjab too. In the 1980s, the task of changing a delapidated police force to a fighting machinery was achieved by selecting the right people for the job, putting them at the choke points and by making effective use of young officers whose minds were not fossilized (Interview of K. P. S. Gill, 2007).

Learning the lesson from these successes, some of these techniques can be applied to the police departments in bringing about the transformation that is required today. In implementing the internal marketing plan, it would also be necessary to segregate policemen into three different categories as mentioned in the Chart II.2.1.

For the pro-changers, key positions should be identified so that they become the catalysts of change. Those who oppose the idea should be sidelined. Care should be taken so that only employees with a positive attitude should reach out to the community and customers. Selecting someone, for public interface efforts, who does not express an interest in working with people, can result in a disaster. In fact, selecting the wrong officer can create the opposite of the department's intended effect and

Chart II.2.1   Internal Marketing

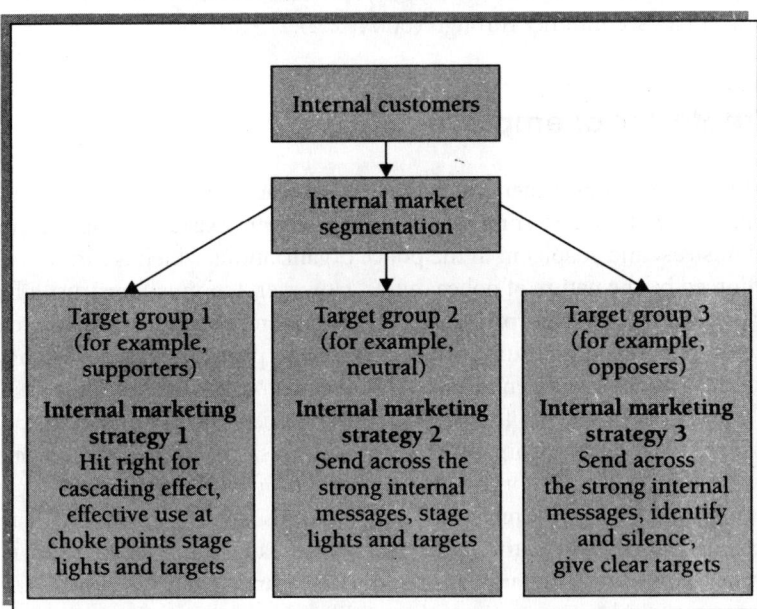

possibly lead to a negative impression about the department and police-men. Regardless of rank, those officers who have positive attitudes, enjoy public speaking. Those who are professionally competent and present a positive appearance for the police department, prove to be ideal candi-dates to work on cutting-edge jobs in the police stations.

As a matter of straightforward and simple principle, the policemen would deliver to the public what they 'receive from the department'. If there is openness and fairness within the department, there is transpar-ency and justice in the postings, transfers and promotions; the policmen will carry a high sense of justice. In turn, this is what they will deliver to the customers. Therefore, it is of utmost importance that the selection of the Station House Officers be done on the basis of merit and that there is transparency in their selection. The police officers should feel that everyone is eligible, provided they exhibit qualifying traits. Another important position is that of *thana munshi*. Similarly, there should be a fair selection procedure for this post in the police stations. A written exam for all willing candidates can be a very good method to create eligibility and the selection list. In South Africa, the selection for the in-charge of the police stations and the districts is done on the basis of open process of shortlisiting and on the basis of recommendations by a selection committee of the senior police officers. This ensures that there in no political or bureaucratic interference and that only the merit of the officer can see him/her through (Box II.2.2).

Treatment of employees

Along with empowerment there is a need to place trust in the policemen. Like many of the government organizations, there exists a strong culture of mistrust and suspicion in the police organizations which is further re-inforced by the nature of police duties. However, too much mistrust kills initiative and is counterproductive for any organization. The police force will need to build a culture of trust, respect and principle-based working, to create an environment where the officers and men can be inspired. The process of change from the culture of mistrust and manipulation to one of trust, friendship and respect can transform organizations from micro-managed high-control, autocratic environments to places of high involvement, empowerment and rapid response to customers. A classic example is GE where the CEO, Jack Welch and other senior leaders transformed the company from a bloated bureaucracy with little in-volvement and trust, to one of the world's most competitive companies

---

Box II.2.2   Assessment Centre Process in the South African Police Service

The South African Police Service's (SAPS) assessment centre can be described as a multi-method and multi-trait technique. Essentially, it is a series of individual and group exercises in which a number of candidates participate while being observed. The exercises are simulations of managerial tasks designed to test various managerial skills.

The selection of the senior managers in the SAPS assessment centre is done over two consecutive days:

1. Day one includes all the written exercises and personality questionnaire which are completed by all the candidates. Psychological services administers these written exercises and the personality questionnaire of all the candidates.
2. Day two includes all the behavioural simulations. All selection panel members must be present to do the assessment of the candidates. Psychological–services personnel facilitate the exercises during day two of the assessment centre.

The following competencies are determined throughout the process:
Strategic perspective, confidence as a leader, achievement focus, judgement, team building and maintenance, communication, negotiating and influencing, information usage, and technical and professional knowledge.

Short descriptions of the techniques are used to measure these competencies:
Draft test: It is designed to test the candidate's ability to draft a tactful reply to a sensitive letter, thereby testing judgement and discretion in a written format.

Written appreciation: It is a test where a scenario is given to the candidate, where a good analysis across all options with the use of factual and numerical data is expected. Short-, medium- and long-term issues must be considered and recommendations must be made in a structured, logical and persuasive way.

Personality assessment: Personality is considered to be important in the workplace as it is a valid predictor for job performance. Specific constructs measured during this stage of the assessment centre are: emotional stability, conscientiousness, resilience and emotional robustness, in other words, coping in general.

Presentation: The candidate must demonstrate an understanding of the widest ramifications of the topic and communicate this with great clarity. The presentation must be well constructed, the arguments must be logical and the advocacy needs to be persuasive. Scenarios such as real-life problems are posed to the candidates who need to handle it on a strategic level with limited preparation time.

Crisis management: It is the form of a crisis phone call, while the candidate is busy with the presentation. The rationale of this test is to determine how

(Box II.2.2 continued)

(Box II.2.2 continued)

the candidates function under pressure; the technical and professional knowledge of the candidates are also determined.

Role play: Police context-specific examples of real-life situations, such as unplanned union meetings, sexual harassment cases, personnel problems, etc., are used for the role play. The panel judges the candidate on the extent to which he/she was constructive and influential to reach the desired result in a firm, though sensitive manner.

Source: E-mail sent to the author on 27 July, 2007 by J.K. Phahlane, Divisional Commissioner, Personal Services, South African Police Service, on behalf of Commissioner of Police, SAP, Mr Jackie Selebi.

with a highly committed workforce (Rogers, 1995: 7–15). The key is trust, but verify and hold accountable for results (Osborne and Plastrik, 1996: 214).

The people who come in contact with the policemen are those who are in distress and turn to them for assistance. Their problems are extremely important to them, though they may seem to be of little significance to the policeman who is used to dealing with sordid and distressing situations daily. It is important that the matters of such vital importance are handled with compassion, understanding and a genuine desire to help others. If we want policemen to respect the people they deal with, they need to be treated with respect, trust and sensitivity.[1] Therefore, 'de-humiliate',[2] and eliminate policies and practices (almost always tiny) of the organization which demean and belittle human dignity (Peters, 1987: 376). For example, the police department supervisors sometimes use harsh words and language against the subordinates when they make some mistakes. In the changed times, this sub-culture of parent–child relationship between supervisors and lower ranks of police officers has to give way to a more matured relationship of mutual respect, clarity and understanding of each other's roles in the organization.

Another practice that is strongly ingrained in the Indian police is the culture of highlighting the mistakes, more to unsettle the subordinates than to provide them with constructive criticism. As a matter of tradition in the department, the supervisory inspection notes are full of negative

---

[1] Stating that the police force should have a humane attitude not only towards all those who come into contact with them but also with their subordinates, the prime minister asked them to 'treat the men and women in your force with compassion, dignity and respect' (http://www.tribuneindia.com/2006/20061027/main1.htm).

[2] This means increase the self esteem of the employees first by removing those practices and policies that make them feel small and are an insult to human diginity.

cliché with hardly any remarks of encouragement, whereas in the new promising and emerging field of positive psychology, 'strengths-based' approach[3] involves focusing on the strengths—selecting employees based on their talents and placing them where they get to do what they do best every day. This has been shown to result in employee engagement and satisfaction with well documented positive impact on customer satisfaction, increased productivity and reduced employee turnover and accidents (Luthans and Youssef, 2004). The basic paradox of police hierarchy is that discretionary authority tends to be greatest and at the bottom of the police organization. This is where patrol officers apply laws, policy and regulations to situations that do not fit neatly into the rulebook. Further, these discretionary choices are made in the field, removed from the direct scrutiny of management (Kelling, 1999). Consequently, in addition to the accountability measures (discussed later), the police managers should consider methodologies that use the power of employee commitment, organizational culture, peer norms and values to shape behaviour and build motivation (Wilson, 1972). (Box II.2.3).

Box II.2.3   Organizational Health Survey of the Singapore Police Force

In the vision of the Singapore Police Force (SPF), it is articulated that people are their most valued assets. To this end, they have put in place systems and structures to continually sense the motivation and morale of their officers so as to ensure that officers remain passionate in their work. One mechanism through which this is done is the Organizational Health Survey (OHS). The OHS is a regular staff feedback exercise in the SPF's journey towards the organizations' excellence. 'Organizational Health' refers to the total well-being of the staff in an organization. It includes 'people' issues such as job satisfaction, working relationships, rewards, etc., as well as those related to the organizations' functioning such as capability, communication, etc. The survey is conducted once every 18 months by their psychologists in conjunction with external consultants and the survey seeks to capture the collective aspirations of the SPF. The regular conduct of the OHS not only allows the SPF to seek continuous improvement, but the results also allow the SPF to benchmark with external organizations.

While the OHS measures motivation, morale, sense of belonging and job satisfaction, these have served as excellent tell-tale signs to the leaders of the SPF and have allowed them to fine-tune initiatives and approaches towards engagement of their officers.

Source: Singapore Police Force, 2007.

---

[3] More discussion on this topic under sub-head 'positive psychology' and 'POB' later.

Motivating policemen

Motivating the policemen is an issue that needs more attention in the police department than it has received till now, in light of today's turbulent environment characterized by economic liberalization and globalization, heightened geopolitical unrest, terrorist crimes spreading its tentacles to all the major towns of the world, 24 × 7 duty demands and the use of never-ending advanced technology in crime by criminals. Only a truly motivated and committed manpower can take an organization to the pinnacle of performance and achievement. In the following paragraphs we look at some of the ways for high sustained motivation, commitment and satisfaction of the policemen in emerging 'new policing order'.

High vision and participation efficacy

Stephen Covey, the management guru, in his book *Principle Centered Leadership*, has emphasized the need for creating an empowered work-force around a common sense of meaning and vision, around a value system that is principle based and then tapping into the power of that workforce in order to compete in the world economy. High quality and low cost, necessary for competitiveness in the world economy, can only come through 'high trust' culture, which in turn comes through principles (Covey, 1992). Increasingly, the managers are realizing that the employees perform most energetically, creatively and enthusiastically when they believe they are contributing to a higher purpose (Peters and Waterman, 1982). As various studies would tell us, people derive great satisfaction from the realization that their efforts make a difference. While the departments are engaged day and night in making a differ-ence to the lives of millions of citizens in this country, the policemen, in-cluding the office staff, should be able to see that they are doing so. The police officers should be able to feel that they are engaged in activities that 'make the society a safer place to live in', rather than just working for solving cases or reducing crime to save their skin. This kind of inspired working was one of the key reasons for the unparalled fight of the Punjab police against the terrorist movement from the mid-80s and the early-90s. The young IPS officers who were in charge of the districts, putting their lives at stake and families at risk, worked for a bigger vision, a greater cause and were a hope for the distressed citizen, in a seemingly hopeless situation running out of hand.[4]

---

[4] Here, only the aspect of motivators for the young IPS officers at that time is commented on. The credit of the fight goes to the entire Punjab police, different sections of the force

Positive psychology[5] and positive organization behaviour[6]

The fault-finding attitude remains an integral and deep-rooted part of the police sub-culture in India. In business and industry, managers are assessed on the basis of overall success but in the police, officers tend to be judged by failure leading to an increasing tendency among police officers to take refuge in unnecessary paper work, excessive monitoring and consultation (National Police Commission, 1977–81: para 44.6). In the exacting demands of the modern-day police work it is necessary to attach greater importance to overall success rather than be obsessed by the fear of a possible failure. In this context, there is a strong case for examining the need of a proactive, positive approach emphasizing strengths, rather than continuing in the downward spiral of negativity trying to fix weaknesses in the police department (Box II.2.4).

The time has come to follow the lead of psychology and take a pro-active positive organizational behaviour approach in looking at the issue of motivating the policemen (Kim and Mauborgne, 2003: 9–10). The positive psychology movement seemed to have considerable relevance to the workplace and potentially may have the ideas and possible solutions to current challenges facing the police department.

To further emphasis the need and utility of POB, Bandura's (1986, 1997) rich theory and considerable research support clearly indicates that the more confident the individual:

1. The more likely the choice will be made to really get into the task and welcome the challenge.
2. The more effort and motivation will be given to successfully accomplish the task.
3. The more persistence there will be when obstacles are encountered or even when there is initial failure.

had different interplay of reasons for their actions and reactions as the events unfolded during that historic period.

[5] Positive psychology movement is a recent development drawing considerable attention during the last five years. M.E.P. Seligman is generally recognized to be spearheading today's positive psychology movement. The aim of positive psychology is to shift the emphasis away from what is wrong with people to what is right with people: to focus on strengths—as opposed to weaknesses—to be interested in resilience—as opposed to vulnerability—and to be concerned with enhancing and developing wellness, prosperity and the good life—as opposed to the remediation of pathology—(Luthans, 2002b). The recent trend can be judged by the fact that two special issues of the *American Psychologist* have been devoted to positive psychology: 55(1), 2000 and 56(3), 2001.

[6] Positive Organizational Behaviour or simply POB, which applies positively oriented human resource strengths and psychological capacities that can be measured, developed and managed for performance improvement in today's workplace. These POB capacities

Box II.2.4   Management of Mistakes (MOM) Framework

To help officers make decisions, the SPF has also put in place systems to foster a safe-to-fail mentality rather than a fail–safe one. The Management of Mistakes (MOM) framework is one such example. Under the framework, mistakes are evaluated based on a two-dimensional matrix of intention versus impact. This ensures that officers are not unduly penalized for consequences not intended in the first place. Besides revamping the 'stick' approach, the SPF has also reviewed its 'carrots'. Rewards, beyond monetary gains, are used to incentivize officers to exercise initiative.

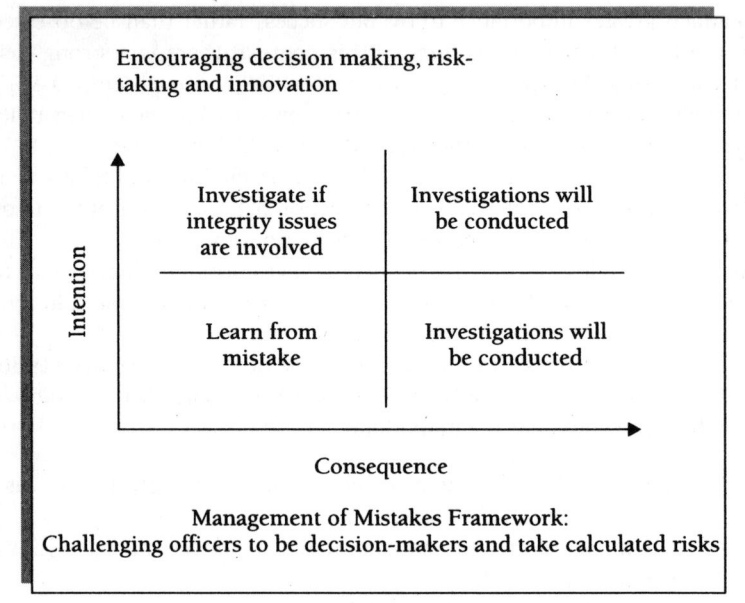

Source: Singapore Police Commissioner, 2007.

This profile of a highly confident employee seems ideal for policeman's effectiveness and high performance on the street today.

Some of the representative techniques that can be useful in police for managing psychological capital (Luthans and Youssef, 2004) are given in Table II.2.1.

include self-efficacy/confidence, hope, optimism and resiliency, are collectively referred to as positive psychological capital. Efficacy/confidence is about believing in one's ability to mobilize cognitive resources to obtain specific outcomes. Hope is about having the will-power and pathways to attain one's goals. Optimism is about having the explanatory style that attributes positive events to internal, permanent and pervasive causes. And resiliency is about having the capacity to bounce back from adversity, uncertainty, conflict, failure or even seeming overwhelming positive changes (Luthans, 2002b).

Table II.2.1   Techniques for Managing Psychological Capital

Developing efficacy/ confidence through	Developing hope through	Developing optimism through
• learning/modelling • positive feedback • physiological and psychological arousal	• clear goal setting • participative initiatives • contingency planning	• leniency for the past • objective appreciation for the present • building opportunities for the future

Source: Luthans and Youssef, 2004.

It would be foolish to assert that there is no place for punishments and pointing out mistakes, and the good old-fashioned methods of making people work are not important. However, the recipe would not be complete without positive organizational behaviour approach. Earlier, it was thought that the positive organizational behaviour approach is a nicety in the organization. Now, we know for the sake of performance these are ingredients essential in the organization.

Healthy competitions in the organizations not only improve the efficiency and quality of performance, but also enhance the dedication, engagement, discipline, self pride and responses of individuals, groups or departments. In the police department there are very few opportunities for appreciation of tangible work, whereas, in policing competition with the performance requirement and award criteria being very clear, tangible results can be shown. Activities such as the 'Good Policing Competition' can be used as an effective tool to implement the identified priority policing activities at the district/range/state level, using a balanced scorecard.[7] The priorities can change from year to year and accordingly the balanced scorecard format also can be tailor-made and used to lay emphasis on different aspects of field policing like—excellence in operations, management excellence and bridge building (see Chart II.2.2). Such a competition-based implementation can be used as means for

[7] Developed by Robert S. Kaplan and David Norton in 1992, the balanced scorecard (BSC), is a popular concept now for measuring a company's activities in terms of its vision and strategies. The BSC method of Kaplan and Norton is a strategic approach and performance management system, that enables organizations to translate a company's vision and strategy into implementation, working from four perspectives: financial perspective, customer perspective, business-process perspective, learning and growth perspective. The system consists of four processes: (a) translating the vision into operational goals; (b) communicate the vision and link it to individual performance; (c) business planning and (d) feedback, and learning and adjusting the strategy accordingly. Originally introduced as a tool for business organizations, the BSC has found considerable support in the public sector also, as a public-sector performance management tool in the countries like the USA, the UK, Canada, Australia and Scandinavia.

**Chart II.2.2   Balanced Scorecard Framework for Policing
Competition Activities
(Adapted from the RCMP Architecture)**

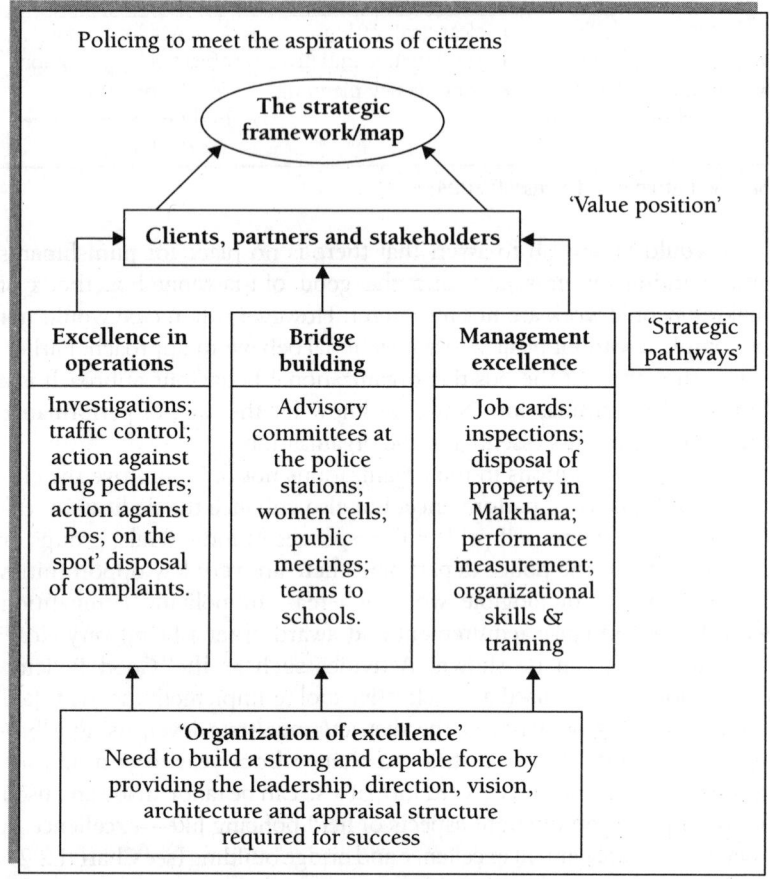

Source: Presentation on 'Non-traditional Scorecards in the Public Sector' available on the website www.bscol.com.

motivation of the employees and benchmarking the performance in a positive manner, while the BSC format can ensure that necessary attention is being paid to different aspects of functioning in any department, with necessary modifications as per the identified needs. In the SPF the units and departments are assessed on their abilities to meet the key performance indicators specified in their BSC. There is a best land division competition among units to surpass the targets set (SPF 2007). In the UK the police forces compete with each other on seven parameters like reducing crime, investigating crime, promoting safety, providing assistance, citizen focus, resource use and local policing. There are similar competitions for the South African Police where the stations with best performance in crime reduction, crime prevention and investigation are awarded with cars and laptops (www.sapsjournalonline.gov.za 2007).

Employee empowerment

As discussed earlier, employee empowerment is an important corner-stone for motivating the policemen, only an empowered employee can be inspired to produce results beyond the routine call of duty.

Intrinsic motivation

There are many managers who believe that financial incentives have the most powerful pull and with poor pay structure, especially in today's economy, the police department can only have demoralized employees. However, this is not true as the financial incentive and benefits are important hygiene factors but not motivators of lasting value. Researchers and psychologists like Herzberg to Maslow have pointed that other things are more important. In the police department today, while we are groping with the issue of lack of motivation due to lack of financial incentives, we may look at these levers of purpose, service, values, sense of belongingness, pride in service, recognition and challenges in the job to energize the officers and the force.

In Australia, when researchers asked public managers about the kind of rewards they would prefer in order to do outstanding jobs, money ranked at the third position—far behind personal recognition from senior managers and career development opportunities (Osborne and Plastrik, 1996). In the US, Police Chief Bratton provided clear achievable targets and used the bi-weekly meetings of all the commanders and top police officers in an auditorium to provide an opportunity to the achievers to make presentations and get recognition for their performance, this motivated the commanders who in turn motivated their men in the same way in the efforts to bring about turnaround in the New York police.

A recent meta-analysis of relevant research studies has shown that feedback can enhance performance on average by 10 per cent and that social recognition can enhance performance on average by 17 per cent. Feedback enhances performance through clarifying tasks and expectations (Luthans and Youssef, 2004). While in the police department in comparison to costly perks and monetary rewards, feedback and recognition are readily available for managers to use at no cost, yet they are often ignored as rein forcers.

Nurturing environment in the organization

Research has shown that employees who are shown organizational kindness are more motivated towards task accomplished (Schulman, 1999; Salzmann, 1997) and are 86 per cent more productive than when in organizations where such kindness is not shown (Lloyd, 1990). Bill George former CEO, Medtronics, took issue with the widely held belief that the company's purpose is to serve its shareholders. 'If you have de-motivated employees you cannot improve shareholder value', he argues (Heffs and Marshal, 2004). Similarly the police deaprtments too will have to ensure that the organization is able to offer opportunities to the policemen to develop and blossom. The SPF places equal emphasis on developing in harmony both the organization and the people in the organization. On personnel development, the force awards scholarships to young officers to study in prestigious universities abroad. The senior police officers of the SPF are valued professionals and are sought after by other government agencies. As a part of the exchange programme, the officers are encouraged to do a stint with other departments and ministries for a couple of years to contribute and develop their horizons (see the section on 'supportive environment in Part II, Chapter 5).

Similarly, the Denmark police has employee development as a part of its core objective, appreciating the philosophy that long-term learning is not a luxury but a necessity and this can only happen with the support from the organization.

Servant leadership for the police

The police department by nature is a service organization. In day-to-day activity itself it offers a number of opportunities to the employees to be of service to mankind, to live up to their ideals, to bring about a change in the society and find challenges in the job. The SPF looks for people who feel engaged and motivated by the call to serve and not by the sense of power that comes with the profession. As the legendary Chief of the Los Angeles Police, William Parker, addressed his officers:

> In order that you and your families may be happy at work, you must develop a philosophy that will suit your service. You do not, I hope, come into our profession with the hope of any great materialistic gain, because the field does not offer that. We expect you to do a good job, and there must be something within you that will cause you to strive hard to perform your work well.... If you develop philosophy of service and of dedication to the welfare of mankind you too will be happy; you will also enjoy the camaraderie of your companions and will serve your nation at the time it badly needs your assistance. (Parker, 1957: 20, 22)

In the West, greed has become less acceptable and there is a movement away from materialism to spirituality, towards intangibles such as honesty, truth, courage, conviction, self worth, the quality of relationship and personal fulfillment. The future corporation will have shifted its self image from that of a primarily manufacturing organization to that of a primary serving organization (Harman, 1982). A sample group consisting of the police chiefs from 50 larger municipal police departments in Michigan, USA, viewed that they enjoyed their job the most when they were able to make improvements and affect the departments and officers in a positive way. A second significant response was helping people, solving problems, and making a difference in the community (Benson, 2004).

There is a developed model that attempts to simultaneously enhance the personal growth of workers and improve the quality and caring of our many institutions through a combination of teamwork and community, personal involvement in decision making and ethical behaviour. This emerging approach to leadership and service is called *servant-leadership* (Spears, 1995). The model of servant leadership (Box II.2.5) would be best suited to mo-tivate the police officers in service of people. No other place is in more need of leaders who put service before self than the Indian police, no other mind can imbibe the concept of service as an end in itself than that of an Indian. Mahatma Gandhi had been the greatest example of this model and later Mother Teresa had shown what power does the intention to serve the people has. The Indian police offers, to its leaders, a readymade ground to serve the public, especially, the disadvantaged and the weaker section of society and an oppropriate environment where the Servant Leadership model can be of immense utility.

Box II.2.5   Servant Leadership Model

The model called the 'servant–leadership' is a practical philosophy which supports people who choose to serve first, and then lead as a way of expanding service to individuals and institutions. The servant–leader is servant first. It begins with the natural feeling that one wants to serve first. Then the conscious choice brings one to aspire to lead. He or she is sharply different from the person who is a leader first, perhaps because of the need to assuage an unusual power drive or to acquire material possessions. The leader-first and the servant-first are two extreme types. Between them there are shadings and blends that are part of the infinite variety of human nature. The difference manifest itself in the care taken by the servant-first to make sure that other people's highest priority needs are being served. The best test which is difficult to administer is: do those served grow as persons; do they, while being served, become healthier, wiser, freer, more autonomous, more likely themselves to become servants? And, what is the effect on the least privileged in society; will they benefit, or, at least, will they not be further deprived? Servant-leadership encourages collaboration, trust, foresight, listening and the ethical use of power and empowerment.

Source: Greenleaf, 1977.

Alignment

Barrett (1998, 2003) proposes that there must be a strong alignment among the personal values of employees, the values of the current organization and the desired values employees consider necessary for a high-performance organization. With alignment people are able to respond to the call from within rather than relying solely on the rulebooks and procedures. If the police department is able to align the personal values of the officers with the core values of the department one can imagine what difference an aligned police officer on the street can make to the service he provides to the citizens. While the training courses and the organizational monitoring and reinforcing mechanism should promote alignment, the recruitment of aligned individuals at the entry point itself, as practised by the Royal Mounted Canadian Police, ensures this significantly.

Spirituality at workplace: organizational HAPPINESS model

We've come a long way since Frederick Taylor, the father of scientific management, asserted, 'What workers want most from their employers, beyond anything else, is high wages.' As Kotter (2001) states in the *Harvard Business Review*:

> Motivation and inspiration energises people, not by pushing them in the right direction as control mechanisms do but by satisfying basic human needs for achievement, a sense of belonging, recognition, self-esteem, a feeling of control over one's life, and the ability to live up to one's ideals. Such feelings touch us deeply and elicit a powerful response.

In his book *The One Thing You Need to Know*, Marcus Buckingham advocates similar arguments for motivating the employees. In today's environment, we have to treat the employees as individuals and not mercenaries for whom just the incentives are sufficient. For them a fair wage and non-horrific working conditions are required just to fulfill the need of getting the act. But it takes more than that to motivate employees to do the best job possible.

Many times managers are not as good at judging employee motivation as they think they are. They assume that 'more' means external incentives such as money, titles and job security. They forget that some employees find greater value in the chance to learn a new skill, the satisfaction of solving a tough problem or a belief in the organization's mission (Moyer, 2005). There is a tendency in all of us to assume that others are more driven by external rewards for work than we are. For example, people tend to think those around them are more motivated by extrinsic rewards like money and less so by intrinsic motivators like meaningful work. Is that kind of disdain for peers and lower ranks not prevalent among the policy-makers and officers in the police department? Yet, research has shown that this widely held assumption is false. Therefore, managers should follow the rule of thumb: assume what motivates you motivates others. By stressing extrinsic motivators—while overlooking intrinsic ones—well-meaning managers may be pushing the wrong levers and developing incentives that don't reflect employee needs (Morse, 2003). While traditional rewards and punishments can, if ill managed, severely damage motivation, they have little beneficial effect under even the best of circumstances. It is the fuzzier things—feelings of purpose, belonging and engagement—that push people to do their best (Herzberg, 1987; Levinson, 2003; Nicholson, 2003). The negative theories that we hold about human behaviour and motivation in the police department need to give way to the positively oriented strength-based management that focuses on developing human, social and psychological capital to achieve their full potential. The emerging trend towards positive psychological capital management in particular can effectively channel policemen's talents, strengths and psychological capacities toward achieving worth-while productive, ethical, sustainable outcomes and results.

The concept of spirituality at workplace is drawing considerable interest among today's progressive organizations in search of excellence. Spirituality is different from religion and should not create any dilemma in the minds of the police administrators about its acceptability in multi-religious and multi-ethnic society like ours. Some of the suggested measures to develop workplace spirituality in the organizations is inte-grating the concepts discussed earlier. Companies like Tom's of Maine and Hewlett-Packard have successfully integrated them in their corporate culture (Decenzo and Robins, 1998). The police department too can easily adopt many of these measures:

1. Employee-centric management: Employee development and properly placing employees, providing opportunities for members to pursue professional and personal growth and to fulfil their own personal mission through work.
2. Develop culture of trust and mutual respect, which can serve as basic building blocks. In the SPF, the culture of mutual respect, openness, sincerity and trust is permeated through the practice of five learning organization disciplines—shared vision, personal mastery, mental models, team learning and systems thinking. The SPF continuously embarks on open communication of these values through generative dialogues pitched at different levels (SPF Executive Summary, 2007).
3. Personal two-way communication, open-door managerial accessibility.
4. Management by walking around (MBWA).
5. Servant Leadership: Leaders and senior members who inspire employees through their leadership and their example.
6. Building cooperation and shared sense of purpose. Developing positive connections among all members and a sense of community in the organization.
7. Focus on Positive Organization Behaviour.
8. Creating working environment where people can do their best realize their potential and be recognized for their achievements. Recognition for creative accomplishment and performance and using an equitable system by matching rewards to performance.
9. A positive workplace culture including a positive physical space for employees to work in. Allowing staff to take exercise breaks to promote physical and spiritual wellness so that the workplace is enjoyable.

10. Creating an evolving mission statement that the employees are proud to live by, an intention to contribute to the overall good of society.

11. Creating a corporate culture that lives that statement by having organizational integrity and work that is aligned with its mission and purpose.

12. Addressing individual differences by focusing on specific needs and accommodating those needs.

13. Developing emotional intelligence of employees.

14. Enriching jobs by increasing employee's responsibility for planning and self-evaluation of their work.

15. Job rotation to make work more diversified.

16. Introducing the concepts of yoga and meditation to the police officers for stress management, personal development and fulfilment. Courses like the 'Health and Happiness seminar' and 'The Decision Maker's Course' run by the non-profit organization Art of Living have shown to bring about significant improvement in performance of employees and managers who have undergone these courses.[8]

By bringing together all the motivational levers discussed above, that are of relevance today and will be increasingly so in time to come, for high sustained motivation and commitment of policemen, proposed herein is a police department HAPPINESS model (Chart II.2.3) for fostering spirituality at workplace in the police department. In this model acronym 'HAPPINESS' stands for:

H—High vision for the organization; emphasis on human values.
A—Alignment of employees.
P—Positive Organizational Behaviour (POB)
P—Participation efficacy.
I—Intrinsic motivation.
N—Nurturing environment in the organization.
E—Employee empowerment, Personal development and fulfilment.
S—Servant leadership.
S—Spirituality at workplace.

The servant leadership (Box II.2.5) is central and binding in this nurturing, fulfilling and strength-based organizational context.

---

[8] These courses are available throughout the world and available at www.artofliving.org.

Chart II.2.3   Organizational HAPPINESS Model for Police

Organizational HAPPINESS Model for Police

High Vision Human Values

Servant Leadership

Alignment

Employee Empowerment

Spirituality at Workplace

Participation Efficacy

Nurturing Environment

Positive OB

Intrinsic Motivation

For high sustained motivation, commitment
and satisfaction of policemen

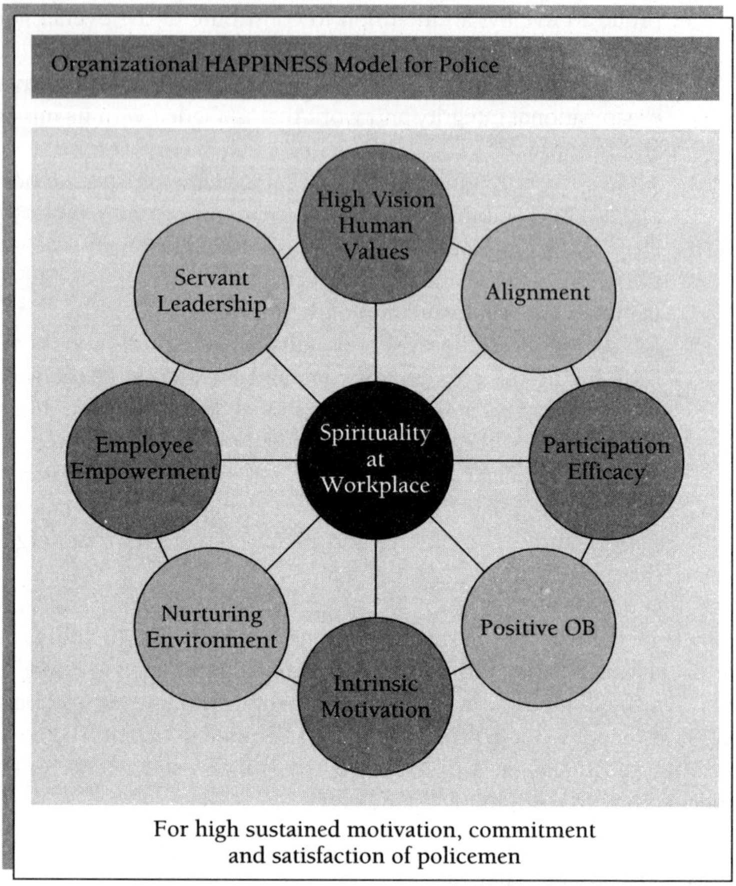

Source: Choudhary, 2007.

Transforming the culture of the Indian police

- Police Leadership to not only desire change but it has to be an embodiment of change.
- Mandatory training on change management for senior- and middle level officers.
- Engage the beliefs and energies of the critical mass of people in the department.
- Pro-change officers with positive attitude, professional competence and integrity to be placed at key positions in the department.

- Give clear targets and put the stage lights on.
- Ensure fairness, transparency and sense of equity within the organization as the policemen would deliver to the public what they receive from the department.
- Eliminate policies and practices in the department which demean and belittle human dignity.
- Foster workplace spirituality following the organizational HAPPINESS model.
- Conduct regular surveys to assess the organizational health and for necessary corrective measures.

Values 3

Ethical conduct

On 17 October 2007, two news items concerning the conviction of police officers, which is currently happening at an alarming regularity, were on the front page of newspapers (*The Tribune*, 2007c). The editorial next day read:

> Horrifying incidents like the Khalra murder and Cannought Place shooting expose the real face of Indian police and show how ugly it is... One wonders whether anything is being done even now to eliminate such barbaric methods from the police list of 'standard procedures'... (*The Tribune*, 2007d)

Undoubtedly, such incidents can erode public faith in the police and significantly damage its image. Public trust in the police is vital for its effectiveness and legitimacy. The public demands of its servants a more exemplary conduct from the very fact that they have entered the public life. Not only is their conduct at the time of duty under relentless scrutiny of the public, their behaviour in private life too has to be such that it inspires the confidence and trust of the people they serve. The members of the police force by the very nature of their job of enforcement of law are bound to a more exacting code than a private citizen. The role of integrity in the department is very important as the values stand at the core of what a policeman works for.

Not only does police deviance hit the people who are already in distress and very often belong to disadvantaged section, but it is also very glaring. One unethical act in the public eye can wipe all the good impression that the department may have formed by the hard work of a large number of officers. However, for the Indian police today, as discussed in the situation analysis, the public trust needs to be regained and the strategies towards achieving this need to be given serious consideration.

Systemic issues

For the Indian police, the answer to the problem of unethical practices has a much deeper undercurrent than just being a matter of enforcing discipline and strict supervision. It grows on the systemic failure, sometimes originating for a just cause and spreads in a ready environment that our society at large and the bureaucratic intitutions in particular offer. These underlying issues are critical to address for evolving a mechanism for promoting culture of integrity and ethical conduct in the department. A serious role conflict always exists in policing—as one between the ideals of crime control versus the ideals of due process. There are many limitations in our criminal justice system which hamper the efficient and effective functioning of the police. Besides, there prevails an attitude in the society which primarily judges the effectiveness of policing on the achievement of goals and there is a performance culture judged on its outcomes. To add to the complexity of the situation sometimes arising out of the prevailing situation itself are the core sub-culture beliefs of the police such as they are the only real crime fighters, no one else understands them, they are loyal to each other because everyone is out to get them or make their life harder, they can't win war against crime without bending rules, and the public is unsupportive and too demanding. The inadequacies in the relevant legislations, the increase and changing nature of the crime, expectations of people in distress from the police, among other reasons, gives rise to practices where ends are often used to justify means and often leads the police to resort to extrajudicial methods during investigations (Box II.3.1).

Confronted by the ethical issues, the response of the department has been strongly reactive rather than a proactive strategy, which would embrace some of the fundamental ethical problems that the police service faces as an organization. It can be said that there has been a significant reluctance or, at best, apathy within the police service as an institution to embrace the ethical challenges facing their organization as a result the police service today is seen as a beleaguered institution which has lost a clear sense of its identity.

Box II.3.1   Noble Cause Corruption

'Noble cause corruption' in policing is defined as:

> [c]orruption committed in the name of good ends, corruption that
> happens when police officers care too much about their work. It is
> corruption committed in order to get the bad guys off the streets... the
> corruption of police power, when officers do bad things because they
> believe that the outcomes will be good. (Crank and Caldero, 2000)

Examples of noble cause corruption are: planting or fabricating evidence,
lying on reports or in court and generally abusing police authority to make
a charge stick. A recent survey demonstrated that officers felt corruption for
personal gain was a much more serious charge than engaging in corrupt
behaviour that appears 'to benefit society at large' (Ivkovic and Kutnjak, 2003).
This sub cultural value system rationalizes constitutional rights violations.
Officers do not normally define 'a bending of the rules for a greater good' as
misconduct or as corruption; rather, they rationalize that such behaviour is
part of the job description, in a utilitarian sense, to get the criminals off the
streets, regardless of the means.

Source: Joycelyn, 2004.

Pitfalls in taking the route of extra judicial methods

An equally important duty to ensure that the guilty are punished is the
duty of the policemen to see that the persons suspected of the crimes are
not deprived of their constitutional rights. In their enthusiasm to secure
the conviction of the suspect, very often, the police officers forget the importance of their obligations as guardians of personal liberty. But is the
use of extra judicial methods by the police really helping society in the
long run, and for that matter, is the police any better off in getting results
by the use of extra judicial methods? Resorting to extra judicial methods
by the police as a means to control crime has its own pitfalls. It takes
away the checks and balances in the system and it also does not account
for plausible mistakes. The system also becomes extremely vulnerable
to the unscrupulous elements within the law enforcement community,
who can bring about untold damage to the society. There are several
reasons why the police should shun the use of extra judicial methods to
meet the ends of perceived justice:

1. In adopting the extra constitutional methods in the treatment of
    a criminal, the policemen create a strange paradox, in a way, the
    denial of the due process of law adds materially to the defence of

the accused. For example, the judiciary hardly believes the FIRs regarding a police patrol being fired upon while negotiating a culvert, which culminated in apprehension of a wanted criminal. Such tactics, in the final analysis, become counter-productive to the effort by the police in seeking conviction. There are other hazards too of premature mind formation, one of them is the premature arrests prompted by other conjuctures of the suspect's possibilty of eloping and of his confessing the crime. When there is little evidence to conclusively prove the guilt, the other set of consequential illegal actions follow, such as the use of torture to get confession, planting of evidence and illegal confinement.

2. Controlling limitations and the issue of setting the boundaries: There is great danger in allowing policemen to decide the situations where they would resort to the use of illegal methods. The police force that has taken to the path of extrajudicial methods of functioning would find it difficult to confine the use of such methods in only justifiable and limited cases.[1] The control of the superior supervisory officers becomes weak when they start overlooking the transgressions. The malady spreads in the department and the question of setting the boundary becomes difficult. Therefore, it has to be accepted that any police force which practices the use of extra judicial methods would be a loosely-controlled and an ill-disciplined force.[2] There are extra-ordinary situations which may need the use of extra judicial methods but if the police force once gets used to these methods, it is difficult to put it 'back to barracks'. Policemen misuse the assumed authority for their own benfit and continue the use of extra judicial methods even when there is no perceived bonafide requirement.[3] Therefore, there is the issue of setting the house in order after the extraordinary situation ceases to exist. The culture in the organization is difficult to change quickly.

---

[1] See *The Times of India*, 2006c. The inspector fabricates case to frame witness to his own crime. A police inspector faced with molestation charge wants to 'fix' a witness, a west Delhi businessman. He contacts a gang of blackmailers led by a Tis Hazari lawyer. A 23-year old woman is hired to play the rape victim for Rs 40,000. Babloo, who has the same blood group is asked to have intercourse with the 'victim'. To make the 'rape' appear authentic, semen is injected into the woman.

[2] See Sen, 2008. In many states within the police forces, now, there are encounter specialists who become the darlings of political masters and police bosses. The heady mix of power seven success turn their heads and many of them become corrupt.

[3] See *Deccan Herald*, 2006. A case in point is that of Daya Nayak, who was hailed as an 'encounter specialist' till the other day, but was recently arrested for accumulation of huge wealth. He is suspected to have got so much wealth that he was accused of financing film

3. Breaking the code of conduct initiates the police officer on to the path of working outside the legal parameters; involvement in this is a kind of conscience overruling. The conscience within each individual is an important guiding light that tells and stops an individual from committing any wrong. The voice is stronger initially, but gets weaker, and eventually deluged, if ignored. The incident of going against conscience is a significant event in any individual personality and behaviour evolution. Any un-acceptable behaviour may be undertaken with some underlying justification, but subsequently, it is easier to repeat, for personal gratification too. The ill-effects of police brutality and the use of other illegal methods in policing do not remain limited, the Mollen Commission (1994: 47), set up to investigate corruption in New York in the 1990s, also argues that the use of excessive force may be a rite of passage into the police subculture and the beginning of 'the slippery slope' that leads toward other forms of police misconduct:

> It [police brutality] strengthens aspects of police culture and loyalty that foster and conceal corruption. For example, brutality, regardless of the motive, sometimes serves as a rite of passage to other forms of corruption and misconduct. Some officers told us that brutality was how they first crossed the line toward abandoning their integrity. Once the line was crossed without consequences, it was easier to abuse their authority in other ways, including corruption. Brutality is also used as a rite of initiation to prove that an officer is a tough or 'good' cop, one who can be accepted and trusted by his fellow officers not to report wrongdoing. Dowd, like other officers, reported that brutality strengthened the bonds of loyalty and silence among officers and thus fostered corruption tolerance.

4. Policemen may form a premature opinion in the case and the investigation carried out with a predetermined mind may exert strong influence on the minds of witnesses. The investigator with a fixed mind is likely to ignore many evidences that may prove the

productions. With 83 killings to his credit, Nayak has inspired two Bollywood films—N. Chandra's *Kagaar* and Ram Gopal Varma's *Ab Tak Chhapan* and a Kannada film, *Encounter Daya Nayak*. After attaining the height of glory, Nayak found himself accused of being in cahoots with the same underworld he had pledged to eliminate and amassing huge wealth. He was arrested by Maharashtra's Anti-Corruption Bureau (ACB) and suspended from service.

innocence of accused.[4] Many miscarriages of justice has resulted in this kind of investigations.

5. Unfortunately, the police officer's effort to apprehend a criminal is often hindered by the very laws that protect the rights of a common man. In the use of extra judicial methods the remedies offered are in conflict with law, such practices are certain to lead to trouble. When such illegal methods are practised by the tacit support and understanding of the seniors in the department there is also the issue of providing protection to police officers who are caught for the use of extra judicial methods. In any situation that may justify the use of extra judicial methods, the law may catch up with those officers. In a sense their actions are bonafide actions and may be for a perceived cause, like national security, and yet they may find themselves being prosecuted for their action.[5] In such a situation the people who had given the tacit support and allowed or directed them to carry out these actions are in no position to help them.[6] Thus, they are also not justified in allowing or directing any action for which they cannot provide protection to the subordinates.[7]

6. The support of the public opinion, in these cases is very fragile. While the whole concept of the justification of the use of extra judicial methods is based upon what is being perceived as good for the largest number, the role and support of public opinion is a very important pillar here. But public support in itself is very elusive and difficult to quantify. It may be there today and may not be there tomorrow—there is also no explicit contract or demand. With only public opinion to support any activity that

[4] See *The Economic Times*, 2000. CBI filled chargesheet against five army officers including one Brigadier, one Lt. Col., two Majors and one JCO and found them accused for acts punishable under 120(b), 364, 307, 302, and 201 RPC after the slain were conclusively proved innocent and innocuous civilians.

[5] As on 12 October 2006, there were 462 police officers facing criminal writs, trials and investigations against them for allegations of acts of omission or commission performed during the period of terrorism in Punjab. Writs faced by officers include two A.D.G.P.s, three I.G.s, two D.I.G.s and 12 S.P.s. There are court trials underway of CBI cases against 20 S.P.s, 21 D.S.P.s, 57 inspectors, 52 sub-inspectors, 53 assistant sub-inspectors, 42 head constables and 51 constables for this period.

[6] See Sen, 2008. Unfortunately, when the trouble deepens they are cast away by their political and police bosses. Recently, in Gujarat the well-known encounter specialist D.G. Vanzara found to his utter dismay that the chief minister and political leaders, who were appreciating his work earlier, dumped him because they wanted to present an untarnished image before Supreme Court.

[7] See *The Economic Times*, 2000. While the armed forces believe that neither of their can be tried without formal sanction by the central government, the CBI insists that impunity under the law cannot be extended to the accused because they were not 'conducting any legitimate military operation in good faith'.

may have legal implications must not be indulged in. It would not be judicious to tread such a path which may land the practitioners into serious trouble in their career. The public is also awakening to the fact that the difference between a totalitarian state and a democratic state upholding principles of personal liberty does not lie in the law, but in the manner in which these laws are applied. Illegal detentions, fabrication of evidence, planting of false cases and witholding from the suspects the right to due process of law is bringing considerable criticism to the police from the courts and public alike.

7. The use of extra judicial methods provide a quick fix method of attending to the problem which requires a rather elaborate and multiple agency redrafting of rules and procedures to logically and truly provide a solution. The use of extra judicial methods may be doing damage to the cause by providing an escape route to the framers of the laws and to the society as a whole. As then the wider issue does not get the attention the society needs to pay, of bringing up-to-date the laws[8] and of thinking about application of science and technology more rigorously to police practices such as the use of lie detectors,[9] narco analysis technique[10] and brain mapping.[11] Therefore, the use of extra judicial methods delays the operation of appropriate channels due to ad hoc solutions

[8] The drafting committee on National Criminal Justice System Policy headed by Professor N.R. Madhavanan has recommended various measures to be taken up by the government for effective management of not only traditional forensic science requirements but also to overall Science and Technology (S & T) needs of the criminal justice system to raise the levels of capability and sophistication.

[9] British scientists claim they have invented the world's most sophisticated lie detector. Named, 'silent talker', it delivers degrees of lying—complete lie and half-lie. The assumption for both polygraphs and the silent talker is that lying triggers a sense of conflict and anxiety in the person being questioned. This leads to physiological change, for the polygraph, and facial movements, for the silent talker.

[10] 'Narco' + 'analysis' which means analysis of the knowledge of the individual in drug induced sleep-like state. The narco analysis during the past was in use only by psychiatrists to find out psychological reality or psychological truth which was achieved by using one or two barbiturates such as sodium amytal or scopolamine. The revelations made during the narco analysis have been found to be of very useful in solving sensational cases of Mumbai serial train blasts, blasts at Delhi and at Malegoan. Narco analysis technique has thus not only revolutionized the causes of crime investigation but also have led various courts to redefine the very scope of the constitutional provisions vest under Clause 3 of Article 20 (3) and Article 21.

[11] This technology scientifically detects the record of crime stored in the brain and the test represents a new paradigm in law enforcement. Increasing understanding of neurosciences will contribute significantly towards piecing together the crime pattern stored in brain. The recent amendments (2005) made to section 53 of Cr.P.C apart from others, is positive and proactive towards the recognition of the importance of scientific tests which include narco analysis and brain mapping apart from others.

providing temporary respite. In the end, in place of getting a legislation to tackle the problem at hand more often it has been the enactment of restrictive legislation and the development of adverse public opinion for police.

Therefore, no police action can be justified in the use of extra judicial methods and the real remedy lies in the amending of rules and procedures to bring them in sync with the times and the society culture, as also strongly recommended by the National Police Commission in its fifth report. Mechanisms like torture warrants (Box II.3.2) can be an answer to the dilemmas faced today by the police officers of the possible moral price of accepting a certain public role—that price being the sacrifice of one's soul or integrity for a greater good. This would also help in weeding out the possibility of misuse of authority of police over the detainees and the use of torture against the accused of crime other than accepted by the society at large and approved through legislation.

Developing culture of integrity and ethical behaviour for the police

Every criminal justice profession and association has codes of ethics, professional responsibility, values and principles of conduct. The police departments in India should also own a set of core values that are aspirational, after developing them through a collective exercise within the police organization. Having done so, monitoring and control mechanisms should be put in place, in the police department, to oversee the

---

Box II.3.2   Torture Warrants

Recently, especially after 9/11 and the US invasion in Iraq, when the issue of national security and terrorism came to the centre stage, the discussions on torture by security forces of suspected terrorist was among the spin offs. The idea of providing some legal sanctity to the torture under special circumstances is under discussion, one such provision that is discussed is the concept of torture warrants. The idea of a torture warrant is that a judge—or perhaps a panel of judges—would be presented with a case for torturing a particular person and would decide whether, on the basis of considerations like those relevant to ticking bomb cases, the person should be subjected to medically supervised torture. In the US, warrants of a relatively similar kind are already required under the Foreign Intelligence Surveillance Act (FISA). In 2002, all 1228 applications were approved by the appointed judges (although two of them only after appeal) and in 2003, 1724 out of 1727 applications were approved in whole or part.

Source: Kleinig, 2005.

conduct of the individuals and the police department as a whole, in relation to these core values.

Three main dimensions influence the process of ethical decision making and a culture of integrity within the police service. These three dimensions, in the order of their influence, are: the environment, the organization and the personal characteristics, values and behaviour of the individuals involved in the process (Chart II.3.1). The second report of the National Police Commission 1977–81 sums up:

> the sustained capacity of the police system to function as an efficient and impartial instrument of law will largely depend on the attitudes developed by the personnel at different levels in the system and the manner in which they respond to different situations in their career. This in turn depends on the training which they get at the time of their entry into the system and even more on the climate and culture they have to work in, specially the examples and values they imbibe from the leadership at various, levels within the system.

Chart II.3.1   Three Dimensions Influencing the Ethical Conduct in the Police Organization

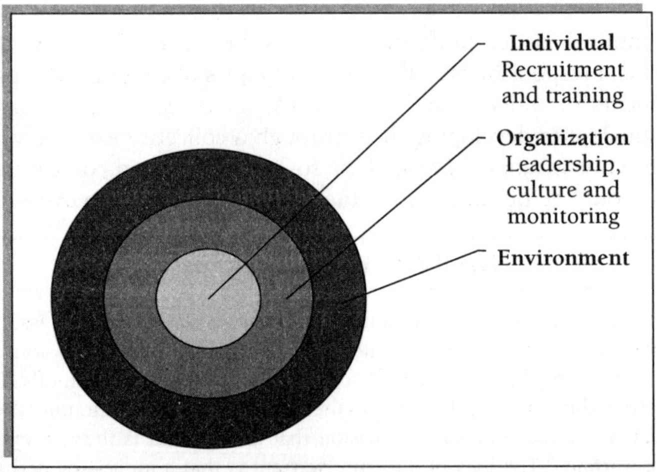

Source: Conceptualized by the author.

Environment

The environment means the number of pressures competing social and political agendas, which influence decision making primarily. A helpful analysis in this context is the application of stakeholder analysis. When making an ethical decision it is important to identify all the interested external stakeholders and evaluate the impact of the decision as it relates to their respective rights and responsibilities. If the process of stakeholder evaluation is conducted in a way that is ethical and transparent, then the credibility of the police can be enhanced in the eyes of the wider public (Mills, 2003: 331).

Organization

The organization itself is one of the most significant influences on the ethical dimension of decision making, from the perspective of both the structure and culture of the institution (Mills, 2003: 331). The Royal Canadian Mounted Police (RMCP) has a set of values that are all important to the organization forming the basis of every decision and policy in the organization. Values are cherished above competencies. These values are well advertised and are highly visible and are not hidden away in some policy statement that no one reads. These values guide their recruitment and training. Part of their training involves scenario thinking and within that the recruits need to demonstrate that they use these values in decision making. Similarly, the discipline system in the RMCP is based on the same values. In the organization, any violation of these values is 'conduct unbecoming'. RMCP is able to demonstrate that with good leadership an organization can, as a whole, adopt a set of values and use these to guide conduct throughout. For the SPF, the core values are courage, loyalty, integrity and fairness while the desired culture in the organization is that of mutual respect, openness, sincerity and trust.

Within the organization, there is a need to address both the structural issues and the culture issues. Ethics codes have an important role to play in this. As the police department has a strong sub-culture of resistance to change, therefore, to integrate the ethics code into the fabric of the decision-making process the appropriate education, training and development programmes should support them. Within the organization, it would be desirable to ensure that the systems of reward and sanctions, organizational culture, education and training together with visibly ethical leadership—leading by example—would enhance the ethical conduct of most police officers in a decision making situation. In the SPF, the core values are first instilled in the officers during their induction programme and translated into desired behaviour through policies, programmes and practices. The rewards and recognition programme than provides the incentives to live out the core values. Finally, the standardization of key services and procedures ensures adherence to policies, practices and behaviours that reflect the core values (SPF Executive Summary, 2007).

Institution of 'ethics committees' to focus on some meaningful debate around the dilemmas that accompany difficult decisions in the organization

is worth considering. Such committee can also steer corruption prevention studies, monitor implementation, effectiveness and identify new
areas of study.[12] Along with the ethics committee in the state police departments, there should be an expert ethics policy body, at the national
level, to which complex ethical dilemmas could be referred for advice
and guidance. Such a body could also disseminate best practice in this
area throughout the various police forces in the country.

A holistic way to foster ethical behaviour in the police organization
could be through promotion of spiritual orientation in the department
as discussed in Chapter 3 (Spirituality at workplace: organizational
HAPPINESS model). If the organization is spiritually oriented, it is more
likely to avoid situations of ethical misconduct. 'Being in touch with spiritual principles and values helps to stimulate the moral imaginations and
can provide greater depth of understanding of many ethical problems
that arise' (Jackson, 1999: 66). As an illustration, the corporate frauds
that surfaced or uncovered in 2001 and 2002 have self-centredness
as their root cause. Those at Enron, Worldcom and Anderson were simply
acting with a desire to satisfy their individual interests. In contrast, in the
spiritually-oriented organization, materialism, determinism and egoism
do not guide decisions; their non-material values are integrated in the
system of orientation, and people are able to see each other as deeply
interconnected (Gull, 2004). With the mission and purpose of the organization being more than material profit, people are empowered to look
beyond self-interest to make a difference in and contribute to society as
a whole (Neck and Milliman, 1994).

Individuals in the department

Ultimately, the ethical conduct resides within the individual. The effective recruitment strategies would weed out those individuals whose behaviour is deemed ethically unacceptable. The new recruits coming into the
police service must exhibit the traits, values and behaviours to enhance
more ethical conduct within the organization. At the level of recruitment
in the police, in the criteria for selection, consideration should be given to
the aspects of the personality and experience of individuals to determine
their values and ethical standards. RMCP's core values are well advertised
and people apply for employment there because they subscribe to these
values. To verify their authenticity they can be subjected to polygraph
testing and conscientious testing, at the time of being confronted with

[12] In Hong Kong, the Police Corruption Prevention Group, from 1981 to 2003, identified
over 50 areas of police functions and operations for review by the corruption prevention
department.

these tests 30 per cent of the candidates opt out. Only those candidates are successful who are aligned to RMCP's core values.

Once an individual has been recruited, the department should be able to nurture and develop the individual. In this context, the role of education and training in ethics and ethical awareness, from induction onward, is especially important. The Hong Kong Police as a part of its efforts to promote integrity launched a series of specific measures in 1996, these included anti-smoking campaign, station fitness rooms, stress management publications, and training and anti-gambling publicity.

The actions taken by leaders to influence an organizations culture include (Jacocks and Bowman, 2006):

1. Attention, measurement and control: Those things a leader consistently notices, pays attention to and systematically deals with will communicate to the subordinates what is valued and what norms the leader deems appropriate.
2. Reactions to critical incidents: How leaders react to organizational crises will uncover and communicate underlying assumptions to subordinates.
3. Deliberate role modeling: The leader sets the example.
4. Criteria for reward allocation: An organization's leaders can emphasize their own priorities, values and assumptions by linking rewards and punishments to the behaviours.
5. Criteria for recruitment, selection and retention: An existing culture can be reinforced or a new culture introduced by the careful selection and retention of members who fit the culture.

Considering the ethical conduct as an essential requirement, several police departments like the Canadian and Dutch have officers as Ethics Commissioners. The Hong Kong police has an anti-corruption steering committee chaired by a senior assistant commissioner. The committee is not just concerned with corruption but also with the related issues of integrity and ethics (Box II.3.3). Australia has an integrity framework in place to promote and foster such culture in the organization and have the office of professional responsibilty and professional integrity.

Ethical awareness and conduct in the department is not just a result of some punishments for deviant behaviour. It can only be promoted in the department by adopting a more structured and multi-pronged approach. Recognition that while the police may determine who enters the criminal justice system, being at the first line of contact, they do not influence the eventual outcomes, needs to be stressed when the overall effectiveness of police in terms of crime control is under consideration.

Box II.3.3   The Hong Kong Police Strategy for Police Integrity

Given the complexity of the problem of police integrity, the Hong Kong police have adopted a holistic four-pronged approach to address the issue of police integrity in 1996. The prongs are:

1. Education and training;
2. Minimizing opportunities for malfeasance;
3. Police and independent commission against corruption partnership and co-operation and
4. Discipline.

The objectives of this four-pronged approach are to:

1. Promote a corruption free working environment;
2. Develop a culture of honesty and integrity;
3. Identify and eliminate elements that may influence susceptibility to corruption and
4. Co-ordinate and monitor police and ICAC initiatives.

The strategy adopted to fulfill these diverse objectives is two-fold. First, to minimize opportunities for corruption and malfeasance. Second, to introduce initiatives and measures to counter, reduce and minimise adverse or unethical influences. The strategy's success could be judged from the figures, in 1974 some 47 per cent of the corruption complaints in Hong Kong were against the police compared with 13 per cent by 2002.

Source: Hong Kong Police, 2007.

By strengthening of the 'ethos' of policing, by heightening the awareness of ethical issues within the service and addressing the challenges of more ethical conduct and decision making in a proactive manner, culture of integrity can be developed and sustained in the department and the police service can present itself to the outside world as a professional institution with credible practices, values and beliefs.

Promoting ethics and integrity in the Indian Police

- Own up core values for the department through a collective exercise within the police department.
- Cherish values above competencies.
- Well advertise the values and make them highly visible within the organization.

- Recruit and promote only those individuals who are aligned to these core values.
- Value, encourage and reward ethical behaviour. Disciplinary code to specify the sanctions associated with the behaviour that does not confirm with the core values.
- Appropriate education, training and development programmes on ethics, well-being and financial prudence, to integrate values into the police department's fabric.
- Foster workplace spirituality to nurture and develop individuals in the department.
- Weed out individuals exhibiting unethical conduct.
- Leaders to be the centre of gravity in sustaining and developing a culture of integrity.
- Minimize opportunities for malfeasance.
- Constitute an 'ethics committee' for corruption prevention studies, implementing measures and for identifying areas to reduce corruption in the police department.
- Form an 'ethics policy body' at the national level, to deal with complex ethical dilemmas facing the police department, for advice and guidance.
- Co-ordinate and partnership with outside oversight bodies.

Measuring 4

Empowering the policemen would also mean the loss of some old forms of controls with the passing of authority. In their place, new systems that help in creating consequence would have to be put. In today's age of information, detailed data collection and analysis is not a problem. Therefore, issuing directions from the top for every matter in order to exercise control[1] can be replaced with management information systems to monitor and control employee behaviour and response. The way to check corruption would be to gain full information, ensure consequence for performance and prosecution for illegal activity (Osborne and Plastrik, 2000: 239).

Performance appraisal

Performance appraisal is a vital component of a broader set of human resource practices; it is the mechanism for evaluating the extent to which each employee's day-to-day performance is linked to the goals established by the organization (Lowenberg and Conrad, 1998). Cardy and Dobbins (1994) define the performance appraisal process as the process of identifying, observing, measuring and developing human resources in the organization (Shen, 2004). In search of establishing a

[1] Some senior officers increase their routine workload manifold in order to see, monitor and approve every activity. They tend to lose contact with problems and issues. This is fatal for any organization (National Police Commission, 1977: para 44.9).

dynamic and progressive work environment in the police department for all employees' performance, appraisal systems can be an effective tool (Lee, 1989). Osborne and Plastrik (2000) have considered perform-ance measurement as important as it constitutes a core competence needed to implement any other reinvention strategy for the organization. The performance appraisal, performance targets, performance-related rewards and punishments and job description form the base for the consequence strategy in reinventing the organization (Table II.4.1). Per-formance appraisal is considered as one of the several key elements of performance management.

Assessment of existing system

The Committee on Police Training, 1973 had the following observation regarding the performance appraisal system in the police:

> The existing systems of assessment and promotions are subjective and in some cases vitiated by extraneous influences, thus leaving room for merit going organisation. A considerable amount of research has been done in recent times into systems of assessment and evaluation of performance. It appears to us desirable that advantage should be taken of such research to introduce objective systems of assessment and promotions at the various levels of the police force.

The state of the present system can be summarized as:

1. *Merely a tool for disciplining:* Current research suggests that the efficacy of performance appraisal systems may be increased through the use of appraisal for feedback and the development of employees rather than for promotion, merit pay or employee dis-cipline (Kozlowski et al., 1998; Murphy and Cleveland, 1995). However, the present form of performance appraisals in the Indian police remain insulated from this modern shift in the basic philosophy of appraisal which ranges from using annual con-fidential reports for disciplining the employees to treating them as a source of information for administrative reforms and organ-izational development, thereby improving the performance of the employees (National Police Commission, 1977: paras 56.3, 56.4).
2. *Annual exercise:* The police department relies on the annual con-fidential reports as the basis for rewards and promotions. As the name itself suggests, this is an annual exercise and little is being thought about the whole process during the year. There are

Table II.4.1 Police Work Charts

Constables	Non-gazetted officers/head constables	Gazetted officers	Community policing officers

• Sentry duty	• Cases registered:
	  1. IPC
	  2. Local and special laws
		• Inspections carried out
		  1. Formal
		  2. Informal
			• No. of complaints handled/solved

• *Naka* duty	• Action under Section 174 Cr.P.C.	• Supervise visit to police stations (number)	• Number of conflicts identified/solved
• Patrolling	• Case diaries written	• *Chowkies* checked (number)	• Number of public meetings held
• Raids	• Cases sent to court	• Village tours/village/meetings held	• Citizens fear of crime in neighbourhood
• Searches	• Cases convicted	• Night rounds	• Rate of crime in beat area
• Gunman duty	• Raids conducted	• Visits to scene of crime	• Crime prevention measures initiated/new groups formed
• Summons/warrants	• P.O.s arrested	• *Nakas*/patrolling parties	• Exceptional work done/innovations introduced in the beat
• Court duty	• Other arrests made	• Departmental inquiries conducted (numbers)	
• Secret/special operation duty	• Prevention arrests made	• Inquiries conducted (numbers)	
• Miscellaneous duty	• Bound down under prevention sections		

- V.I.P./*mela* duty

- Night duty

- Administrative/clerical

- Traffic duty

- Operators
- Drivers
- On job training
- Critical incidents

- Recoveries made
  1. Local and special Laws
  2. Property
  3. Arms
- *Naka*/patrolling duty

- Operational duty

- Traffic duty

- Night duty
- V.I.P. *bandobast* duty
- Administrative/clerical duties
- BCs checking carried out
- Complaints disposed off
- Critical incidents
- Training

- Operations planned and supervised (numbers)

- Malpractices exposed and punishments recommended against (numbers)
- V.I.P./*mela* duty (days)

- Training (number of courses attended)
- Exceptional work done

Source: Conceptualized by the author.

instances where the reports are written much after the period of reporting. While today, there is a need for remodelling the police organizational systems to meet the demands of the twenty-first century society, traditional performance management systems do not mesh with today's lateral oriented, fast-paced organizations.

3. *Leaning on personality traits:* When experts disagree about whether performance should be measured in terms of the results produced by employees (Bernardin and Beatty, 1984; Kane et al., 1995; Swank and Conser, 1983) or in terms of work-related behaviours (Latham, 1986; Murphy and Cleveland, 1991), there is no dispute that personal traits-based system has several drawbacks. The present system of the performance evaluation in the Indian police is not job oriented for any rank, it leans heavily on personality traits than on performance (National Police Commission, 1977: para 56.12). Therefore, in the police departments, at present, there is a pressing need for an objective performance appraisal system for the policemen.[2] The absence of such a system has resulted in a valence of zero for the department since the majority of employees have become indifferent to the outcome. The inequity in the organization became high as the group of the overachievers felt that though they worked hard, they got the same importance as others who scrapped by or were under achievers.

4. *Subjective assessment:* The ACR writing relies on the subjective assessment—an officer's judgment—rather than on indisputable performance data. Under the present system, it is perhaps impossible for the officers to be consistent in the way they rate the policeman. Although there is a five-point rating scale (outstanding, very good, good, satisfactory and unsatisfactory), rating officers have different interpretations of what it meant. A manager probably cannot be trained to effectively evaluate an employee's performance based on subjective characteristics (Markowich, 1994). Consequently, at present the reports are totally subjective; these tend to erode the confidence of the employee in the system and cause considerable harm to the organization and the official reported upon. By asking the managers to judge, they encouraged the people to please the boss rather than serve the organizational needs (Mohrman and Mohrman, 1995).

5. *Lake Wodegon syndrome:* Subjective appraisal system also puts officers in a difficult position as it makes it difficult for them to tell the non-performers that they are not performing well. They feel

---

[2] The Congress felt that there is a need, above all, to bench-mark clear and measurable performance evaluation standards (www.bprd.gov.in).

less confident in justifying why they are rewarding one person and not another. More often the result is not 'rating inflation'. Officers finish up rating everyone good/very good resulting in 'Lake Wodegon syndrome'.[3] On the other hand, the rated police officers have all the reasons to suspect the rating if it is not favourable. Accusations like personal bias and misuse of the process are made in such cases.

6. *No feedback and counselling:* An important component of effective performance appraisal relates to the frequency and nature of supervisor feedback and to be most effective, a continuous performance-based feedback process should exist between the superiors and subordinates (Henderson, 1984; Meyer, 1991). However, in the Indian police departments, proximity between the person reported upon and the reporting officer is generally absent resulting in distorted perceptions (National Police Commission, 1977: para 56.19). While the present system provides no feedback to the police officers except for conveying the adverse remarks, there is a legitimate need for the employees to know how their performance is viewed. Undesirable work habits may be formed and good habits may be modified if there is no communication. Periodic counselling is a concomitant corollary to continuous appraisal as correction and reassurance are the main objectives of continuous appraisals. An effective system of performance appraisal is a major component of an organization that allows every employee to feel that his/her contribution has been made to the success of the organization and a desire to add to that success (Boice and Kleiner, 1997).

Suitable appraisal system for the police

For an effective system the performance appraisal experts have recommended measuring employee behaviours instead of traits, more than one source of rating information, conducting evaluations more than once per year and proper training of the raters (Edwards, 1990; Kozlowski et al., 1998). In light of the research findings and the present state of affairs, the Indian police needs to evolve a system of assessing their performance (efficiency and effectiveness) objectively and analytically instead of banking on limited personal knowledge, stray critical incidents, media and public opinion to gauge performance.

[3] Duke professor Robert Behn called this phenomenon 'Lake Wodegon syndrome', after Garrison Keillor's mythical town where 'all the children are above average'.

The National Police Commission (1977) recommended that the performance appraisal system in the police should be broadly classified into
the following two areas: (a) a continuous appraisal which is correctional
and developmental in its impact and (b) the annual performance appraisal report meant for organizational purposes in the matter of training,
placements and promotions. In the opinion of the commission it will not
be difficult to introduce a system of continuous assessment in the police as
the nature of the police work requires, even today, a continuous maintenance of the records of the duties performed at various levels, especially
in the operational areas like the maintenance of beat book, case diary,
personal diary, the general diary crime register, court register, and so on.
(National Police Commission, 1977: para 56.11). When you view your
performance management responsibilities as an ongoing process, rather
than a once-a-year event, you will informally praise or criticize worker
performance on a continual basis, and provide prompt, corrective feedback and reinforcement whenever necessary. You will then have far
fewer employees spending half the year trying to forget their last formal
performance review and the other half dreading their next one (Pratt,
1991). When job objectives and their measurements are clearly specified,
the evaluation does not surprise the employee, and both are clear about
how it will affect performance review. When the review of performance
is an end-of-the-year event, even if the goals are clearly stated, employees
and managers think about it a week or two before evaluation; such a
process does not achieve any purpose. Therefore, the performance
appraisal process should be made a way of life and continuous and not
be made into a dreaded judgment day (Sahl, 1990).

For the police department the adoption of the graphic rating method,
where the traits and performance heads are spelt out clearly in a format,
would be able to provide the necessary objectivity in appraisals (National
Police Commission, 1977: para 56.17). The graphic rating method should
in general cover the essential items of job rating and this would mean
a thorough job evaluation for different ranks and posts. In this way
traits and performance heads that have a direct relevance to the efficient
performance of the particular level of job can be identified and form a
part of the format.

The continuous appraisal aspect of the appraisal system for police can
be built in by formulating work charts for different ranks of police officers. Some of the performance parameters for different ranks can be
given the form of a work chart. Some of the sample formats for constables,
head constables, non-gazetted officers, community police officers and
gazetted officers are listed in Table II.4.1. Further, the personality traits
like physical fitness, sense of responsibility, initiative, tact, willingness to
learn and integrity, attitude towards public and how the officer has been

helpful and the type of relations he had maintained with the citizens and his attitude towards the weaker sections of the community can be combined with the work charts to cover the continuous appraisal of the police officers across the department.

The police department should also think of doing away with the old system and make a quantum jump in adopting some of the latest computerized appraisal systems available. Thought could also be given to try an online performance appraisal system that is able to provide analysis data on daily basis. Such an information system will produce integrated personnel performance reports and group performance reviews for different desired periods of time and aid more objective decisions on training needs, placements and promotions in respect of individuals or in respect of group operational strategies (National Police Commission, 1977–81, para 56.29). It would be a leap, but if one has to move on then a better option is to take a leap (Box II.4.1).

Box II.4.1. E-performance

We are in the information age today. Computer software is one of the ways in which performance appraisals can be dealt with more proficiently (Spink et al., 1999). Performance appraisals today are more dynamic and interactive than ever, especially with variety of web-enabled software with multiple features, such as job profiling, assessments, goal setting, training management and 360° feedback in use by many organizations.[4]

While streamlining the organization of processes, the web-deployed performance management solutions enable the managers, employers and the human resources administrators to collaborate on performance evaluations and goals, review performance process.[5] In built in these software are the notifications that keep all the interested parties up to date throughout the performance cycle. While these products do not solve all the problems encountered in performance appraisals, they do give structure to the process and make this sort of appraisal easier to conduct (Spink et al., 1999).

Benefits of an objective system of appraisal

The main goal of an appraisal system is to improve performance. A well-designed, well-communicated system helps achieve organizational objectives and motivates employee performance (Sahl, 1990). Some of the reasons for this are:

---

[4] Performance appraisal software, www.hr.guide.come/data/209.htm.
[5] Oracle's Peoplesoft e-performance. www.oracle.com/applications/peoplesoft/hcm/ent/module/eperformance.html.

1. *Better control to supervisors:* The performance parameters listed in Table II.4.1 can give better control to the supervisory officers in finding the utilization of manpower in different fields of working and in issuing directions for any reallocation, to fulfil the strategy adopted to combat crime and efficiently use the manpower. Frequent reviews also enable clarification and revision of objectives. It also helps in long and short term manpower management of the police force.

2. *Focuses on performance variables:* Such a system can provid for means to measure performance rather than personal traits as the existing system reflects heavily. One factor that contributes to an effective performance appraisal system entails ensuring that the system focuses on performance variables as opposed to personal traits (Smither, 1998).

3. *Creates a sense of equity:* The implementation of such a system give the impression to the policemen that all their actions are being accounted for and this can result in a sense of justice and equity in the department. The outputs from the system provided for the basis for rewards, punishments and recommendations for medal cases. As noted by Gilliland and Langdon, without the perception of fairness, 'a system that is designed to appraise, reward, motivate, and develop can actually have the opposite effect and create frustration and resentment'. Another benefit is that such an objective assessment can withstand public and political criticism. One may debate over which measure is to be used, but no one can then contest that rewards and punishments are related to demonstrable performance.

4. *Continuous evaluation and feedback:* The review of the performance and feedback with such a system can take place on a monthly basis, and rewards and punishments can be issued in the monthly meetings.

5. *Analysis:* Maintaining work-related records helped in establish patterns of work behaviour and allowed statistical analysis of the overall time spent by the policemen on different duties like patrolling, checking, night duties VIP duties, and so on. Equity in allocation of pleasant/unpleasant duties could be established.

Performance evaluation for community policing

Community policing principles have broadened the role of police officers from that of law enforcers to problem solvers who address disorder in an effort to improve the quality of life in communities (Trojanowicz et al., 1998). Therefore, traditional internal administrative processes designed to measure and evaluate the performance of officers as law enforcers are no longer adequate to measure the work done in the area of community policing. Additionally, performance appraisal tuned to measure community policing parameters can be used as a tool to communicate changes in agency goals and objectives, and orientation towards community policing to employees throughout the organization. Strategically, the need for rapid and effective organizational change requires that employees continually realign their performance with the evolving goals and objectives of the organization. For example, this need to continually realign performance characterizes police departments which continue to struggle with getting their members to embrace the philosophy and practices of community policing (Clairmont, 1991; Scrivner, 1995; Vinzant and Crothers, 1994). While there are many reasons for the difficulties experienced by the police departments in their transition to community policing as discussed in the second chapter, the absence of an effective employee evaluation and feedback process is an important contributing factor. As noted by Kane, an appraisal system 'must be considered a major organizational change effort which should be pursued in the context of improving the organization's effectiveness' (Kane et al., 1995: 285). Therefore, if community policing is to be successful in the police department, they must ensure that their performance appraisal processes are supportive and inclusive of new objectives consistent with that paradigmatic approach (Lilley and Hinduja, 2006).

For any community policing, the evaluation processes a different format from the one used for evaluating traditional policing units should be used, going beyond adding few more parameters to the list of traditional measures (Table II.4.1), with the following common recommendations incorporated (Lilley and Hinduha, 2006: 6):

1. Community policing evaluation process to give importance to officer traits that supports the community policing paradigm—such as leadership, innovation and public-speaking ability—when compared with traditional policing units. As the desired officer performance in these agencies emphasizes leadership, creativity and public speaking ability more than traditional law enforcement roles (Reiter, 1999), essential for problem solving and working with communities.

2. Community policing units should have more frequent evaluation of officers compared to traditional policing units as this would then act as developmental and feedback tool for the unit members.

3. Community policing units provide more training of evaluators when compared with traditional policing units. Though this part is totally neglected for the filling of traditional policing evaluation, it needs much more attention here as the parameters for evaluation will present a greater challenge for the rater in the community policing units.

4. More control-based system inhibit action and initiative, for example, if the idea is to look for zero error then the focus of the team will be to make no mistake even at the cost of inaction. To prevent the officers from falling into this trap, community policing evaluation process should give higher importance to the use of evaluations for officer development and lower emphasis on officer control and discipline when compared with traditional policing units. Since the agencies which are community oriented in their philosophy must encourage independent, intelligent, problem-directed thought if officers are to succeed in making strong connections to their communities (Reiter, 1999).

5. Community policing evaluation process to give greater importance to feedback from sources other than the direct supervisor when compared with traditional policing units. As the community policing emphasizes problem solving and assisting citizens in addition to carrying out traditional law enforcement actions, some police departments are beginning to incorporate more measures of performance such as measures of the character of relations with co-workers, citizen satisfaction with officer contacts and contribution to the pursuit of teamwork (Oettmeier and Wycoff, 1997; Whisenand and Rush, 1998).

Developing performance measurement system for the police: Useful suggestions

There are a number of lessons that can be learnt and kept in mind for developing a system for performance measurement in the police department:

1. Begin with policy outcome goals and work downwards, watching out for overkill of trying to measure everything. The Oregon police department made the mistake of starting with 270 measures leaving the employees confused and they could not connect the measures to the policy of the department (Osborne and Plastrik, 2000: 261). It can be useful to involve the customers in deciding on performance indicators for a department like the police.

2. Reliance only upon distal performance indicators may be particularly problematic in police work because the specifics of the process are often as important as the end result (Lilley and Hinduja, 2006). An arrest, for example, though counted in terms of the work done by an officer may be rendered meaningless if proper investigative procedure is not followed. Public dealing skills are as important. Officers that have high statistical outputs but infringe on civil rights or treat citizens rudely cannot be said to be performing well overall as in the process they are alienating citizens and damaging departmental credibility. Nevertheless, this system does help in identifying the people who work; this can form a useful combination by coupling with other information like the reprimands and issue of warnings. Therefore, measure all the terms—effectiveness (customer satisfaction can be a useful measure), quality and cost effectiveness—not just efficiency. The statistical reports are to form the basis for the assessment of the subordinates, yet the supervisory officers have to continuously guard against the over emphasis on just the data—qualitative work has to be rewarded as much. Balanced scorecard method provides for an all round perspective and can be a useful tool in creating parameters.

3. It is prudent to implement the system in a phased manner rather than putting it in practice in single phase. Let it be implemented in one police station first for a few months as a pilot project. Train people vigorously on the system. The trained staff from there can further work as change agents in subsequent implementation. This also provides an opportunity to make corrections and improvements in the system before it is implemented at other places.

4. The help of experts and the involvement of both the top managers and the employees is necessary at the design stage. While the top managers would be the users, the employees can also provide useful inputs at the design stage, on the measurables. The system should be standardized and computerized, but should have adequate scope for adjustments from district-to-district depending on local requirements.

5. Watch out for perverse incentive especially in the area like the figures of arrests made. As this would be one of the indicators, there is danger of policemen affecting early arrests without proper verification.

6. Also, it would be pertinent to mention that any system is as good as the utilization made of the system by the manager or the officer in charge. Use the outputs from the system on regular basis to make decisions about rewards and punishments, redeployment

of force and corrections in duty allocations as such decisions can
be taken with the available data objectively. In the 1970s, New
York City generated thick volumes of data on performance of
city agencies every year but they gathered dust till Giuliani administration started using them to manage performance (Osborne
and Plastrik, 2000: 248). Till then, most public employees ignored them. The performance measurement outputs if sought,
seen and acted on timely would have tremendous impact on the
functioning of the force. To be seen acting on the information
collected, monthly meetings or the welfare meetings can be the
best time to announce performance-based rewards on regular
basis. In this system the data captured is right from the grass-root
level and thus require efforts and commitment on the part of
those who collect the same. On the other hand, if the impression
goes that the outputs generated are not seen or the data collected
is not analysed critically, the system can soon turn into one of the
many redundant data collection exercises carried out by the government agencies.

7. The most commonly cited reason for non implementation of
improvement in the appraisal format indicates either failure to recognize the importance of this change or the lack of commitment
on the part of the top managers in the police. To say that the
police officers have no control over the format is untenable as no
government will turn down the plea by the police department to
affect the necessary changes. When top officers in the police are
unconvinced about the efficacy of performance appraisals, only
then do they stand in the way of devotion of time and resource to
change the process.

Measuring the Indian policemen

- Use evaluations for officer and organizational development and
  not just as a disciplining tool.
- Develop work-related performance parameters after carrying
  out job evaluations for different jobs.
- Measure employee activities instead of traits.
- Continuous performance-based feedback process should exist
  between the superiors and subordinates.
- Provide more training of evaluators.
- Use of objective computer-based appraisal system.

- Watch out for overkill of trying to measure everything.
- Measure all the terms—effectiveness, quality and cost effectiveness—not just efficiency.
- Involve both the top managers and the employees at the design stage.
- Provide adequate scope for adjustments from district to district depending on local requirements.
- Watch out for perverse incentive.
- Use the outputs from the system on a regular basis to make decisions.
- Top officers in the police should be convinced about the efficacy of performance appraisals.

Training 5

Training the police

The Gore committee set up in 1971 by the government to look into the aspect of police training came to the unflattering conclusion that police training had been badly neglected over the years and training arrangements, by and large, were unsatisfactory, both in quantity and quality. The committee found that the training institutions failed to take note of the changing situations and develop realistic training programmes. According to the committee, the most important reason for this unhappy situation was a lack of conviction about the value of training on the part of the administration. The committee shifted the focus of the training from drill and regimentation to the development of proper attitudes through the study of social and behavioural science and modern management norms and techniques. The situation remains so till today. As described in the report, police training is 'a ritual where unwilling and ill-equipped instructors are performing the rites of training and drilling to the unwilling trainees. The syllabi were outmoded and oriented mainly to the paramilitary culture of a crime-control agency and the lecture methods of teaching'.

The police department remains stuck with antiquated and uninspiring training methods, contents have little applicabilty in the field and to the future needs, and the organizational environment has little support for training (Chart I.3.2). According to Peter Drucker, the management guru, the success of IBM's Thomas Watson, above all, can be attributed to the fact that he trained, and trained, and trained his people. Training is a second important component of consequence strategy (Table I.3.1). The training of the policemen should be of utmost importance along with mock drills, surprise checks and inspections—both formal and informal—in the reinvention efforts.

Andragogy model of learning

An A, B, C analysis done on the duties performed by a constable has shown 49 per cent of the duties call for the exercise of higher degree of initiative, discretion, judgement, and so on, and 37 per cent fall in duties involving combination of mechanical with application of mind and exercise of judgement—together they constitute about 86 per cent of the duties (National Police Commission, 1977–81, para 56.22). For the empowered police officers to be successful they have to develop initiative and become self starters in solving the problems of community with the co-operation of various groups. If we review our training process we find that in our teaching we still lay emphasis on the lecture mode suited for children, whereas adults need a learning process drastically different from lecture method. Furthermore, adults learn new knowledge, understandings, skills, values and attitudes most effectively when they are presented in the context of application to real life situations (Knowles, 1990). The basic approach to police training should highlight self-directed learning on the part of the trainee's. The andragogy model of learning,[1] which argues that adults learn differently than the children and therefore should be taught differently, should be adopted by the training institutes and schools in police. Self-directed learning or problem-based learning (PBL) can be done with the help of group exercises and other activities like debate within the context of training classroom (Box II.5.1).

   This can be extremely important for the police officers when they are relating to problem solving, conflict resolution, cultural, religious and social diversity at work. While the police recruits at present—even at the level of assistant sub-inspectors and constables they are highly

[1] Andragogy is the theory which is vastly different from the traditional pedagogy model; it advocates both the self-directed learning concept and the teacher as the facilitator of learning. The message of the self-directed learning and learning based upon the experience of the student is the key. Adults are motivated to devote energy to learn something to the extent that they perceive that will help them perform tasks or tasks or deal with problems they confront in their life situation. Scholars have found self-directed learning to be the principal guiding force in the practice of adult education.

Box II.5.1   Problem-based Learning in Police Training

The Napa Valley Academy in California provides an example of how the PBL is being used across the United States. 'The Napa Valley College Police Academy... believe[s] that in order to train effectively, we must engage the recruit in real-world ill-structured problems that interconnect the curriculum and cause the recruit to think', according to a statement on the academy's website. 'PBL is a teaching method that incorporates just that. The PBL model is the exact process that law enforcement officers use (naturally) every day to solve problems. Then why not begin this process of learning in the academy?' (Napa Valley website).

Numerous law enforcement agencies are moving to the PBL training model. Academies in Washington, Kentucky and California are changing their instructional style to reflect current learning and teaching needs. The Royal Canadian Mounted Police has used the PBL in their training academy for years and are the leaders in self-directed training (Palmiotto et al., 2000). The University of Delaware uses the PBL in its continuing studies programme for law enforcement personnel. In 1999, the COPS office provided funding to PERF and the Reno (Nevada) police department to develop an alternative national model for training new officers that would incorporate community policing and problem-based learning techniques. The resulting Police Training Officer (PTO) programme addresses the traditional duties of policing in the context of specific neighbourhood problems and includes several segments on the use of force. The PTO programme is an alternative to their 30-year-old San Jose Field Training Officer (FTO) programme. Many agencies in the US are using the outlines of the PTO programme to develop their own in-house programmes adapted to their particular needs. The programme is available through Regional Community Policing Institutes (RCPIs).

Source: Cleveland and Saville, 2007.

qualified—police training must be active, engaging and relevant for the recruits and in-service personnel who attend professional development courses.

Emotional intelligence and multiple intelligence

Two important components of adult learning are multiple intelligence and emotional intelligence. Multiple intelligence recognizes that not everyone learns information the same way and that training must be provided in different ways to accommodate the various learning styles. Emotional intelligence includes the way police officers manage their emotions, contacts and relationships with others. Effective leaders are alike in one crucial way: they all have a high degree of emotional intelligence, 90 per cent of the difference in their profiles was attributable to emotional intelligence factors rather than cognitive abilities. When the managers had the critical mass of emotional intelligence, their units outperformed yearly earning goals by 20 per cent, while the leaders without that critical mass underperformed by almost the same amount (Goleman, 1998). Five components of emotional intelligence at work are: self-awareness, self-regulation, motivation, empathy and social skills.

Emotional intelligence has an enormous role in policing, particularly in developing new officers and solving the most common issues that create problems for the department and the individual. These problems develop when the police officers are unable to empathize with others or to control their impulses and emotions. Both multiple intelligence and emotional intelligence should be a critical part of every teaching and learning environment in a police department. These difficult and emotional topics should not be dismissed; these are the real-life issues that the police officers must deal with on the street and in the police station every day.

Alignment of field work and training

Police training is rigid; it evolves from the law, policies, procedures and rules that are followed in strict conformity by the law enforcing agency. However, studies and practical experience show that traditional police training curricula are designed to instruct the recruits in what they will be doing 10 per cent of the time while on duty, that is, their law enforcement functions (Brand and Peak, 1995). Topics and contents must be adapted to the practical daily police work. Goldstein (1990) found that the traditional police training does not deal with specific problems the police are expected to handle and the methods for dealing with them and this is one of the major reasons why recruit training has so often been criticized as having no relevance to the job. Specifically for the Indian police, the situation is grimmer as the training remains far from the realities of the ground situation. As soon as a police officer reaches the police station, first of all, he has to unlearn what he had been taught in the training institutions (National Police Commission, 1977–81: para 62.7).

Another neglected aspect in police training is that it is weighted towards technical aspects of police work (Dunham,1988) and does not prepare the officers for the everyday interactional tasks that they perform (Walker, 1992). For this the training should be designed with inputs from the staff in the police stations so that there is a 'connect' between the teaching and practices. For example, too much of drills may not be required for the trainees now, instead more inputs on personality development, describing and analyzing police misconduct, training on ethical standards and police myths and cynicism may be useful.

Mayhall et al. (1995) make a very relevant comment that the lack of training in such subjects as introduction to social theory, basic psychology, human development and behaviour, police history, interpersonal relations, ethnic studies and communication skills allows communication blocks to remain intact. Instructions on community relations, crisis intervention, and sensitivity training should become part of the academy's curriculum order to improve police officers in dealing with complicated problems of society (Shaw, 1992). In order to align individuals' learnings and the departments' objectives the Singapore police force determines the training needs through a top-down and bottom-up approach. In the top-down approach the strategic education, training and development needs are identified and converted to training plans to support the SPF's objectives and goals. In the bottom-up approach the learning needs analysis process is adopted to ensure the alignment with field requirements.

Developing the necessary skills for maintaining quality standards that the public has begun to expect, would be dependent critically on the skills developed in the empowered employees. Not only the training institutions at the state and district level, but also the training schools in the police lines of every district should work on these guidelines; they should also be given their due importance and earmarked funds. Regular, short and focused capsule training courses of two to three days in the police lines, with the help of the faculty from outside police, could also be of immense benefit to polish the skills in interface activities with the public. The training programmes should be used to herald a commitment to a new strategic thrust and to teach the police department's mission, vision and values.

Strategic partnerships

With the advent of the Internet, increased flow of manpower, trade and crime even the training needs are becoming globalized. In the globalized world, exchange of ideas, information and expertise can play an important role in the training of police officers. The International Police Expertise Platform (IPEP) is a global learning network for the exchange of information between the law enforcement institutions and individuals, of police training, academic and police knowledge networks. It is also a storehouse of resources, consolidating all aspects of law enforcement activities, police assistance, training techniques, funding opportunities and virtual communities of police experts, but also contains information on job opportunities and new publications. Similarly, the European Police College (CEPOL) is a network of national training institutes for senior police officers in the member states of the European Union (EU). It was established in January 2001 for the purpose of training law enforcement officers and to support and develop a European approach for the prevention and combating of crime and the maintenance of public order and security from a cross-border perspective. CEPOL also welcomes co-operation with national and international training institutes outside the European Union.

Based on the ideas of the Police Learning Network, Scotland and the Netherlands took the initiative in 2000 of developing the European Police Learning Network (EPLN), based on the three pillars of study, knowledge and discussion. EPLN is being developed within the CEPOL. EPLN is the platform on which the e-learning activities of CEPOL will be developed in the future. The network is primarily intended for the exchange of information and expertise between policy-makers, researchers and managers within police organizations and training organizations in Europe. In this way they can bring together the knowledge and experience of the different national organizations. Thirty countries are taking part in the project, including all the EU countries, the candidate countries, Norway and Iceland. The navigation structure, which has been established in accordance with the domain structure used by the Police Knowledge Network (PKN), is the backbone of the European Knowledge Network.

In the Netherlands, the PKN, which is a form of digital databank, occupies a special position among the centres of expertise. The databank serves as a repository of the knowledge of the police training and knowledge centre, the police forces and the external partners, and can be consulted online by the police officers. The data consists not only of documented knowledge taken from textbooks and training modules but above all of practical information that can be used in the situations with which the police officers are confronted with on a daily basis.

A similar approach can be adopted by the police academies in India to meet the training needs and for resource pooling and optimal utilization in the future. India can also integrate with such wider networks to draw from the internationally available resources, to supplement the POTNET network setup at the National Police Academy at Hyderabad[2].

---

[2] The S.V.P. National Police Academy has established the Police Training Network (POTNET), a network of all police training colleges and academies of sates/CPOs in India. This network will act as the backbone for communication between various police training institutions in the country. This will allow sharing of all the course material, training information, training calendar and online communication with each other (www.svpnpa. gov.in).

Supportive environment

The organizational considerations of training remain one of the most important issues. If the police department itself remains hostile or indifferent to the purpose the officer are trained for and does not provide a supportive environment, any amount of good training will not have a significant positive effect (Mastrofsky and Ritti, 1996). In the Indian police departments, presently, the training remains a neglected wing and very often, the people who are sent for training are those who are considered spare, near retirement and many a times, they are working in a unit not related to the training theme. On return from training, the skills acquired by the police officers are seldom put to use as their job responsibility is rarely decided on the basis of training programmes attended.

Since 1997, the SPF has been a fervent practitioner of learning organization concepts. Therefore, human capital is the most valued asset of the SPF. Recruiting only the best talents, the majority of the SPF recruits are degree or diploma holders and this ensures intellectual propensity for learning. They also offer scholarships to top high school graduates, sponsoring their tertiary education. Subsequently, the mental models of officers are then shaped through training.

Future training needs

Kirkpatrick's model is an effective way to evaluate the effectiveness of the training in relation to organizational goals. In this model, the effectiveness is measured in terms of reaction from the participants, learning from training, behaviour and results. The training programmes for the police should be reviewed and continuously improved adopting such a model to maintain their relevance and efficacy.

While taking care of the current needs it is essential that the training also looks at the preparedness of the police officers in terms of what demands future would place on them. For a future police training and planning, the following external factors as listed among the threats in the SWOT analysis have to be taken into account (Feltes, 2002):

1. The increase of the police product in volume, gravity and complexity, aggravated by the expanding international dimension requiring new resources, connections and information exchange.
2. The development of new technologies.

3. A greater mobility and the abolition of borders, clearing the way to larger markets with easier escape routes for criminal organizations and making effective communication systems available to them.
4. The economic and political situation with social and political unrest, economic crunch, massive unemployment, juvenile crime and further migration waves.
5. The challenge to tackle terrorism, underworld and spreading Maoist Naxalite movement, which today is affecting one-third of the districts in the country.
6. The budget restrictions imposed by the government or local authorities cutting down on additional human and material resources.

The new culture of empowerment and transparency in the department would mean not only training the employees, but also the managers to use the right levers. As a result, the supervisory skills need to be taught to the supervisory officers to use controls in tune with the new evolving culture of the department, such as, the customer contact, the power of the market, self-discipline and self-control born out of involvement and empowerment. For the senior police officers, an innovative way of combining exchange with individual learning is the new initiative of the action learning method was recently adopted by the Australian, Canadian and the Dutch police. Participants were invited to work together on a real assignment in a worldwide law enforcement learning set as reflective practitioners. It meant learning by action and reflection, supported by professional trainers. The participants also communicated and worked together through virtual exchange discussions realized through the IPEP.[3]

Community policing training[4]

Community policing training is different from the traditional training. It involves learning to think critically, to solve problems, to share responsibilities with citizens and is not fostered by authoritarian or non-interactive training techniques (Dantzker et al., 1995: 50). A department that plans to undertake the implementation of community policing will have to shift police training, at the academy, field training and in service training, from the current model of mastery of technical skills and

---

[3] International Pearl Fishers Action Learning Group held three seminars during 2007–08 in Canberra, Canada and Hague with on going discussions on IPEP.
[4] Adapted from article by Palmiotto et al., 2000.

obedience to a focus on empowerment (Trojanowics and Bucqeroux, 1994). The training method recommended is the andragogy model of learning. When the recruits are allowed to engage in self-directed group discussions with the trainers, allowing them the liberty of expressing their view point freely, the classroom in itself begins to reflect the picture of community with different voices presenting different perspectives, such experience in training would help the recruits. The training curriculum for the police officers should include familiarity with the community they are to serve, techniques of crime prevention and conflict resolution, police philosophy and culture, techniques to handle the physical and mental stress, self-awareness, ethics and development of human values.

Knowledge of the police history can provide an overview of policing. The police recruits with no knowledge. The police history may not be aware that the police have been involved in social service activities in the past and that a large portion of their job is service oriented. This will also help them to understand most of the issues and problems confronting policing today, and about storehouse of past knowledge and existing practices for generating creative solutions. The recruits need to have training on the police mission, police objectives and the value system of the police agency to be able to see how an individual police work fits into the larger department and community. Classes in police culture, police cynicism, police myths and discretion are extremely important to understand the operating environment of the police agency.

The recruit should be familiar with the community. This includes the socio-economic make-up of the community, its power structure, potential partisanship on important social issues, the community's cultural and social diversity. Problem-oriented policing has been considered an important part of community-oriented policing and without an understanding of problem solving activities and applications and an emphasis on creative thinking, police officers will not be successful in grappling with the many social and community problems they will face. Therefore, the recruits should be trained to have an understanding of crime prevention concepts, including Crime Prevention Through Environmental Design (CPTED), crime triangle, Scanning, Analysis, Response and Assessment (SARA) model and Situational Crime Prevention,[5] along with training in specific applications and strategies should be provided. Such training would enable the police recruit to use practical techniques that he or she has learned, for example, organizing neighbourhood watches, doing security audits and promoting property identification procedures.

---

[5] See 2.1, Chapter 6, Part II—Proactive Policing for more on CPTED and situational crime prevention.

Ethics training

Given the close connections between the police and the community envisaged by community-oriented policing, the police recruits should be
required to take classes describing and analyzing such misconduct and
given training in ethical standards so that they recognize and successfully
handle potential misconduct situations. In handling the situations, conflicts, disputes and public dealing, the role of self-awareness, inner clarity
and human values in an individual is very important. Without attending
to this aspect the genuine concern for community in the recruits, which
is very important for any community policing officer, will be missing.
For a community policing recruit, awareness of oneself and others,
living in physical and mental health, good relationship with all, love
and compassion for all and responsibility to be of service to others are
very important. Therefore, programmes on yoga, *pranayam*, developing
human values, spirituality and concern for the community should be
included in their training for the sense of service to society and the love
for mankind to blossom from within. Police training should ensure that
the physical, mental and spiritual well-being becomes the part of the
lifestyle of the police personnel.

The Hong Kong police, as a part of their strategy to promote integrity
in the department, have been imparting training to their officers to even
manage their personal financial situations.

Ethics training for police professionals should help them do the
following (Jacocks and Bowman, 2006):

1. Readily recognize an ethical problem or dilemma.
2. Identify various options to address the particular issue involved.
3. Make a rational and ethically sound choice of which option to
   choose.
4. Take prompt action based upon that choice.
5. Accept responsibility for the outcome.
6. Develop healthy life style among officers by encouraging and facilitating physical and mental well-being and financial prudence.

Once the recruit has a solid foundation in areas such as police history,
community culture, ethics, human values, sense of belongingness to society, self-awareness, problem solving and crime prevention, he/she will
be prepared to better understand and implement the community policing
philosophy and be able to incorporate community-oriented policing
into his/her professional value system during the formative period in the
academy.

Training for the Indian police

- Basics approach to highlight self-directed learning on the part of the trainee.
- Align individuals' learning and the departments' objectives.
- Determine the training needs through a top-down and bottom-up approach.
- Both emotional and multiple intelligence should be a critical part of every teaching and learning environment in the police department.
- Strategic partnerships between training institutes, police knowledge networks and individuals for exchange of ideas and expertize.
- Specialized training for community policing and courses on ethics training.
- Provide supportive environment within the department for training.

Aiming 6

A long with the implementation of control strategy with employee empowerment as discussed earlier (Part II, Chapter 1), the implementation of the core strategy of developing an inspiring vision and leadership for the police department is equally important. The empowerment of policemen without any sense of direction can lead to anarchy. While the employees want the freedom of empowerment, they need the sense of direction also. The vision and leadership are like the light and the edifice of a lighthouse that can guide the police department in the ocean of conflicting and ever changing currents from all sides. Given these two, the police in India has demonstrated the capability to produce spectacular results.

Vision or 'strategic intent'

In the year 2005, the Dutch police developed a memorandum entitled 'The Police in Evolution', setting out a mission, followed by a vision and then a strategy for the coming years. In the document, the mission clarifies the identity of the Dutch police and affects the positioning of the police and the working methods of the organization. The vision is presented for the Dutch police indicating how police, now and in the fututre, will give substance to their mission. The strategy in the document explains the concepts involved as regards the tasks, the organization, the issue of public safety and operations. The managerial aspects, collaboration and the administrative embedding of the police are also discussed (Box II.6.1).

Box II.6.1   Ten Points on the Horizon for the Dutch Police

The main components of the vision memorandum 'The Police in Evolution', that gives the directions in which the Dutch police service wants to develop in the next few years, have been expressed as ten points on the horizon:

1. The Dutch police want to contribute to safety.
2. Reporting and giving advice is an explicit task of the Dutch police.
3. Subordination with authority determines the direction of the Dutch police.
4. The community focus will remain a guiding principle for the Dutch police.
5. A nodal orientation is a necessary supplement to the local orientation in the community focus.
6. The Dutch police are focussed on policing of communities.
7. The Dutch police want to work in an information driven manner.
8. The Dutch police consider programme management as an adequate means of collaboration.
9. The Dutch police form an organizational entity.
10. The Dutch police consider close collaboration with the European police services as a self-evident element of the joint EU safety policy.

It is a framework memorandum that needs further elaboration and the School of Police Leadership, Netherlands, further worked on the vision for development of a methodology to translate this into practical terms.

Source: Netherlands Police Institute, 2006.

For the Belgian police, vision is linked to the image of building a house; it provides, in society, an 'outstanding police function' which is the vision for the police. In enunciating the basic principles and the coherence between them, the foundation of this house is laid. In the implementation of the concept 'outstanding police function', building stones and critical success factors are dealt with and the building plans for the house are described. Beyond the building plans and foundations, the police decide 'what' they put inside and 'how' they furnish it, which means that police has the necessary local autonomy for carrying out their operations and functions (Bruggeman et al., 2007) (Box II.7.3).

The vision or 'strategic intent' is something more than a war cry; it is a dream that energizes the organization and provides for direction, destiny and discovery (Hamel and Prahalad, 2002: 142). Employees today are driven by something more than the paychecks—by the desire to make a

difference to the lives of the people. Police job, by its very nature, provides such an opportunity. The strategic intent of the department should
capture this sentiment. The SPF has the mission statement to uphold the
law, maintain order and keep the peace in the Republic of Singapore.
The shared vision is:

> We are the force for the nation, ensuring the security, survival and success
> of Singapore, and helping to built it into our best home. We are a police
> force that inspires the world. We are united with community. We care for
> and serve the community that we work in and with. We are feared by those
> inclined to crime and disorder. We are always ready to deal with any threats
> to the safety and security of Singapore. We are a harmonious family. Each
> of us serves and leads, contributing to the objectives of the team we are part
> of. Our workplace is enjoyable to be in. Our people are our most valued
> assets. (SPF, 2007)

The strategic intent should not only be emotionally compelling, but
it should also be personalized for every policemen, which means that
they should understand the linkage between his/her job and attainment
of the goal. Leadership in the department has to look inwards and work
with everyone to develop and live an enabling and empowering vision,
something more than an incrementalist, annual routine bureaucratic exercise. The strategic intent should be specific enough to be acted on, and
general enough to leave room for taking bold initiatives in a department like
the police where the working needs meeting challenges from time to time.

The first task in personalizing the strategic intent is to set clear
challenges that focus everyone's attention on the capability to be built
next. To chart a direction for the department, each year the director
general of the police, after taking extensive opinion, can enunciate the
next key challenge for the department. One year it could be focused on
the quality of investigations, another year it could be focused on the
police–citizen interface; it could clear the backlog of pending inspections,
increase professionalism or promote the culture of integrity and ethics
in the department. One of the benefits of enunciating challenges is that
everyone in the organization is focused from top to bottom on the identified task as achievements are made by the organizations working as a
team in one direction and not as cross-purpose units. The SPF's organizational direction that has been mentioned is guided by its three strategic
thrusts so that all the efforts are geared towards the achievement of its
shared vision. The three strategic thrusts are: enhancing organizational
capability, strengthening community partnership and building organizational resilience. These thrust areas are translated into long-term
and short-term strategies and plans at the SPF corporate retreat. These

strategies are then cascaded to every SPF unit which then conduct their respective retreats and formalize their work plans (SPF, 2007).

Strategic architecture (Hamel and Prahalad, 2002)

One way of doing this can be by building a strategic architecture for the present and perceived future threats for the police department. Such strategic architecture only identifies the capabilities to be built and need not be a detail plan of how it is to be built. The strategic architecture is a high-level blue print for the deployment of new functionalities, the acquisition of new competencies or the migration of existing competencies and the reconfiguring of the interface with the customer (Hamel and Prahalad, 2002: 118). For example, threats like the huge youth population in coming years, emerging area of economic and transborder crimes should make the department determine the competencies that will have to be accessed, acquired or strenghtened to counter these threats in future.[1] This would mean anticipating and identifying the need for the creation of specialized wings with tecnologically advanced equipments, special programmes to reach out to the youth, mechanism for quicker information sharing among the important trading nations and neighbours, attachment of experts in finanace with the investigating teams for economic crimes, proposals for amendment in the law of evidence and court trial procedures and the training need to equip the staff to deal with such crimes and situations.

The Royal Canadian Mounted Police (RCMP) is an agency that ensures public safety in Canada. Aggressively fighting crime in Canada since 1863, the RCMP also plays a role in fighting international terrorism. Many of the provinces and counties where it operates are on a contracting basis. Therefore, the RCMP has to compete with the business to provide public safety to citizens. Managers in the RCMP were not people who were devoted to security and social welfare of the Canadians. Faced with growing dissatisfaction from the public in the year 2000, the RCMP took the initiative to develop a strategic architecture to co-ordinate and align its diverse initiatives, ranging from community policing to an internationally co-ordinated fight against terrorism. The strategic architecture gave shape to the RCMP mission of 'safe homes and communities' (Box II.6.2). Today the RCMP leads Canada's counter-terrorism efforts, while demonstrating excellence at 'on-the-ground' community-based policing across Canada.

---

[1] This year the National Police Academy is starting a course on investigations on international crimes to develop competencies in investigators to deal with increasing trans border crimes (Kandula, 2007).

Box II.6.2   The RCMP Architecture*

As the focus of the RCMP revolves around the citizens, stakeholders and part- ners, the strategic architecture starts with a system focus and then drills down to processes and people. The architecture of the RCMP (see also Chart II.2.2, adaptation of the RCMP architecture as applied to the Indian police) has four elements, which are consistent across the organization. The first element is the RCMP strategic framework or strategy map. The strategy map defines what the organization is trying to evolve into and what the organization wants to be from the perspective of its clients and stakeholders. Articulating such a strategic framework helps the organization see where it is going and helps its people to visualize the key drivers that they need to have in place to get the organization to achieve its objectives.

The second element is the RCMP value position, which specifies very clearly who they have to deliver value to. They need to deliver value to (a) clients who are people with whom te RCMP contract,[2] that is, the local authorities who want the RCMP to be their policing agency, (b) partners who are those with whom the RCMP works together and (c) stakeholders who are the citizens in that particular province or municipality that the RCMP is in the business of protecting.

The next stage, that is, the strategic pathways, sets clear objectives for the internal processes, which the RCMP must achieve in order to deliver value to its clients, partners and stakeholders. The first objective of the internal pro- cesses perspective is 'excellence in operations', that is, achieving excellence in its activities of policing, investigation, public safety and enforcement. The second objective of 'management excellence' stresses on doing all these activities in an excellent way and in a cost-effective manner. It focuses on the management excellence, accountability and resource management objective. The third strategic pathway being 'building bridge with community'.

The fourth stage is to identify and put in practice the processes to improve the quality of the RCMP human capital and enabling technology that are re- quired to become an organization of excellence. Performance management processes linked by the balanced scorecards are used for implementing these measures in the organization.

Note: *Information provided in these paragraphs has been sourced from Clarke, 2002.

Strategic planning cell

However, at present in the Indian police departments, the strategic plan- ning remains neglected and there are no functional strategic planning cells or any senior officer given the assignment of strategic thinking. There is an attitude of helplessness that not much can be done by planning in the department, given the constraints and dependence of the police on the

---

[2] The RCMP is unique in the world as it provides policing service at national, federal, pro- vincial and municipal level. It has policing services contract with about 200 municipalities.

environment, towards building up a road map of future direction.[3] But to be successful in today's law enforcement environment, police executives must set the course with strategic management by appointing a senior officer of the rank of inspector general/additional director general of police as strategic officer and creating a cell for strategic planning and implementing plans and organizational change measures. Progressive police departments like the Dutch police, Norwegian police, Hong Kong police and the SPF, to name the few have appointed strategic managers for their department. Strategic managers integrate strategic planning with other management systems. Ang Hag Seng, the Director of Strategic Development and Information, has been one of the brain behind the new vision of 'from police to policing' of the SPF. Core competencies require the strategic manager to do any of the following (Charrier, 2004):

1. Conduct research to support and co-ordinate the department's strategic intent and architecture.
2. Identify adjustments in organizational designs.
3. Identify potential barriers or gaps created by human system resistance.
4. Monitor and assess departmental progress toward strategic planning goals.
5. Serve as the department liaison with external stakeholders in planning projects.
6. Review programme research to determine applicability to departmental needs.
7. Identify proactive approaches to issues through trend analysis and predictive indicators.
8. Work to drive organizational change through marketing and educating personnel on best practice methods.
9. Assist middle managers in navigating the change process.
10. Enhance efficiency by evaluating operational systems across organizational lines.

Strategic planning can not only lead to efficiency but also effectiveness in department's functioning by constantly assessing the requirements and the competencies of the department and their alignment with the customer needs. Future scenario planning is tool often used by the private

[3] We have observed that for quite some time now the police officers tend to abdicate their role, initiative and responsibility. Some of them have convinced themselves that they are helpless due to scarcity of resources, problems of staff and the overbearing control of/and interference by the political leadership. Things would not have degenerated so much if the deficiencies of the politicians had been made up by the ability, courage, vision, competence and leadership of the senior civil servants and police officers (National Police Commission, 1977–81: para 44.9).

sector giants such as the oil industry and the defence organizations. This tool could be useful for the police too, as an aid in strategic planning, since it is aimed at planning long term over a time span of more than 10 years. This involves identifying key developments to tackle such as population explosion, urban growth, global warming or mass migration. The next step involves data gathering and from the data gathered, the scenarios driving forces are identified. Driving forces could be important technological advancements, political, economic or social developments. Also, the predetermined factors, the factors that do not change, are identified. The critical uncertainties are then identified for which little is known in the present. Having identified these different variables, futuristic scenario planning can be done for the police giving the optimistic and the worst scenarios to develop police strategies and response for different events. The police in Germany use a strategic early detection system and utilize scenarios not just to look at geographical patterns of crime or insecurity, but also to assess their impact on the organization. Knowing the threats ahead, the German police are able to decide which people, what kind of specialist knowledge, networks and training they require. Having made that assessment they are able to formulate appropriate strategy. This can sometimes lead to altering the fundamental approach in the way the police department functions (Box II.6.3).

Box II.6.3   Strategic Plan of the Aurora Police Department

In 1998, members of the Aurora Police Department, US, began developing a strategic plan for the department's future. The strategic planning committee was tasked with developing a plan to increase the department's effectiveness and efficiency and improve the quality of customer service. The committee addressed many important aspects of agency operations, including future technology acquisition, employee career development and the physical decentralization of departmental resources to better serve the community. The committee emphasized providing a more efficient and effective delivery of police services through an enhanced problem-solving approach. This required a change in the physical structure of departmental resources, developing a new philosophy and implementing a new approach to address community concerns with an emphasis on customer service through problem solving. The new approach was to concentrate efforts on three main police mission areas that negatively affect the neighbourhoods and businesses of Aurora: Crime, Quality of life and Traffic or CQT. Under the new philosophy, the traditional pillars of law enforcement—random patrol, fast response and turning all cases over to the detectives for follow-up are replaced with teamwork, problem solving and accountability. In January 2002, the Aurora Police Department embarked upon the new CQT philosophy to provide better customer service to the community as a result of its strategic plan.

Source: Bennet, 2005.

The police board of the Victoria police in Australia is another example. In cooperation with the Victorian police and the department of justice, it undertook a new direction with the development of a 'long range strategic plan' for policing (Interview with Wilson 1997). Being 'long range' in nature required that strategies be effective for at least 10 to 15 years, which meant extensive review and analysis of worldwide environments, and forthcoming trends was necessary. At times, the board also undertook some independent research, releasing several documents—one of which was titled 'broken windows, zero tolerance and other policing styles' (Box II.6.4). Such research and analysis of other systems was a continued attempt at rectifying any outdated or redundant practices on the behalf of the Victorian police.

Box II.6.4   Broken Windows Theory

The political science professors, James Q. Wilson and George Kelling, originally developed the 'broken windows' theory during 1982 after several years of field study (Wilson and Kelling, 1982). His theory is based on propositions developed through extensive observation. If for instance, there is an abandoned building with one broken window, within a short period, all the windows will end up broken. Precautions need to be taken to ensure that the first window never gets broken to begin with. To be able to do this, police officers must take even the slightest sign of disorder as extremely serious—this would include such things as graffiti. They argued that an ambience of unrestrained petty crime creates the impression that 'no one is in control' and that more serious crime can be committed with impunity. In other words, unchecked disorder and incivility in a given locality send an implicit invitation to more predatory criminals. The policing strategy that were based on this theory is also termed as 'zero tolerance policing'.

Source: Wilson and Kelling, 1982.

Leadership

Visionary and inspiring leadership was found to be a critical trait in the top 100 best companies in the USA (Leiber, 1998). For the police, leadership is even more critical and demanding. Ideally, the job requires a person who understands the complexity and urgency of urban and rural problems, who sympathizes with the way these problems affect the daily lives of the people, who is devoted to democratic procedures and principles, who is tolerant to unconventional modes of expression and behaviour, who is ready to experiment and innovate, who can keep up the enthusiasm of the department in the face of inevitable frustration and setbacks, who can plead the police's case persuasively to the government; who acts vigorously against dishonesty and corruption; who can look ahead in future and who can administer an extremely intricate organization (Cizanckas and Hanna, 1977: 7). Given this broad competency profile, the key challenge for police organization operating with an ever-changing scenario is a modern leadership. The SPF has realized that conditioning ground response based on prescriptive and exhaustive standard operating procedures is no longer sufficient for going forward. The grey of today's environment has to be matched with discretion and instead, therefore, principles and rationales are laid out clearly to the SPF officers. By understanding the out-of-bound markers (OB markers), officers are then equipped with skills to assess the situation and to make their own judgement. To hone individual leadership skills, a leadership competency framework was established. The framework seeks to instill ownership in personal development and places emphasis on the role of supervisors as mentors. The SPF spares no expense in leadership investment. As a part of the training, all senior officers embark on a two-week overseas leadership programme in Nepal. The stint draws officers out of their comfort zone and allows them to capitalize on experiential learning in the great outdoors to hone individual leadership skills (Singapore Police Commissioner, 2007).

The Netherlands police have a separate school for police leadership and in India, the National Police Academy does the job of preparing the probationers of the prestigious Indian Police Service (IPS) for the leadership role. However, in the Indian police an officer moves up the ladder through time-bound promotions within an uninspiring bureaucratic set-up. Today, many a times, the officers are not adequately equipped to handle difficult responsibilities due to the complex functioning of the police department.[4] Therefore, like any other bureaucratic organization in the police department, the energies of majority of senior officers are directed on just the supervision work and control, to prevent people from doing what they are not supposed to do, by a system of checks and balances. Given the complexity of police work and intricacies of the organization, the job of the top officers' demands much more than the routine bureaucratic office work.

---

[4] No thinking and planning are in evidence because the senior administrative ranks are perpetually insecure and are exhausted by the continual effort to survive, in an atmosphere where their assessment by the executive—administrative and political—is not always based on merit (National Police Commission, 1977–81: para 62.8).

Living by the vision

Effective leadership—at all levels—is marked by a core philosophy (values) and a vision of how the department wishes to make its mark (Peters, 1987). Once the vision is created, the leadership then has to become the biggest living example of this vision through the actions and should make it a point to emphasize the vision time, and again, to the frontline policemen. For the frontline policemen to be able act at an instant, which they have to act most of the time, they must have clear understanding about what the department is trying to achieve and in what manner. Jack Welch says:[5]

> Good leaders create a vision, articulate the vision, passionately own the vision, and relentlessly drive it to completion. Above all else, though, good leaders are open. They go up, down, and around their organization to reach people. They do not stick to the established channels. They're informal. They are straight with people. They make a religion out of being accessible. (Charan and Tichy, 1989)

Management by walking around

The most effective leaders, from Mahatma Gandhi to Sam Walton of Wal Mart, lead from the frontline where the action is. Any police officer, at any level, who hopes for even limited success must lead from the trenches. One effective way to do this is by practicing visible management or 'management by walking around'. K. P. S. Gill, as the director general of Punjab, went around in the nights with his men, in the most disturbed areas of Punjab, as a part of operation named 'Operation Night Domination', to send a strong message to his men and instil confidence in public. Richard Roodman, CEO, Valley Medical Centre (VMC) was able to turn around the medical centre plagued with problems like indecision, lethargy, demoralization, insecurity and feeling of betrayal among the employees. Within two weeks of being hired, Roodman went to 700 employees and wrote each one of them a letter, met with medical staff and formal and informal leaders. Such is the effectiveness of visible management that VMC got the prized Innovation awards for 1986. It

---

[5] Interview of Jack Welsh, the famous and very successful CEO of General Electric, who is known for giving new strategic direction to the flaggering fortunes of one of world's largest corporations. After a decade of his taking over as CEO, GE was rated number one or two in all its businesses. GE today is also known as the nursery for the future CEOs.

all started with powerful dose of getting out and about (Peters, 1987: 423–32). Policing, unlike many other bureaucratic positions, entails field working, though paper work and reports which have their own role to play in supervision and control, nothing energizes and spurs the force as the presence of a leader among the ranks. The best of the ideas also have come to the leaders while moving about interacting with their officers.

Credibility

Kouzes and Posner's research for their book, *Credibility: How Leaders Gain and Lose It, Why People Demand It*, strongly supported the benefits of having leaders who are honest, competent and inspiring. In one study they compared employees' sense of teamwork, alignment of organizational values, work attitude and organizational commitment with leader's honesty, competence and abilities to inspire. They found that employees who worked for leaders viewed as being more honest, competent and inspiring were more likely to feel a strong sense of teamwork and alignment with organizational values and exhibit a positive work attitude and organizational commitment (Roger, 1995). Research has also established that the employees are willing to forgive the lack of professional knowledge and even failure of their leader, but not a lapse of integrity in their conduct. When it comes to the issue of ethical leadership, its significance cannot be over emphasized.

It is therefore not surprising that honest, competent and inspiring leadership, whenever given the opportunity, in the police, also has been able to work wonders. Such leaders have been able to inspire the policemen to perform deeds that go well beyond the expectations and the poor image that the department enjoys, the are many such examples of police leadership in different parts of the country at different times. The senior officers, particularly the director general and the senior superintendents of the police must be prepared to set an example of diligence in their offical as well as personal conduct by exhibiting exemplary overt behaviour to demonstrate visibly and transparently what is and is not ethically acceptable within the organization. Their personal conduct and values are so much under the scrutiny of their own men and public alike that if they allow even an iota of slip in their conduct, they should surely be expected to face far-reaching consequences due to the importance and influence associated with these positions.

The Virginia Beach, Virginia, Police Department in the US, had embarked on an ambitious programme to develop and sustain a culture of integrity in the organization. The department's command staff realized that the traditional emphasis on the ethical conduct of police officers in the field would not fully develop a culture of integrity in the organization. An analysis of the situation by senior leaders concluded with the observation that the department's leaders must be the centre of gravity in developing and sustaining a culture of integrity (Jacocks and Bowman, 2006).

Conversely, leaders lacking integrity tend to drift with the flow and approach problems designed merely to appease or to please. Characterized further as avoiding responsibility and exhibiting ever-changing loyalties, such officers lack acceptance by the rank-and-file and by the people, they have no grip over the situations and the organization. Such hollow leadership eventually leads to neglect, mismanagement, escalation of crises and the perpetuation of unacceptable behaviours, responses and relationships throughout the organization (Plummer, 1995).

Leadership model for the police

The retention of autocratic management styles in the Indian police departments is largely due to a glorification of the past and a belief that restraint and control is the key to 'real' policing. The department takes pride in their responsiveness to commands and a disciplined workforce. There is no culture of treating subordinates as partners in working towards a common goal in the police departments. As we near the end of the twentieth century, we are beginning to see that traditional autocratic and hierarchical modes of leadership are slowly yielding to a newer model. If in the past our ideas about leadership tended to revolve around the solitary heroic figure, the leadership of our future will be defined by inspired teamwork. Leaders will oversee organizations that are flatter, with fewer levels of management and fewer clear distinctions between them. As the lines of demarcation between leader and follower continue to blur, empowering strategies and inclusive decision-making styles will not just be recommended management practices; they will be essential competencies of police leadership (Wuestewald and Steinheider, 2006). The traditional mechanistic management approach in the Indian police too often resort to fear as a means to obtain employee obedience and compliance. However, it is increasingly being realized that the 'era of managing by dictate is ending and is being replaced by an era of managing by inspiration' (Dehler and Welsh, 1994).

Robert Greenfield's servant leadership model as discussed earlier (Part II, Chapter 2 and Box II.2.5) appears best suited for the police department today and more so in times to come, when the problems would be even more complex and the job even more demanding, and that would call for inner strength in a leader to see through the situations.

Vision and leadership for the Indian police

- Formulate a strategic intent and strategic architecture for implementing the intent in the department.
- Appoint a strategic officer for the police department.
- Leadership to become the biggest living example of this vision.
- Leadership to follow servant leadership model—principle centred, honest, inspiring, participative and empathy for the weaker section of the society.
- Leadership to set example of diligence in their officials as well as personal conduct to become centre of gravity in developing and sustaining culture of integrity.
- Practice Management by Walking Around (MBWA) for being in touch with public and policemen in the department.
- Lead from the front.

Customer Offering 7

T he services offered to the citizen and other stakeholders and the
duties discharged to enforce the law of the land is the second
P—'product', for the police department, as discussed in the characterstics
and categories of police service earlier. The primary purpose of the police
is the preservation of peace and protection of life and property against
attacks by criminals and injury by the careless and inadvertent offender.
In addition, the police departments are charged with the enforcement of
a wide variety of state and local laws, ordinances and regulations dealing
with all sorts of subjects, some of these are designed to safeguard the
morals of the community, and through their enforcement, the police department becomes the principal agent of society in eliminating the opportunity for immoral conduct (Wilson, 1972). Undoubtedly, then, in the
discharge of these duties, it should be not be forgotten that ultimately
these duties are entrusted to the police in service and for the benefit of
the society and the public.

The idea that the police must be closely associated with the public
was suggested by Sir Robert Peel in his 1829 rules and regulations for
the London Metropolitan Police. He stated: 'The police are public and
the public are the police.' The core philosophy of policing, then, should
be unmistakebly citizen centric. In that, the effort should be that the
citizens must feel that the police and the criminal justice system put them
first. Citizen-centric policing is a way of policing in which the needs and
expectations of individuals and local communities are always reflected in
police decision making and service (Box II.7.1). Citizen-centric policing
does not only apply to the public-facing parts of the organization, but

---

Box II.7.1   Citizen-focused Policing

The UK police have adopted the concept of citizen-focused policing. Here the efforts are that the citizens must feel that the police and the criminal justice system put them first. Citizen-focused policing is a new way of policing in which the needs and expectations of individuals and local communities are always reflected in police decision making and service. There are five key workstreams to the citizen-focused policing programme:

1. improving the experience of those who have contact with the police,
2. rolling out a neighbourhood policing approach across all forces by 2008,
3. effective community engagement which includes consultation, marketing and communications, and public involvement,
4. public understanding and local accountability of policing,
5. organizational and cultural change to bring about increasingly responsive services where feedback from frontline staff and the public is used continuously.

Source: www.homeoffice.gov.uk.

---

to everyone within all forces, at all levels, whatever their function. That requires a cultural and operational change, like proactive policing, customer empowerment, systematic identification of citizen needs and some measures like the quality of service commitment and citizen's charter which are discussed in Chapter 11.

Looking at the SWOT analysis (Chart I.3.2), while for the Indian police the weakness is its colonial mindset of focus on serving the political masters, the common man finds an insignificant say in the matters of policing and the police remains rigid, insensitive and detached from the public. Old laws and political masters' interests govern their activities and orientation, the rise of new type of crime, rapid urbanization, cross state and border crime and technological advancements pose a grave threat to the organization. Despite that the police remains the only face of governmet in many far-flung areas of the country, is in continuous contact with the community and the opportunity exists today in increased awareness among the people about their rights and need for police reforms.

With the above in mind, in order to provide the kind of police people need, we consider appropriate strategies and metatools given in the following table.

Customer strategy	Customer needs
Culture strategy	Proactive policing
Control strategy	Customer empowerment
Core strategy	Shape the future

Customer needs

Britain's Audit Commission preliminary report titled 'Enhancing Police Patrol' concluded that in a police force with an average strength of 2,500 police officers, only 125 (about 5 per cent) could be expected to be committed on street patrol at any time. In addition many of those involved in beat patrols were inexperienced, badly briefed and ill-trained. It was also concluded that the street patrolling job, demanded the most by the public and was the least desired by police officers (*The Guardian*, 1995). The police must understand the make-up of their communities, as well as the needs and expectations that citizens have of their police services. For example, if a locality has a high school population of 1,500 girl students who come from many different neighbouring communities, law enforcement must consider providing for their public safety needs while they are on the way to school, at school and when they leave school. Just the relocation of duty points can have a big impact on the utility of policemen on the street. Holding of regular public meetings in both the rural and urban areas can be one way in identification of customer requirements.

Different methods by which the citizen voice can be heard (Osborne and Plastrik, 2000) by the policy-makers/implementers in the police department are summerized in Chart II.7.1. Customer surveys help to know what customers think and want, an interesting example of one such survey conducted in Russia is shown in Chart II.7.2. Customer surveys can cover an entire community or it could be targeted customer survey, random survey or exit survey of the people who have just used the police services. Surveys can be conducted through mail, email, exit survey, and so on. Telephone lines and helpdesks help customers not only get required information, but can also act as a source of feedback. Customer suggestion boxes help collect written feedback from customers, which can be an effective tool to ensure quality assurance to the customer. Feedback from frontline employees who are in direct contact with customers can provide useful information on what frustrates customers and what changes they desire.

Customer panels are groups of customers who agree to be surveyed repeatedly and participate in focus groups, interviews and other consultations over a period of time to provide the department regular feedback. Focus groups are the small groups of customers brought together for an hour or two to discuss a particular service or issue. Police station advisory committees can be used as focus groups by the police. Most intense customer feedback can come from showing up unannounced at the police stations, when still unknown, and go through the system as

Chart II.7.1   Citizen Voice

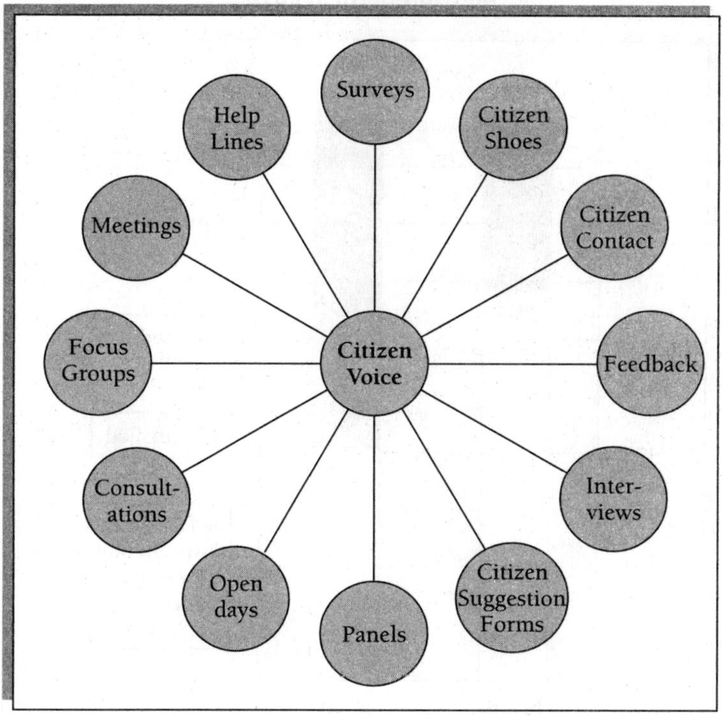

Source: Osborne and Pastrik, 2000.

a customer would (Box II.7.2). 'Mystery shoppers' is another concept used by the private sector but the citizen's charter has made its use more popular in the government too. The Royal Mail of the UK employs a private firm of mystery shoppers to check its 200 delivery offices (Osborne and Plastrik, 2000: 382–87). The police in Singapore gathers insight into customer needs with the help of meetings and dialogue sessions, focus group discussions and surveys, feedback forms, emails, faxes and letters, telephone hotlines and media.

One of the roles of the Victoria Police board, Australia, is to conduct market surveys to identify the needs and satisfaction of people, and to make recommendations to structure service delivery and management systems in the police organization. Such research is seen to be essential to understanding 'core functions, efficiency and resource allocation' of the police and will be used to review the corporate planning processes and the police business plan. The key areas currently under examination include customer demand and satisfaction, delineating core and non-core activities, management systems and decision processes.

**Chart II.7.2   Citizen Satisfaction Survey: Performance
Measurement in Russia**

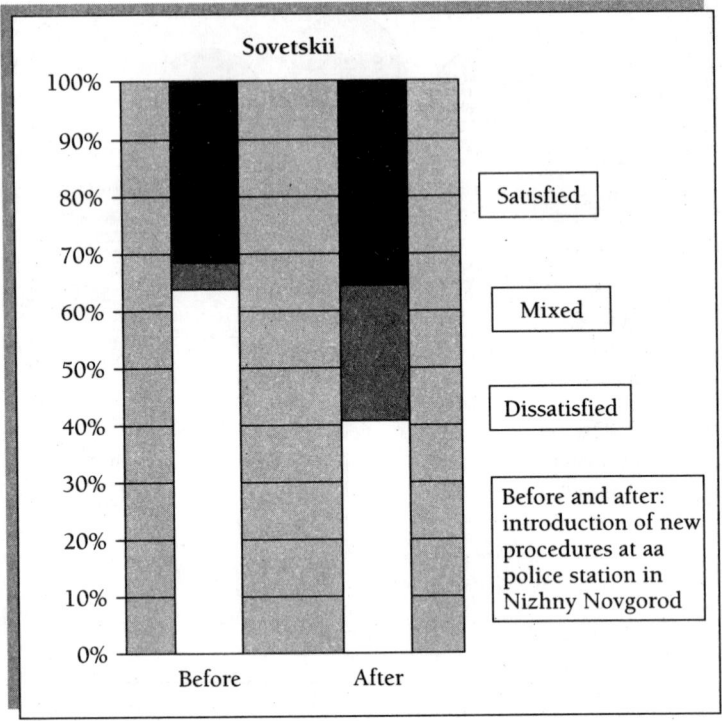

Source: www.altus.org.

Box II.7.2   Lodi Police Department Satisfaction Surveys

The Lodi Police Department, New Jersey, USA, used a survey instrument to measure resident satisfaction with the agency's services. Lodi police log about 3,000 calls a month. Of these 3,000 calls, approximately 10 per cent require a written report. The completion of a written report is a strong indicator that the citizen had more than a casual contact with the police officer. Each call for service receives a case number. Each month, police choose two numbers at random, and any case ending with either of these two numbers would be flagged to participate in the evaluation process. From among the participating cases, the police would identify cases with written reports and mail a resident satisfaction survey to anyone who was involved with that case, including victims, witnesses and even the accused. The survey measures satisfaction with several aspects of the police agency, including respondents' perceptions of officers' demeanor, helpfulness and professionalizm. The survey inquires

(*Box 11.7.2 continued*)

(*Box 11.7.2 continued*)

> about the level of service provided, how the dispatchers treated the caller, how well the detective division responded to their needs. It also invites the respondent to write comments about how the police department could improve its service, what factors in their lives the police can influence and other concerns. The Lodi Police Department continually receives an average rating of 'excellent' on the monthly surveys. Approximately 80 per cent of those who respond write comments on the survey. The comments and suggestions provide ideas about how the agency can improve its service and what other service the department should provide. From the written comments there is an extraordinary amount of information ranging from vehicles speeding in particular areas to suspicious people in an area of known drug dealing.

Source: Scimeca, 2004.

Once the needs of the customer are identified, the policing activities should be oriented towards meeting these needs. Customer Relationship Management (CRM) is perhaps the most important concept of modern marketing.[1] Police agencies easily can adapt these concepts of business marketing. The CRM framework in the SPF ensures that the insights garnered from its customer interactions are translated into customer requirements (SPF Executive Summary, 2007). CRM would mean creation of customer value, maintaining customer value and appropriating customer value, thereby increasing the overall favourably inclined citizen equity (Chart II.7.3). While reaching out to new people, it is important to keep those who come in contact with the police as satisfied citizens by improving service delivery. The creation of customer value would mean providing quality service; maintaining customer value would mean keeping a positive relationship with those who already have had contact with the department (discussed in Part II, Chapter 11). Appropriating customer value for the police would mean that in return for providing these services, the police department would receive more positive contacts, information relating to crime and antisocial activities, co-operation from people and an improved image from the community that it serves. This proves true no matter what type of population (for example, college campus, city, rural or state) is considered.

Having identified the needs and tailoring the policing activities to meet these needs, the issue of implementation with sustainability is very important. The common complaint that people make is that the officers come to listen to the grievances from the public and thereafter, for few

---

[1] It deals with building and managing profitable customer relationship by delivering superior customer value and satisfaction. It deals with all the aspects of acquiring, keeping and growing customers (Kotler and Armstrong, 2006).

Chart II.7.3   Customer Relationship Management (CRM) for the Police

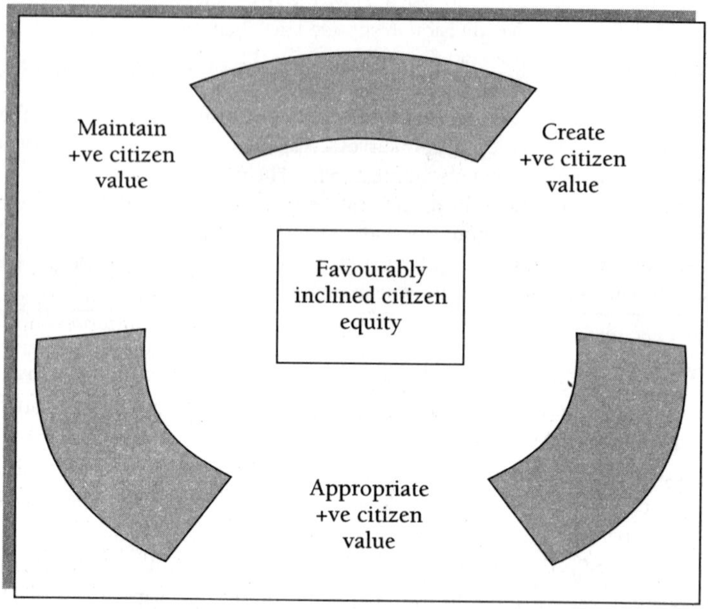

Maintain +ve citizen value

Create +ve citizen value

Favourably inclined citizen equity

Appropriate +ve citizen value

Source: Conceptualized by the author.

days, there are policemen attending to the issues raised and then the matter is forgotten. With such response, the faith the people have in the police is affected. To translate public concerns into sustained action of police duties and to overcome the problem of inadequately briefed and ill-informed policemen on the street, the police can benefit by issuing 'job cards' to police officers (Chart II.7.4). These job cards can be replaced by hand-held computers with 'wimax' connectivity for policemen with technological advancements in times to come.

Proactive policing

While the enforcement duties have strict laws and procedures defining the police role and that leaves little discretion on the part of police to follow, it is the equally important aspect of crime prevention that has a lot of scope of innovation.[2] Here, the police need to move beyond

---

[2] Also see characteristics and categories of the police service for distinction in approach for law enforcement and order maintenance functions.

Chart II.7.4   Job Cards for Policemen

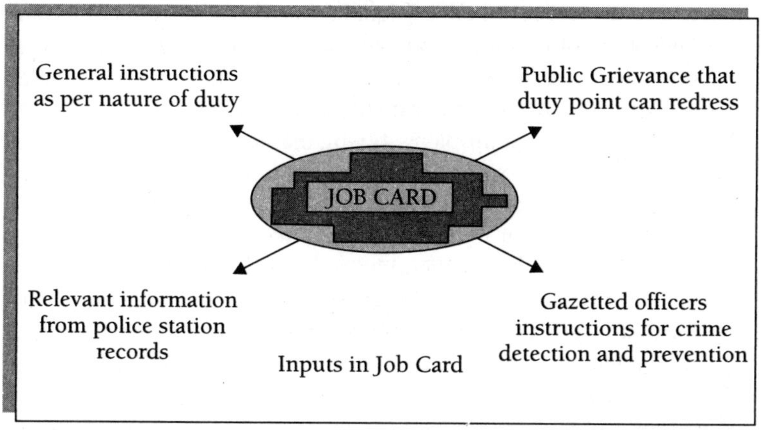

General instructions
as per nature of duty

Public Grievance that
duty point can redress

JOB CARD

Relevant information
from police station
records

Inputs in Job Card

Gazetted officers
instructions for crime
detection and prevention

Source: Conceptualized by the author.

making 'preventive arrests', patrolling, checkings and can start playing a more proactive role. One formal definition of crime prevention is—anticipation, recognition and appraisal of a crime risk and the initiation of some action to remove or reduce it (Crowe, 2000). Though interestingly, quick detection of earlier crimes and the apprehenion of the criminals is one of the best ways to prevent a future crime, yet the present allocation of only 1 per cent of the officers (Non-gazetted officer [NGOs]—in the Indian context) for crime prevention as compared to 40 per cent for crime detection (Nash, 1998), calls for some correction and improved emphasis on crime prevention strategies. Some of the current approaches that can be used for crime prevention are:

1. Crime Prevention Through Environmental Design (CPTED), which implies that the crime can be prevented by shaping the physical environment in a manner that it becomes difficult for the offenders to commit crime (Palmiotto et al., 2000). This involves creating an environment in which people are free from the fear of crime.
2. 'Situational crime prevention' approach to reduce opportunities of crime. This is directed at highly specific types of crime and involves the management and design of immediate environment in a systemic and permanent manner so as to increase the effort and risks of crime and reduce the perceived rewards by a wide range of offenders (Clarke, 1992: 4). The use of burglar alarms, ID cards, CCTV systems and screening are some of these methods.

3. Signal crime perspective is an approach in which attention is paid to certain crimes called as 'signal crimes' that make us think and take stock of existing security measures. This approach helps in distinguishing between the crimes that impact upon people's sense of security and other incidents that do not.

4. A commonly used problem-solving method is the SARA model.[3]

5. The 'problem analysis triangle' (sometimes referred to as the 'crime triangle') provides a way of thinking about recurring problems of crime and disorder. This idea assumes that crime or disorder results when (i) likely offenders and (ii) suitable targets come together in (iii) time and space, in the absence of capable guardians for that target. Effective problem-solving requires understanding how offenders and their targets/victims come together in places, and understanding how those offenders, targets/victims and places are or are not effectively controlled (www.popcenter.org/about/?p=triangle).

6. 'Intelligence-led policing', originally articulated as a law enforcement operational strategy that sought to reduce crime through the combined use of crime analysis and criminal intelligence in order to determine crime reduction tactics that concentrate on the enforcement and prevention of criminal offender activity, with a focus on active and recidivist offenders. This approach emphasizes information gathering through the extensive use of confidential informants, offender interviews, analysis of recorded crime and calls for service, surveillance of suspects and community sources of information. These sources are analysed so that law enforcement managers can determine objective policing tactics in regard to enforcement targets, prevention activities and further intelligence gathering operations. In the last few years, the interpretation of 'intelligence-led policing' appears to be broadening in scope. While still retaining the central notion that the police should avoid getting bogged down in reactive, individual, case investigations, intelligence-led policing is evolving into a management philosophy that places greater emphasis on information sharing and collaborative, strategic solutions to crime problems at the local and regional level (www.homeofice.gov.uk) [Box II.7.3].

Apart from the mandatory functions, carried out strictly as per the law and the preventive functions, there are a host of service-oriented

---

[3] The SARA model is used frequently by the practitioners of the community policing in the US. Available at Center for Problem-Oriented Policing SARA.htm.

Box II.7.3   The National Intelligence Model

The National Intelligence Model (NIM) in the UK provides the framework for gathering and using intelligence, and driving strategy in all areas from road safety to organized crime, targeting active criminals and tackling problems on the basis of intelligence. The NIM is quite simply a system for managing intelligence that will ensure uniform practices across the country. It means that different forces and diverse law enforcement agencies are able to share intelligence and mount joint operations without encountering the problems that can hamper such activity, for example, computer databases that are not compatible or information that is processed differently. It also demands that intelligence be shared properly within forces and ensuring that cross-border problems are always spotted early. It is also a blueprint for effective and efficient policing at any level because it specifies how intelligence should be progressed and linked into policing priorities. It intends to make all police activity focused and relevant, based on a much more scientific approach. The NIM is structured to impact on three levels of activity:

1. local issues (level 1)
2. cross-border issues (level 2)
3. serious and organized crime at national and international levels (level 3).

The NIM is made up of four prime components that are all crucial to making the process work. It is best explained in two parts. The first is how intelligence is formed into useful tools for decision making. The NIM calls these tools 'intelligence products'. The second is how these are used to inform police activity. This is referred to as a 'tasking and coordination' process. In simple terms, this is a framework for tasking or deploying resources to a problem and coordinating the police response:

1. The tasking and coordinating process: necessary to give managers a good view of the real nature of the problems they face in order that priorities can be established and resources linked to tasking decisions.
2. Four key intelligence products (strategic assessments, tactical assessments, problem profiles and target profiles) by which intelligence-led policing can be implemented, and its impact measured in terms of crime reduction, arrests, disruptions and enhanced community safety.
3. Knowledge products: a range of national and local components that define the rules for best practice by which skilled processes are completed, for example, data protection and regulation of Investigatory Powers Act.

(Box II.7.3 continued)

162   POLICING

(Box II.7.3 continued)

> 4. System products: facilities for the collection, reception, recording, storage and use of information.
>
> More recently, some UK police forces have tried to use the NIM as a way to manage and integrate the intelligence-led policing paradigm of information evaluation and decision making with the community policing philosophy of addressing community concerns.

Source: http://specials.homeoffice.gov.uk/Good-practice/national-intelligence-model.

duties carried out by the police. Ironically, many a times these duties are performed assuming the requirements of the customer without consulting the intended beneficiaries. Then, there are police duties that are carried out as a matter of routine and with a mindset which makes the policemen believe that policing has to be performed in a particular fashion only. Even the manuals that detail the activities have not been updated for the last several decades. All such activities carried out by police needs to be reexamined by putting the customer at the centre. Before Bratton became the commissioner, the New York narcotics unit was given than less than 5 per cent of the police force though it was felt that about 50 per cent of the crime were related to drugs, the police officers in the unit worked on weekdays, while the major drug dealing took place on the weekends. Bratton made these corrections and his call for major reallocation of staff and resources within the New York Police Department (NYPD) was quickly accepted (Kim and Mauborgne, 2003: 7).

These different strategies, as discussed, are not mutually exclusive rather considerable opportunities arise in making the police successful in controlling crime by the introduction of such strategies in tandem.[4] Many countries therefore have developed integrated plans by combining these strategies (Box II.7.4).

Community empowerment

In the US, the Chicago police holds a so-called beat meeting once a month in every neighbourhood, where local residents themselves report and prioritize problems. People feel that the good thing about taking part in a

---

[4] Police failure in controlling crime has been analysed and attributed to the over-reliance on a single strategy.

Box II.7.4   Belgium's 'Excellent Police Function'

The Belgium police have recently integrated strategies combining community policing, intelligence-led policing and organizational development to achieve their vision of an 'excellent police function'. The vision on an 'excellent police function' is based on four basic principles, especially:

1. the government policy in the field of 'societal security';
2. the specific police model in the field of 'community policing police' or the 'community oriented police function';
3. also the specific police and essential working method 'information-led police function'; and
4. a general basic principle 'optimal management' (as a combination of management models or theories made especially applicable to the police organization).

The 'societal security' as a government policy is the dome under which the police make their contribution. 'Community policing police' and 'information-driven police' are the basic police principles in this vision on an 'excellent police function'. The 'community policing police' defines the type of police Belgium wants and refers to the cultural context of the Belgian police and the attitude of their assistants. The information-led police is a working-method, throughout the entire police processes (operational, policy and supporting processes). Without data being converted into information and hence, into knowledge, police can't provide either a basic or a specialized police function. This know-how also results into the formulation of goals, the guiding of actions and the evaluation of effects and performances in order to readjust and redefine goals afterwards. The general basic principle 'optimal management' is a supporting management model. It allows the realization of the specific basic police principles in a purposeful, step-by-step and well-thought way.

Source: Bruggeman et al., 2007.

---

monthly neighbourhood meeting is that it builds up trust. Moreover, they get a more realistic idea of what the police and other agencies can do.

Identification of public needs would have to be supplemented with customer empowerment which transfers the control to people. Without any doubt, working with empowered and communicative communities is likely to remain the bedrock of everyday policing. Just like employee empowerment, implementing the concept of community empowerment can also pay rich dividends to the police department. This happens because people are more involved, energetic and responsible when they control their own environment than when some authority outside the community does. While the department needs to cater to the needs of the communities they serve, the community in itself can be the best ally for the police. The department needs to appreciate the benefits of this relationship, as the communities score over service bureaucracies for their (Osborne and Plastrik, 2000):

1. Commitment to their members.
2. Understanding their problems.
3. Offering of care rather than just service.
4. Flexibility and creativity.
5. Cost effectiveness.
6. Enforcement of standards of behaviour more effectively.
7. Focus on capacities than on deficiencies.

Therefore, within the local environment, mutual trust, relationships and interactions between the police and empowered local communities must be strengthened. The police need to participate actively in building the chain of social, administrative and judicial processes. However, many studies indicate that the three components of justice system, the police, courts and corrections, are reluctant to involve citizens in their operations and many employees view such participation as an attempt to minimize their professional expertise (Trojanowicz and Bucqueroux, 1994).

Community empowerment involves handing to communities substantial control over the decisions, resources and the tasks of the police. Some tools for community empowerment in practice today are community governance bodies, collaborative planning, community police partnership and community-based compliance (Osborne and Plastrik, 2000).[5]

Community governance bodies

These are the community oversight bodies for the police, such as the police authorities, to ensure police accountability and responsibility towards the community they serve. There are different arrangements in place in different nations as the police systems in the world vary from one country to another. Based on the characteristics of police systems in various countries, police experts have categorized them into three distinct models: fragmented model, centralized model and integrated model. The fragmented model is characterized by its extremely localized organizational structure. Police agencies are organized locally and are accountable to local authorities. Police systems in the USA, Canada, The Netherlands and Switzerland are typically classified under this model. In

[5] Also see Chapter 7—Community policing.

countries with the centralized police model, there is usually a centralized national police force directly under the control of the central government. The national government is held accountable for the success or failure of law enforcement. The centralized police model is used in such countries as France, Italy, Finland, Ireland, Denmark, South Korea and Sweden. The characteristic of the integrated model, which is also referred to as the 'combined system' or 'composite system', is that the organization and administration of the police are a shared responsibility of the central government and the local authorities. Police agencies are accountable to both the central and local authorities. Police systems in the UK, Germany, Australia and Japan are categorized under this model (Bayley, 1985; Becker, 1980; Hunter, 1990; Terrill, 1992). To understand how the issue of police accountability is addressed under different systems of policing, it is interesting to take a look at the regulatory mechanism prevalent in the UK, the US, Australia and South Korea, one country each from different policing models as discussed in Part II, Chapter 12.

Collaborative planning

Collaborative planning is another useful tool of community empowerment. Some of the ways of doing this is with the help of police advisory committees (Box II.7.5) or the neighbourhood watch groups. Both these tools can lead to excellent participation from the people and police can get ground information and useful suggestions for improved service and efficiency.

Not only the police, but also different public service departments, like the town planning department, are exploring consultative committees as a way to provide better service to customers.

Neighbourhood watch groups not only augment the resources of the department but also provide easy to implement and cost effective solutions to the local security issues.

During the time span of nearly 30 years, before the implementation of the policy of economic modernization, the Chinese police had developed extremely effective policing strategies. The main components of Chinese policing were a closely monitored household registration system and an extensive surveillance system of mass-line organizations. Under the household registration system, everyone must register his or her residence in a locality with the police. To ensure the enforcement of the household registration law, a tightly knit police and mass-line supervisory system was set up. Neighbourhood committees were established in all neighbourhoods. Corresponding to the mass-line organization network, a police sub-station was set up in each larger community. The

---

Box II.7.5   Police Consultative Committees of the UK

In the UK, consultative committees offer a formal way for the community to raise concerns about the policing in their area and to offer their views on what the police priorities should be. These committees are made up of local councillors, police authority members, representatives of the police and people from voluntary, statutory and community groups. In most cases, Members of Parliament (MPs) are automatically offered membership. In some areas the police have also arranged for consultative group members to be present at major police operations, such as drugs raids, so that they can see at first-hand how the police carry out the wishes of the community.

A crucial objective of the local policing arrangements recommended in the patten report on the Ireland police reforms was to encourage a move from reactive to problem-solving policing. At the local level, community partnerships and liaison committees were to be put in place to achieve this as well as achieving transparency through monthly public meetings between the District Policing Partnership Boards (DPPB) and the local police commander. The local boards would also have the power to buy in extra policing to address their own local problems. This proposal was intended to go some way towards establishing democratic control of public safety and to allow economically deprived communities to address their own particular policing problems.

Source: www.homeoffice.gov.uk.

larger community was divided into sub-sections, with each sub-section containing several neighbourhood committees. A police officer, known as the household registration officer, was assigned to each sub-section. The officer visited the neighbourhoods within his jurisdiction on a daily basis and was informed by the neighbourhood committees about all happenings in the community. In addition to making sure that all residents were properly registered, the household registration officer also maintained the security and order in the neighbourhoods and investigated minor offenses (serious offenses were handled by higher public security bureaus). Since an officer usually worked in a community for a long time, he soon became extremely familiar with the residents, as well as the conditions of life in the community. The advantage of the system was that it enabled the police to keep close contacts with community residents and to keep a tight surveillance on everything and everyone in a neighbourhood. No strangers could come to a neighbourhood without being noticed immediately and reported promptly to the police. Under the system, people were restricted in their freedom of travel and movement (Ma, 1997).

As China entered into a new era of social and economic development, the police could not rely solely on the past policing methods to remain effective in combating crime in an increasingly modernized society. To meet the need for crime control in modern cities, for instance, the Chinese police have introduced in larger cities the routine motorized patrol, a typical policing method in the Western nations. While it is true that the Chinese police are striving hard to professionalize and modernize the force, it is a mistake to assume that they are abandoning the traditional policing. As in the past, the household registration officers continue to visit their assigned neighbourhoods and work closely with the neighbourhood committees. The traditional system, though no longer working as effectively as it used to do, is still a key component of China's crime prevention and security network. China has chosen to effectively combine the traditional with the modern to implement a system of neighbourhood security (Ma, 1997) (see Box II.7.6).

Box II.7.6   Neighbourhood Security Committees of China

To combat the current rise in crime, the government advocates an overall strategy that is referred to as 'comprehensive management'. The strategy calls for mobilizing all possible social forces to strengthen public security and prevent crime. The traditional co-operation between the police and mass-line security organizations is a key part in the strategy. For that reason, the government is taking all possible measures to strengthen the neighbourhood security system. To attract more residents to participate in the neighbourhood security work, the government does not only rely on the traditional methods of recruiting volunteers, but also resorts to economic inducements by giving participants a small allowance for their services. Because of the government's auspices, the number of neighbourhood security committees in urban areas is growing. For instance, between 1986 and 1989, there was a 10.8 per cent increase in neighbourhood security committees in cities and towns, which translated into an additional 16,414 committees.

Source: China Law Association Editorial Board, 1991.

Community–police partnership

There is no doubt that effective community policing can occur only in partnership with this community. Law enforcement needs to address both crime and the causes of crime through co-operation with partner organizations by preventing and deterring offending behaviour and to catch, convict, rehabilitate and resettle offenders. The joint ventures by the police in partnership with the community that share common goals and operations can lead to both the community involvement, resource augmentation, expertise sharing and improved results (Box II.7.7).

Box II.7.7   COPS Programmes in the US

Stalking involves a pattern of overtly criminal and/or apparently innocent behaviour that makes victims fear for themselves or others. It creates uncertainty, instills fear and can completely disrupt lives. It sometimes involves severe, even lethal, violence. By hosting informative conference calls and distributing specialized publications, the COPS is working with the National Center for Victims of Crime (NCVC), the Office for Victims of Crime (OVC) and the Office on Violence Against Women (OVW) to both raise national awareness of stalking and to encourage the development and implementation of problem-solving responses to stalking in local communities.

In addition, through the School-based Partnership program (SBP), the COPS office has provided funding specifically to develop problem-solving partnerships between local police, schools and community-based organizations. These partnerships focus on developing co-operative solutions to specific crime problems through the use of the SARA problem-solving model.

Source: http://www.usdoj.gov/cops.

Strategically speaking, the police can be positioned as an organization that helps to increase safety, working in partnership with other groups, rather than an organization that provides safety solely. The police force in Singapore is hardly seen on the streets yet there is lot of work going on behind the façade. Officers spend time visiting all kinds of associations and citizen groups like the 'senior apartments dwellers' and religious leaders from the mosques and temples in this way forge partnership and educate the public. The concept that is developing there for the last eight years is that of 'from police to policing'. Their Coporate First Responder (CFR) scheme aims to forge win-win partnership between the government and the business community in dealing with the aftermath of terrorist attack. The CFR scheme allows key business personnel from CFR members to access the restricted sites post incidents to take mitigation measures to help expedite return to normalcy.

Stimulating community-based compliance

Co-operating with the population also means stimulating that population's social autonomy. Stimulating the social autonomy means mobilizing citizens by making them partly responsible for the problem. It is mainly about promoting a certain extent of awareness that the authorities cannot, will not and should not be responsible for each individual problem each citizen encounters. The police should not make population dependent upon them. They should rather stimulate the potential of the individuals and neighbourhoods to solve their own problems. An opposite attitude would confirm the idea that co-operation with the police is unnecessary and that this concern for security and quality of life is only a mission of police services and authorities. To that end, the police must support population, act as a mediator and put their professionalism at population's disposal to control conflicts and solve problems.

Community-based compliance is an emerging trend which has been tried successfully by shifting of control over compliance functions to communities in activities such as neighbourhood groups for traffic compliance. This can lead to increased transparency, empathy, augmentation of manpower and can reduce bitterness between the police and the community that the compliance activities inherently breed.

However, in empowering the community it should be ensured that the communities get a clear charter, there is accountability, there is some training input to the community members, and the culture of the police department is also changed so that they collaborate effectively with the community.

Shaping the future

Listening to the community is central to the police, yet important organizations like the Indian police departments cannot be satisfied just by following the customers. They have to go beyond and have to lead the citizens to where our society and nation need to go, to seize the opportunity to 'shape the future'. This would require the police to get out of the mindset of organization that has only to play the role of preventing and regulating people from deviant actions, to that of also in pursuit of shaping the future course of our society and nation.[6]

Unarticulated needs

Traditionally, police departments are expected to function within the limitations of broad policies established by legislative, executive or judicial agencies. However, many times when such policy guidelines are not in place, the police are criticized for their failure to initiate such policy on their own initiative. Most of the people know about their immediate problems but lack awareness about the larger issues that may affect them

[6] The police force will play a pivotal role in the transformation of the country into a developed nation. New vision, technology and methods have to be invented and implemented in the service of the nation (AIPS Congress, 2006).

in indirect manner. One example of this is the global internet threat called the botnet problem. Botnets are very real and quickly evolving problems that is still not well understood.[7] The police needs to take lead in such areas at their own initiative and show the way.

On the Internet, there is already a trend of establishment of virtual communities such as the interactive world of 'second life', the sphere of policing has to be expanded too since the current enforcement apparatus is inadequate to cater to these needs. The first law firm has just established itself on 'second life' and the German police has recently arrested a male while investigating allegations of rape on it for selling a child avatar for sex. An avatar is the player's physical representation in the game world in the form of a customized two or three-dimensional icon (Kealty, 2007).

Another way to address the unarticulated needs by the police is to help the framers of laws in formulating the laws that the society needs for its betterment, though people may not be aware about these issues as their future requirements. In the US, police departments become active partners in identifying laws that need to be amended or enacted. They work with lawmakers and organize citizen support efforts to change the laws. Majority of social issues have direct fallout on the peace of individuals, families and society and any disturbing trend brings police into picture much before the issue assumes larger unmanageable and damaging proportion. Donohue and Levitt (2000) offer evidence that legalized abortion has contributed significantly to recent crime reductions. Crime began to fall roughly 18 years after abortion legalization. The five states that allowed abortion in 1970 experienced declines earlier than the rest of the nation, which legalized in 1973 with Roe vs. Wade. States with high abortion rates in the 1970s and 1980s experienced greater crime reductions in the 1990s. In the high abortion states, only arrests of those born after abortion legalization fall relative to low abortion states. Legalized abortion appears to account for as much as 50 per cent of the recent drop in crime.

Here, proactive policing with foresight can do a lot of service to society (Box II.7.8). Future engineering proposals for the regulation of traffic can be another such area where police can play a proactive role.

---

[7] At the centre of these threats is a large pool of compromised hosts sitting in homes, offices and schools around the world. These systems are infected with a bot that communicates with a bot controller and with other bots to form a zombie army or botnet. With hundreds or even thousands of bots at its command the attacker can choke the bandwidth of any target server, thus denying the services of the server to the legitimate requests. Hosting illegal data and collecting valuable information from the infected machine can be some other malicious uses of botnet. The total number of bot-infected systems has been measured between 8,00,000 to 9,00,000 in the year 2004. It is reported in the year 2007 there has been 10 times increase in malware in just one year (*The Economic Times*, 2008).

Box II.7.8   LAPD Rehabilitation Centres

Following the recommendation of their planning unit, the Los Angeles police responded to the task of handling 100,000 common drunks per year through their jail system by acquiring 588 acres to handle approximately 1,500 prisoners in a new rehabilitations centre. Such rehabilitation centres allowed the department to continue its efforts in rebuilding alcoholics physically, morally and mentally. Healthy outdoor farming activity is available to those who might benefit from such activity. The centres operated at less cost than more formal institutional facilities and they returned a part of their cost by providing food to the entire jail system. Finally, they offered a superior opportunity towards rebuilding alcoholics into useful citizens, eventually saving the cost on repeated imprisonments.

Source: Parker, 1957: 43.

But this foresight can only come when the police begin to empathize with the basic needs of the people and constantly strive for the betterment of society. It comes when top leadership in police is able to identify with a poor man, from the village belonging to weaker section of society and with no political connections, who is seeking justice in a remote police station, against vested interests. The foresight required to shape the future will come from this kind of empathy, with being in constant contact with people, by moving up and down the department and more than anything else it will come from the will to make a difference to the lives of the people. As Hamel and Prahalad write:

> Only by changing the lens through which the corporation is viewed, only by changing the lens through which the markets are viewed, only by broad-ening of the angle of the lens (by being more inquisitive) only by cleaning the accumulated grime on the lens (seeing with a child's eyes), only by peering through multiple lenses (eclecticism), and only by ocassionally dis-believing what one actually sees can the future be anticipated. (Hamel and Prahalad, 2002: 114–15)

Unserved articulated needs

Apart from the unarticulated there are many articulated needs of the customers which the police are not able to cater to as they should. Take the example of electricity thefts, in many states the cases are either not registered by the police and if at all they are registered they are given low priority. In such a situation, the electricity boards also dispose thousands of such detected theft cases with the imposition of penalties at their own level. Andhra Pradesh took the initiative in this area by setting up police stations to deal exclusively with electricity-related crime. With this step an unserved customer was served and this resulted in benefits to the electricity board, by way of huge improvement in the collection of electricity bills. Another example is phishing[8] where globally about 30,000 attacks are reported each month, of which 80 per cent are directed at the financial institutions. India is among the top 10 countries where the sites are hit by phishing. While the issue remains largely unserved extent of this problem can also be gauged by the fact that more than 74 per cent of IT managers across India reported that their employees have received phising attacks via emails. Alarmingly, these attacks have grown by 41 per cent in the last 12 months (*The Economic Times*, 2007c). Phreaking[9] and frauds involving voice over Internet protocal are also there. Similarly, Airline fraud is costing the global aviation industry over USD 600 million a year, growing five fold in last six years.[10]

There are many such emerging trends in crime today for which the police needs to update itself. The whole police system in India is governed by the laws that place heavy emphasis on crime against the body compared to those against property. However, the economic crimes have grown exponentially in proportion and sophistication. Some of the new emerging crimes like stock market scams, cyber crime, non-banking frauds, stamp paper scam, intellectual property rights, lottery frauds, rackets pertaining to employment abroad, frauds by builders and land developers, corporate frauds, misappropriations and frauds in various anti-poverty programmes like integrated rural development programme, tribal development programme, and so on, telecom frauds, insurance frauds, procurement frauds, hawala and money laundering, credit card frauds, counterfeiting and forgery, exports and imports duty evasion, crimes and banking frauds need attention from the police today (Box II.7.9).

For these emerging areas, policemen need upgrading the necessary skills and competencies and in the scheme of things these important yet hitherto neglected areas of crime should be given importance (Box II.7.10). These areas correspond to the needs which have been articulated by the

---

[8] Phishing is a term used for fraud where the perpetrators send out spoof emails to random databases to fool the recepient into divulging personal information like credit card details, usernames and passwords, that can be used for identity thefts. Smishing is another form of phishing where fraudsters use the vicitms mobile phone to fish out sensitive information, though the medium is different the aim remains the same. It begins with the fraud sending an SMS to a gullible and ignorant customer tricking the vicitm to log on to a particular website.

[9] Phreaking is a term for fraud where people make free calls by illegally breaking into telephone networks.

[10] Report by Deloitte and the International Assocation of Airline internal auditors (*The Economic Times*, 2007d).

Box II.7.9   Identity Thefts

In the US, one out of four people buying products online is a victim of identity theft. The Federal Trade Commission (FTC) estimates that identity theft struck nearly 10 million Americans in 2003, with an estimated total annual cost of USD 5 billion to consumers and USD 48 billion to businesses, along with costs ranging from USD 15,000 to USD 25,00 for law enforcement to investigate each case. Add to that the time and money that the victims must spend to straighten out their lives. According to the FTC's consumer sentinel database, which receives and maintains statistics about identity theft and fraud, the most common form of identity theft is credit card fraud, followed by telephone or utility fraud, bank fraud, employment-related fraud, government document or benefit fraud and loan fraud.

Anti-identity theft model strategy: To help local law enforcement deal with identity theft and support federal prosecution efforts, the COPS office provided funding to the Johns Hopkins University for a project aimed at developing a national model strategy based on the best or most promising anti-identity theft practices and for developing policy recommendations. The model strategy was completed in 2005.

Source: http://ww.usdoj.gov/cops.

Box II.7.10   Joint Internet Centre (Gemeinsames Internetzentrum—GIZ)

It has been established that in the field of international terrorism as well as in other crime phenomena, the Internet is being increasingly used as a means of communication and to prepare offences. More and more, the world wide web is playing a decisive role in the dissemination of Islamist propaganda. This is substantiated by numerous websites. So far, the German police have registered approximately 5,000 such websites on the world wide web in the field of Islamist terrorism. The offenders of many terrorist attacks were inspired by the ideology represented by Al Qaeda. There is evidence that the Internet was very intensively used in the attacks committed in the US, Bali, Istanbul, Madrid and London. According to the information of the German police, the two suspects in the attempted suitcase bomb attacks on two local trains in Germany at the end of July 2006 were also decisively influenced by the Internet in their radicalization. In this case, the Internet also played a key role in the preparation of the offence. The offenders found the instructions to make the bombs and a fatwa justifying the attacks on the Internet. In view of the growing criminal activity on the Internet, the German police particularly focus on intelligent, that is, targeted, searches as well as close co-operation and consultation with other security authorities. In order to improve information on this matter in Germany the Joint Internet Centre (GIZ) was set up at federal level. The Federal Office for the Protection of the Constitution (BFV),

(Box II.7.10 continued)

(Box II.7.10 continued)

> the Federal Criminal Police Office (Bundeskriminalamt—BKA), the Federal Intelligence Service (BND), the Military Counterintelligence Service (MAD) and the Federal Prosecutor General (GBA) have been working together in this Joint Internet Centre since 1 January 2007. The tasks of the Joint Internet Centre are information gathering as well as the monitoring and analysis of websites. It is the aim of the experts working there to find and analyse websites of individuals or organizations, newsgroups, forums and chatrooms more effectively than ever in order to detect extremist and terrorist activities on the Internet at an early stage. For this purpose, specialist and technical expertise of the authorities involved is compiled and language competence and knowledge are consolidated, thus avoiding communication deficits, duplication of work and friction.

Source: Contribution from Dr Jurgen Stock, vice-president of the Bundeskriminalant, Germany.

citizens yet police has not been able to meet these demands satisfactorily for the customers to be considered as served.

On the basis of what has been discussed above if we consider a 2 × 2 matrix (Chart II.7.5), on y-axis we have the needs of the customers— those they are capable of articulating and those they cannot yet articulate. On the x-axis is the class of customers—those classes that the department currently serves and those it does not. Blocks I and III will cover the unarticulated and articulated needs of the customers served by police functioning under different laws, social legislations and as per the current practices in the department.

Blocks II and IV represent the unserved customers of police department. Examples for unserved customers, where the needs are articulated (Block IV) are many of economic crimes as discussed, electricity, telecom, intellectual property, data thefts, quality of life issues like noise complaints, disorderly behaviour and so on.[11] Financial crimes in particular are targeted at seniors with alarming frequency, and are all too often successful. In 2000, the US Senate special committee on aging reported USD 40 billion as loss to the telemarketing fraud.[12] In Block II

---

[11] In December 2004, Quark Media House was faced with a unique dilemma. While the company had just begun to explore Mohali, Punjab's proposed IT Mecca, a crucial piece of proprietary software under testing was stolen from its premises. The unco-operative attitude of the police officials irked the company enough to revoke its investment of Rs 5,000 crores promised for developing world class city project at Mohali (*The Economic Times*, 2007a).

[12] Elders are the fastest growing segment of society and they are also an important part of country's economy. America's growing senior population is uniquely vulnerable to a broad range of exploitation and abuse. Over the past year, the COPS office has invested nearly USD 2 million nationwide to address this major crime problem (http://www.usdoj. gov/cops).

Chart II.7.5   2 × 2 Matrix for the Needs of the Citizens

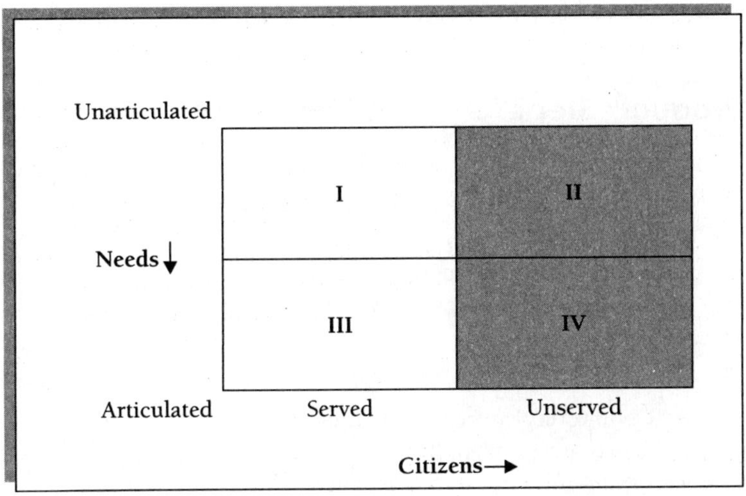

Source: Hamel and Prahalad, 2002.

Notes: I—Unarticulated but served needs; II—Shape the future; III—Articulated and served needs; IV—Unemployed opportunities to serve.

are the unarticulated needs of the unserved customers, large population belonging to weaker, backward and disadvantaged section of society remains unserved and unable to articulate many of their needs. Also, there are certain needs like those relating to the social issues, the environment, and so on, which are not articulated by people and also remain unattended by the police. Therefore, in the present domain of functioning of the police department, Blocks I and III, the job remains unfinished without the service of unarticulated needs and the unserved articulated needs, Blocks II and IV. Block IV represent the area of un-exploited opportunities for the police to extend its service and Block II represents the opportunity to shape the future of the society and the nation.

The Dutch police has added the task of 'reporting out problems and giving advice' to the task description laid out in the Police Act, 1993 which is maintaining public order, investigating public offences and providing aid in emergency situations. The idea is that based on their operational experience, the related information position and their professionalism, the police observe and point out safety-related problems and wherever possible give advice on these problems to other actors, especially as regards the responsibility of these other parties for their contribution to public safety (Hoogewoning, 2006: 60). The police here assumes the role of the authoritative teacher and pacesetter, Block II of shaping the future. The SPF policy statement on societal responsibility is another example where an organization that has positioned itself as the force of the nation that inspires others has shown its commitment to corporate societal responsibility.[13]

'Product': Steps for the Indian police

- Systematically identify customer needs by listening to customer voice (surveys, feedbacks, interactions, and so on).
- Customer Relationship Management (CRM) framework to translated them into customer requirements.
- From reactive policing to proactive policing.
- Community policing.
- Empower community through:

  - Community governance bodies;
  - Collaborative planning;
  - Community police partnership;
  - Community-based compliance.

- Shaping the future by attending to public's:

  - Unserved articulated needs;
  - Unserved unarticulated needs.

[13] The SPF policy statement on societal responsibility: 'We are an organisation that is responsible to the society we operate in. We embark on initiative and activities that are beneficial to the society, and community, and those that are in line with community and nationalistic goals, through leveraging on our resources, strength and capabilities' (Singapore Police, 2007).

Community Policing 8

Apart from the institutional arrangements mentioned in Chapter 7, 'community policing' also introduces a new 'level' between public authority and the scattered individual citizens, notably district or neighbourhood consultation where dialogue or participation is organized and accountability takes place naturally. Consequently, a new source of requests to the police and of bringing the police into action gets created. So far, the police were politically responsible to the government/authorities and responsible to the individuals from an operational point of view. Community policing realigns this traditional sharing of power over the police and establish a new relationship in the social contract between the police and society. If communities define the content as well as the priorities of policing, a new political centre of power over police comes into being—a missing link is formed.

Limitations in implementing community policing initiatives

There are certain differences in the Indian social, economical and political environment and that of the Western nations, where the community policing is practised successfully, and these differences have to kept in mind to modify the implementation strategies for India. The countries in the West, like the UK, have a long tradition of local governance in police and other spheres of life. Historically speaking in the UK, in buroughs and urban districts the control exercised by the watch committees was complete. Even in other local governing bodies, the traditions and activities of most of these reach back to the dawn of the English history; local autonomy has been as much a part of Englishmen heritage as has been the right to personal freedom. In India no local governing system of advanced type was developed. Countries like the UK and the Netherlands are an entirely homgeneous units. By contrast, in India, the vastness and the variety of work is enormous. The local conditions change drastically, sometimes, from district to district. Then in terms of numbers there are 429 people per policeman in the UK, while there are merely 712 people per policeman in India.

In practice, community policing does not develop according to a single one-dimensional process; several factors such as a lack of political and management support, management priorities, internal communication problems, a shortage of police capacity and resources, emphasis on emergency situations may hamper, or even set back, the development of community policing.

The experience of Israel presents an interesting case[1] for learning in adopting community policing. Policing in Israel is organized as a national police force with six geographic districts (each with two or three sub-districts) and 70 police stations. A community policing unit was established by the Israeli police in 1995. The idea of community policing did not come out of the demand from the citizens but it was something the police decided to adopt. The responsibilities of the community policing unit included: training police officers, citizens, public officials at the city level and employees of other community services; development of community policing projects in police stations, based on multi-agency work and problem-oriented policing methods and encouragement of an organizational culture that would support community policing within the Israel National Police.

To start with, four stations were chosen and the programme was implemented to all the 70 stations by 2003. Community policing unit called for empowering the street-level police officers, who would be contacts between the police and the public. They were to act like statesman than as obedient clerks. It also emphasized problem-oriented approaches to policing. To start with, community policing advisors were assigned to each police station. However, by 1997, as the programme expanded, these advisors were not sufficient for the police stations and the responsibility of implementation then fell on the district commanders. In the meantime, a new approach, 'policing by objective', was emphasized

---

[1] Case study on Israel in next three paras adapted from article by D. Gimshi (Gimshi, 1995).

by the top management, especially the new commissioner. In his new directive, while 'policing by objective' was emphasized, there was no mention of community policing. The message went around in the force. Soon after this the community policing unit was merged with the civil guard department and the responsibility of implementation fell on the civil guards who had little idea about the initiatives. Therefore, the broad idea of community policing was not successfully implemented in Israel and community policing lost ground in Israel overtaken by an emphasis on other programmes such as 'policing by objectives'.

The reasons could be many for its non implementation; however, some of the main reasons were: adopting a very broad goal at one go which involved total metamorphosis of the organization; lack of resources to implement these wide sweeping changes; the dependence of the programme on the personal efforts of the commissioner who introduced it; the message had also gone that the changes are not inevitable and one can continue to work in old ways; rapid expansion of the programme without consolidation of phase one. Last, the Israeli National Police remains strongly committed to a military style of management which emphasizes the importance of control and the role of commanders and supervisors in managing police work. This mindset presented strong resistance to the granting of such autonomy and authority to lower ranking police officers in Israel. Nevertheless, some of the community policing programmes still function there like the domestic violence unit, a community policing mini unit in all police stations. More than anything else the Israeli National Police imbibed the idea of providing service to community, which few years back would have been difficult to think.

It is desirable, though not easy, for a department like the police to adapt and adopt initiatives like community policing, some of the primary reasons are discussed in the following sections.

Conservative police culture

Certain problems in community policing seem to have remained the same over the years, particularly, the conservative police culture which has been a major obstacle in implementing community policing, also, coping with basic dilemmas such as hard/repressive/reactive versus soft/ preventive/proactive policing. Those dilemmas clearly have an organizational aspect, but they also relate to the police role—'what functions should the police perform?'—and to the police and the community— 'what philosophy should determine their relationship with the public?' (Punch et al., 2002).

While the old timers and the traditionalists in the department believe that the core job of the police is to 'catch the criminals', the community policing officers feel although their work is important, they still have somewhat marginal position in the department. Studies of proximity policing in Denmark showed that these units were often alienated from the rest of the police, they found it difficult to define their role towards citizens, their work was often derided as 'social work' and not 'real police work' (Reiner, 1985). Similar observations can be seen in a study in Belgium. The traditional crime-fighting culture does not regard problems between people as real police work, but as social work. Most senior officers managing the new neighbourhood teams come from the intervention department (911) and are tried and tested in the traditional crime-fighting culture.

Resistance to change

Just as for anything new introduced in a traditional and rule bound rigid organization like the police, there is an organizational resistance to community policing. In his book, *Community Policing (Can It Work)*, author Skogan observes that the police have a remarkable ability to wait out efforts to reform them and the police resist the intrusion of civilians into their business. The author appear to be in accord in the belief that community policing requires competing for the 'hearts and minds' of police officers who are naturally suspicious of untested social experiments, and distrustful of those who would insist they engage in social work.

Justice Oppal summarized the state of community policing with insight and candour in 1994:

> Virtually every Police Department in North America claims to be committed to, and involved in, community-based policing. They make the claim based on some of their programs. These include school liaison programmes, victims service operations, storefront stations, community relations units, bicycle patrols and Block Watch. These programmes may be important to particular communities, but their mere presence does not ensure the presence of community-based policing. The programmes are still managed by, and run for, the benefit of the police.

Rigid paramilitary structure

There remains considerable distance between what is preached and what is practised about the openness of police organizations. Although police agencies have adopted the rhetoric of community policing, they remain organized to do traditional policing (Weisburd et al., 2002) as it happened in Israel where there was a resistance by the top management to delegate powers to the frontline policemen. A military structure of control was maintained with little local discretion. Whenever strict community policing priorities are centrally directed from the police headquarters, this may seriously misdirect the efforts in the field, as the essential requirement of community policing is that the solutions are tailor-made in the field, rather than a fit all kind of template handed down from the top.

Police scholars have observed that community-oriented policying which is observed as a philosophy in the USA is wholly insitutionalized in Japan. David H. Bayley began this trend with *Forces of Order: Policing Modern Japan* (1976). Others were Ted Westermann's *Crime and Justice in Two Societies—Japan and the United States* (1991), Erika Fairchild's *Comparative Criminal Justice Systems* (1993) and Ed Ebbe's *Comparative and International Criminal Justice Systems* (1996). In his work, Bayley argues that inherent advantages of the Japanese system over other systems are: The Japanese police are decentralized which allows them to be accepted as an integral part of the Japanese community; they routinely engage in counselling, advising and mediating functions; engage in 'problem-oriented' policing and recognize the 'permeability of the boundary between police and citizen roles'. While the American police, followed by the rest of the world, are still experimenting with the concept and implementation of community policing, Japan is seen as a viable role model, a 'paradise' for the typical police officer (Chwialkowski, 1998; Ebbe, 1996; Westermann, 1991).

Underpaid and undertrained staff

For the developing nations when officers are grossly underpaid as well as undertrained, the job of reforming policing is even more difficult. Resources both material and with regard to salaries completely under-mined any individual motivation (for example, the local Community Liason Officers (CLO) were not selected on the basis of training or commitment). For example, in Uganda, where police salaries were very low and often late in arriving, officers could not survive on their pay and, hence, relied on bribes. A female CLO claimed that some of her colleagues are not supportive and not interested in community policing because it assists the public to become aware of the law and their rights. Some do not wish the public to know about community policing issues such as bond and bail. They say community policing is spoiling our things (Raleigh et al., 2000: 87).

Matthew-effect

The community policing concept is easy to implement in a homogeneous community with limited range of problems. This may induce a 'Matthew-effect': community policing will be implemented where it is least needed while those in most need of appropriate protection and support will get, for example, 'zero-tolerance' policing.[2] There are various big cities that present specific dilemmas for the police in terms of an accumulation of big city problems, a widely diverse range of residents, large number of floating population, constant negotiation on policies in a highly political environment with a great deal of media attention and the need to balance service delivery with a public order capacity.

Multiplicity of police wings

Inner-city problems invariably mean that the police will have to give multiple answers, as was the case in policing the inner city area of Amsterdam, Holland. Sometimes, the beat constable can give the answer, sometimes the problems have to be tackled by groups of police officers and sometimes, the issues have to be solved at the strategic level. For citizens this seems to be quite confusing: they sometimes make arrangements with beat constables that are later overruled by other policemen. It becomes obvious that the police are not 'one' single organization, but a diversity of sub-organizations where at times no one seems to be fully in control of the processes (Punch et al., 2002). Generally community policing is interpreted to be the development of a special neighbourhood constabulary. The intervention police of the police stations, by contrast, is usually not involved in community policing reforms. The officers who respond to emergency calls do not have much time left to get involved in community policing. As a result, community policing becomes a new 'specialization' within the existing police force. The public, however, does not make any distinction between the departments. Since they have the most contact with the intervention department, whose members outnumber the neighbourhood constables, the traditional crime-fighting policing style of the department continues to determine the public image of the police. As a result, for every neighbourhood police officer who genuinely wants to incorporate community policing, there are far more constables who prefer to continue the traditional crime-fighting pattern.

---

[2] 'Zero-tolerance' policing has been conceptualized by American experts and implemented in the US as well as in the UK. Its objective is to prevent lawlessness by targeting and repressing any deviant behaviours.

In the end, the citizen does not know what kind of behaviour or policing style to expect from their local police service (Broeck, 2002).

Documentation of results

One of the most important problems for the future of community policing is the documentation of results. Traditional policing may not infact prevent crime (Bayley, 1994), but at least it yields tangible figures in the form of cleared crimes and apprehended perpetrators; such figures, to quantify the work done, are not so common in the community police. It is far more difficult to document a crime prevented than a crime detected. These difficulties put the community police in a precarious position, not only in relation to rest of the police force, but also in relation to the general public (Holmberg, 2002). Then, the prime concerns of the public such as interpersonal conflicts and minor complaints are not reflected in the criminality figures. As a consequence, problems such as burglaries are given priority.

Attitude of 'We' know what 'They' need

Due to what Skogan (1990) characterizes as 'the over-professionalization' of themselves and their (crime-fighting) mission, police departments lack the ability to analyse citizen-provided data (Mastrofski, 1998: 178) and as a consequence, systematically overlook many pressing community concerns because they lie outside of their narrowly defined mandate (Broeck, 2002). Sometimes, the implementation of little considerations seem to have been given to differing community needs and priorities or to local conditions, customs and traditions. This happened when in Uganda, community policing was introduced, based and aided by the UK initiatives. Training for the different local conditions and values seems to have been simply based on British determination of what was appropriate. The police regard community policing primarily as a means of instructing local populations, rather than of listening to them. They thus learn less than they might while doing little to mitigate their authoritarian image (Raleigh et al., 2000: 54).

Finally, community policing represents a new policing paradigm, in terms of shifting from a militaristic and bureaucratic style of policing, where police thinks in terms of 'they' and 'us', officers are impersonal officials, wary of involvement in any social task, to a more proactive, empowered and approachable group of public servants with a service orientation. The general feeling among the people is that they want a visible, recognizable local police that are available, takes their problems seriously, and treats them with respect. Today, people in a community want their own cops and there can be no doubting that policing as a service has improved considerably at the delivery end (Punch et al., 2002), wherever community policing has been implemented with committed policemen.

Strategies for successful community policing

As discussed earlier, in situational analysis there are several reasons why community policing has been difficult to implement in the police department, despite the attention it has received from the police leadership and the people. Very often the initiated programmes fade away with the initiating officer and sometimes they continue to run at the periphery. Any police department that endeavours to embrace community policing philosophy will have to look beyond just initiating some public police programmes and will have to undertake department wide measures.

Community policing efforts can work anywhere, though the methodology of implementation would differ from country to country. Therefore, for a country like India, it is important to understand what are the present-day policing policy initiatives in countries like the US, the UK, Canada, the Netherlands, Japan and China. This can provide many lessons for the Indian police force which is looking for new direction and is already viewing community policing as means to address the problems of citizens in today's working.

Drawing from the experiences in other nations successfully practicing community policing some of the strategies for success of community policing are:

1. *Institutionalization and reengineer other components*: Police departments in India today, like any other bureaucratic organization, are ruled by old rules regulations with a strong resistance to change which does not encourage innovation. Important findings of the Oppal Commission to go into the working of the Canadian Police were that the:

   [m]ajor impediment toward community policing is the police organizational structure itself. It requires a flatter organization without the multiple tiers of rank. It requires decentralization and the individual empowerment of line officers so they can work effectively within their communities. (Oppal Commission, 1994)

To transcend community policing from the traditional public-relations 'grin and wave' approach, police forces must be willing to undergo change, especially deep, organizational shifts from the rigid paramilitary structure to one where accountability and public consultation are the operative philosophies (Anderson, 1995).

For department-wide adoption of community policing, the police will need to reengineer other components of the organization by the integration of philosophy into mission statements, training (see Part 2, Chapter 5, 'training for community policing'), crime analysis, department policies, procedures, performance measurement systems,[3] evaluation tools and vision sharing strategy within the organization. For community policing, police forces need to empower the frontline police officers and bring about necessary changes in the organizational culture as discussed earlier. Police forces practising community policing have given it place in their mission statements and have accordingly amended their reporting and evaluation procedures to align with the activities undertaken under the aegis of community policing.

The US department-wide adoption of community policing is evidenced by the integration of the philosophy into mission statements, policies and procedures, performance evaluations, hiring and promotional practices, training programmes and other systems and activities that define organizational culture and functions. Among the US cities, the San Diego Police Department adopted organization structure, training and officer's appraisal system to support community policing. The Boston Police Department changed organizational process to support a new patrol strategy and creation of neighbourhood beat teams as part of a organizational change process. The Boston Police Department has decentralized itself by creating 11 districts within the city. This allows them to use different neighbourhood policing strategies tailored to its needs. Within the districts community policing, officers patrol specific beats and hold meetings with the community members. The department created strategic planning and community mobilization project to implement community policing and a city wide safety plan. A total of 400 participants from 16 teams were tasked with creating goals, objectives and concrete strategies to support department's mission to fully integrate community policing into Boston's neighbourhoods. The 16 teams comprised of officers, clergy, educators, business leaders and other members.

[3] See Table II.4.1 for the recommended performance evaluation parameters for the community policing officers.

Using the strategic map as the strategic guide, scorecards have been developed for implementation of community policing efforts by RMCP in Canada. These scorecards have measures, targets and initiatives required to execute the community policing efforts. The final step in the implementation of balanced scorecard is the performance reporting. An Excel spreadsheet has been developed to enable the reporting of progress against the objectives and their corresponding initiatives measures and targets identified in the scorecard. Community policing efforts in Canada are therefore not only institutionalized they also find place in mission statement and are monitored effectively and are reflected in the performance of the implementing police officers and the department (Clarke, 2002).

The cornerstone of the current community policing strategies in England and Wales can be traced back to the report of Lord Scarman, who was charged with investigating the riots of 1980 in British cities. The Scarman Report (1981) recommended greater community involvement in the formulation of policing policy and police operations (Reiner, 1995). The structure to realize this aim was to be a system of consultation between the police and the public, provision for which was made in the Police and Criminal Evidence Act (PACE) of 1984. The Act postulated that police authorities, in consultation with the chief constable, should set up structures for the purpose of 'obtaining the views of people... about matters concerning the policing of the area and for obtaining their cooperation with the police in preventing crime' (PACE, 1984: Section 106).

In the year 1993, a government White Paper proposed re-organizing the police to enable them to work more effectively by giving police managers greater freedom to manage their forces and to strengthen the partnership between the police and the public. In consequence of this paper in 1994 the Police and Magistrate's Courts Act updated police organization and management as set out in the White Paper. The document 'Building Communities, Beating Crime': A Better Police Service for the 21st Century' presented to the Parliament by the secretary of state for the home department in November 2004, sets out the current direction in policing in Britain. This paper has three broad objectives at its heart:

(a) the first is the spread of neighbourhood policing for the twenty-first century to every community with improved police responsiveness and customer service;

(b) the second is further modernization of the police workforce to ensure that the service is fully equipped and able to deliver these changes; and

(c) the third is the greater involvement of communities and citizens in determining how their communities are policed.

As enunciated in the document, the community policing efforts are to be central to policing efforts in Britain with their integration into regular policing and with solid financial support from the government. This paper sets out a clear direction of change— to deliver community policing for today's world and face the new challenges of changing criminality. The plan is to spread dedicated neighbourhood policing teams across the country. This programme of investment and reform has achieved real results such as the introduction of 4,000 Community Support Officers (CSOs) with a commitment to recruiting 25,000 CSOs and wardens by 2008. The government intends to embed a genuinely responsive customer-service culture and make the police and their partners more accessible, visible and accountable.

Fully trained officers using modern techniques and updated powers, working with CSOs with a minimum set of powers, will make up the neighbourhood policing teams. They will take an intelligence-led, proactive, problem-solving approach to enable them to focus on and tackle specific local issues. They will involve their local community in establishing and negotiating priorities for action and in identifying and implementing solutions, feeding community intelligence into crime prevention, detection and reduction. This is not a substitute for, rather an underpinning of, solid, professional police work to investigate crime and catch criminals—necessary to tackle systematic and organized criminality.[4]

The formal institutionalization of community policing in Japan is not significantly altered by a change in upper administration. For the Japanese police officers, crime prevention is a function equivalent in importance to criminal investigation, security, and order maintenance functions. While many police departments are doing community policing but their organizational structure and mission remains unchanged, the Japanese decentralized managerial system encourages delegation of responsibility, increasing the social distance between superiors and subordinates, and engaging in social activities outside of work while maintaining deserved respect in the workplace (Alarid and Wang, 1997).

[4] Source of information in last three paragraphs is official UK Government Home Office Website.

2. *Internal research and planning*: The systems of advancement of internal research and planning to modify and improvize the implementation of community policing in the US is worth emulating. The National Institute of Justice which has an annual budget of USD 300 million is the primary federal agency that promotes police-related research. It funds research by the academic and corporate world in diverse areas of police interest, ranging from crime-control method and community initiatives to technology applications. Several projects that have served as model for the future developments in police have been funded across the breadth of the country, in different police departments.

From the 1970s, the crime situation in the Santa Ana city in the US became worse. The Santa Ana Police Department began to implement community policing strategies in 1974 to fight violent, youth and gang crimes. The police department adopted geographical approach to police patrols. Performance standards were developed in 1989 to support community policing methods and procedures. Problem-oriented policing is at the heart of the police department commitment to community policing. In the same year, the police department developed neighbourhood policing task force to identify areas of common concern and develop neighbourhood policing strategies to resolve those concerns. This police–community partnership included 24 community members. On the recommendation of neighbourhood policing taskforce, the police department created Westend Development policing district in 1991 as a field lab for community policing and problem-oriented policing strategies. This site served as model for police departments around the country.

Charlotte Mecklenburg brought in Herman Goldstein, who is considered the father of people-oriented policing, to the department as a scholar in residence over a period of one year. He was available to work with the officers and helped units define their roles in community policing environment. Most interesting aspect of the project was the application of problem solving philosophy and the SARA model to policing activities.

At present in India, very little attention is paid to this aspect, though National Police Academy and Bureau of Police Research and Development are encouraging research, however, the funding for research work and appreciation for the same is dismal. There is a need to improve systems and processes that facilitate communication and flow of information. Though computerization and networking is underway, the Indian police is way far off in terms of collecting data on communities and proactive data analysis and its use for problem solving and crime prevention strategies.

3. *Internal marketing*: In implementing community policing in the Netherlands, everything did not proceed as smoothly. Soon there were issues of the beat officers being perceived as being too soft and not up to the task, when it came to solving the problems and were labeled as the loners, both by the public and the peers in the department. Various terms like 'social workers', 'beat nurses' and 'police psychiatrists' were used to describe them, which did little good to their image and effectiveness. Soon, there were efforts to find an alternative model and the answer came in the form of neighbourhood teams. These teams were to be installed to promote integration—external integration between the police and the public would improve legitimacy; by internal integration between parts of the organization and task integration where each constable should be sharing in more or less all kinds of daily police work. The teams would deal with nearly all 'routine police affairs' and it was envisaged that this externally focused and problem-oriented approach would improve legitimacy and effectiveness at the local level. However, the implementation of this kind of scheme did face considerable amount of resistance, especially from the Criminal Investigation Department, and except for the city of Haarlen, where the police chief was committed to the concept, the scheme stopped functioning after a while. While the surveys in the city of Harleen indicated that people did perceive significant improvement in police functioning and people did even miss the beat constable, who was earlier replaced by the teams (Punch et al., 2002).

There is a tendency within the department to look down upon community policing measures as going soft and futile exercises; it would take good deal of internal marketing to change this attitude. The focus of initial programmes to promote community policing within the department should be the process of organizational change to support, advance and sustain a new philosophy that runs counter to traditional working in the department and not immediate results. Not only the structure but the culture within the organization needs to change and this is important in a traditional organization like the police.

Dealing with the role which organizational readiness has to play in community policing, Oliver (2000: 211) said:

If a police agency attempts to implement community policing while retaining the traditional Para-military structure, chain of command, procedures and continues to utilize an authoritarian style of top-down management, community policing will be destined to fail. Because community policing is a philosophy and is value driven, hence driving the changes in the way police conduct their business and relate with the community, so too should these values drive change in the way management conducts their business and relates with the line officers. For community policing India should promote progressive and creative leadership and management approaches. Within the department, middle level mangers should also be convinced about the idea of community policing. While top manager is important, the middle level is the one that can encourage these practices in the department.

4. *Identify change agents*: Dennis Rosenbaum and Deanna Wilkinson examined two midsized cities (Aurora, Indiana and Joliet, Illinois in USA) that attempted to adopt and implement community policing programmes (Skogan, 2004). What they found was that the best strategy for adopting community policing, at the initial stages, was the formation of specialized community policing units staffed by skilled volunteer officers. The work of most officers doing routine patrol activities did not change, nor did their hearts and minds when community policing initiatives were introduced. But within the specialized community policing units, there existed a large group of officers for whom community policing, creative problem solving and data-driven planning was appealing and easily adopted. Dennis Rosenbaum and Deanna Wilkinson suspect that these officers may become the critical mass that eventually drives policing and organizational change. The Cleveland Police Department created a community policing bureau in the year 1977. This section now includes mini stations, school programmes and other community policing initiatives. The police department implemented an innovative Residential Area Policing Programme (RAPP) giving specialized training to officers by community policing unit. RAPP worked on the concept of developing mini stations. The mini station approach has resulted in a number of initiatives such as neighbourhood watch, home watch, child watch, stop auto theft, gang awareness seminars, senior citizen seminars, business and residential security surveys, bicycle patrols and beat/foot patrols.

5. *Local initiatives*: The implementation experiences of community policing initiatives suggest that the key requirement must be that the initiative is local in character. While the support for community policing should come from the top, the practices and concepts should be developed/evolved at the cutting edge. The initiatives that get evolved from the grass root level are

lasting and implementable in terms of what works and what does not. Second, they must only be implemented when they are constructed through the benefit of local knowledge and sensitivity to local conditions and legal realities. Programmes should only be borrowed from the West when two conditions are satisfied.

The Chicago Police Department developed a community assessment centre. This centre collects data on the communities that the police officers serve and help them to keep in touch with the evolving nature of communities officers serve. In 1996 the entire department was officially decentralized giving more discretion to sergeants and the district commanders to solve the neighbourhood crime and disorder problems. This bottom-up planning process ensures that the police department resources are focused on the problems that are of most concern to the community.

The most recent step in the development of community-oriented policing in the Netherlands has been the introduction of the new-style community beat officer during the 1990s, whereas the former beat constable was 'just an ordinary cop', the community officer is held responsible for 'organizing security' in his area in a much wider sense and they represent the 'the face of the police' (Punch et al., 2002). The community officers take a spearhead position; if he/she needs assistance from colleagues in specialized departments then they are formally obliged to help. Unlike the beat constables, who usually operated in the margin of the organization, the community officers are generally well embedded in the organization, where they are supposed to aid in directing the work of others. This means that the traditional top-down approach in setting police priorities is, at least partly, replaced by a bottom-up approach. Very significantly then, the community policing is no less than the 'pivot' around which the rest of the force is organized.

The specific tasks of the new community officers include:

(i)   Building and maintaining networks with external partners, such as local government and social agencies.

(ii) Effectuate an integral approach to local safety problems, to support and encourage citizens to rely on their own ability to do something about security problems they experience and to improve the quality of life in their own neighbourhood.

(iii) Seeking permanent solutions for recurrent problems that are a continuous burden to the police and a constant source of irritation and unrest to the community.

Today, the Dutch police have drawn on its own past, and on models from abroad, to combine a tradition of social policing with order maintenance and crime control (Punch et al., 2002).

6. *Build broad public and political support*: Finally, the implementation strategy should focus on public ownership of policing, not state or police control. Community policing is not cheap and it is labour intensive and when money and resources are tight, it may be at risk. But if supporters can build broad public and political support for it, the budget for community policing may survive. In a bureaucratic setup, no initiative can survive long unless it gets the necessary support from the top and community policing is no exception. In the US, the COPS programme had a strong federal support and the support of the US President, the policy elites at the federal, state and the city level to take roots across the nation. This is a big asset in introducing policy initiatives of such a nature. The top leadership in the country supported the programme as a mean to fight crime. Massive funds to the tune of nine billion dollars were provided by the federal government to implement the community policing schemes all over the country.

    Political support for community policing can also become a tool to overcome resistance to community policing within a department. Political support also signals other agencies within the government that this is not just the police department's programme; it is service delivery on a grander scale and requires their participation and involvement from all agencies. Community policing can work; but, in order to work, community policing must be the city's programme (Skogan, 2004).

7. *Concluding remarks*: People and police interact to form the service process called policing with community policing it is more so. Community policing is, inherently, a philosophy of policing and cannot be seen as its separate branch. A firm commitment by the local police departments to community policing is more important than having the federal government pay large funds. Funds are a necessary vehicle but the most important aspect is the conviction and belief, in community policing, in the minds of policemen on the street, who can 'work both as policemen and community officers at the same time'. For this eventually the police department will have to move away from special unit/specific programmes-based strategies, which are useful for establishing the concept in the department, though, they many

times die out with individuals or governments, and ultimately work towards the goal that eventually every policeman has to work as a community policing officer. Every officer in the department must genuinely accept the idea that crime prevention and service functions are just as important as law enforcement; on the other hand, the community members must also be committed in realizing their essential role in crime prevention. Any policy on community policing in any nation has to keep this concept at the core. The Knoxville police, US, throughout the 1980s worked internally to change their infrastructure and improve their officer deployment strategy. They do not have a separate community policing unit rather the whole department is committed to practicing community policing at all levels. The police department has built their processes on the SARA model. This has improved police response to community needs, raised the standard of work through greater worker involvement and has established a structure for continued development.

Community policing lessons from other nations for the Indian police

- Re-engineer other components of the organization for department-wide adoption of community policing by integration of philosophy into mission statements, training, crime analysis, department policies, procedures and performance measurement systems.
- Modify organizational structures to support decentralized decision making and responsibility with accountability.
- Support from the top while the practices and concepts should be developed/evolved at the cutting edge.
- Involve middle-level manager.
- Focus on culture change within the organization.
- Encourage research and planning to modify and improvize the implementation of community policing.
- Draw on local experiences and practice in terms of what works and what does not.
- Focus on public ownership of policing, not state or police control.
- Build broad public and political support, community policing must be the city's programme.
- Identify change agents.

Cost 9

The police department is an important department that interacts with people on a day-to-day basis and has an important role to play in the lives of the citizens of this country. There can be no price tag attached to many of the activities that are carried out by the police. However, in times when there is an ever-growing demand on the services and resources of police, the governments suffers from the resource crunch and are unable to provide requisite funds to the police to carry out its functions as per the demands of the day. This is not true only for India, but even in nations like the US and the UK, the police feel the resource crunch. Few years back a booklet released in the US—*60 Steps to Problem Oriented Policing*—mentions about the resource crunch in the police department, the money allotted being used up in the personnel costs and the need to rethink the police functions. In the US, of the 92 police departments surveyed, 73 indicated that there was a perception of fiscal stress within their cities (Levine, 1985).

Police forces are not only stung by the financial constraints, but are also under pressure like never before to use the available finances effectively. The National Police Commission 1977 (para 14.52) says that the police organization should keep the organization at a high pitch of efficiency particularly through effective personnel and financial management for effective role performance. In the UK, the audit commission has published several reports on policing and the criticisms of financial management in the police service have frequently attracted headlines in the national press. Reports of increase in recorded and unrecorded crime are regularly accompanied by criticism of the effectiveness and efficiency of the police and skeptical comment on the efficacy of conventional methods of policing.[1] In Australia, the Management Improvement Initiative programme required the police to pursue cost-saving and productivity improvements measures.

In this scenario not only the department needs to project the funds requirement to the government with painstaking homework (Box II.9.1), but it is duty bound to give the maximum customer satisfaction for the tax payer's money that is allotted to them in the budget.

Box II.9.1   Successful Budgetary Strategies

The police budgets are more often than not a subject of intense discussion and are rarely increased without opposition. To add to this, the department has a very routine approach to this issue ranging from apathy to ignorance about the process. However, the police needs to adopt a more active approach in getting necessary funds. The successful strategies employed by some of the police departments are:

1. Use crime and workload data judiciously.
2. Capitalize on sensational crime incidents, preferably those outside the state to drive home the point.
3. Get the message out effectively.
4. Carefully mobilize interest groups.
5. Strategically plan.
6. Work closely with the chief minister's office and elected officials.
7. Involve all departmental levels in the preparation of budget.

Source: National Institute of Justice.

Today the top police managers are bound to address one of the key questions—Is there a better way to deliver police service that costs less? While the police administrators look for ways to reduce cost of policing, the economics of police working indicates towards an inherent trend which is diametrically opposite to what is desired. As Reenen in his article, *The Unpayable Police* concludes: Law enforcement as we know it today will continuously increase in price and might do so to such an extent that in the long run policing becomes unpayable. It will doubtless take longer in one country than in another before this point is reached. The

---

[1] See *Management Accounting: Magazine for Chartered Management Accountants* (1994). Over the past decade and a half a considerable number of reforms have been promoted in the UK public sector in the names of accountability and value for money—reforms which look set to continue well into the 1990s. Delegated budgets, internal markets, efficiency scrutinies, financial or resource management initiatives and performance indicators are just some of the readily identifiable labels of the 'new' public-sector management accounting function.

application of Baumol cost disease (Box II.9.2) is as applicable to the police as to activities like theater, opera or music. Rubinstein writes much earlier as:

> The policeman's principal tool is his body. He shares with many persons the use of their body as a piece of equipment essential to the performance of their trades. He is similar to a mountain climber; to athletes whose success is rooted in physical prowess rather than the skillful use of equipment; to runners, circus acrobats, sexual performers, laborers and peasants. (Rubinstein, 1973)

Box II.9.2 Baumol Cost Disease

The American economist Baumol discovered that some services and products are incompatible with cost reduction. A dance production, for example, depends so heavily on people that costs can hardly be reduced and become more and more 'expensive' without producing more. This phenomenon is known as the 'cost disease' of Baumol. In general, in the market sector an increase in wages is linked to a rise in productivity. The decrease in cost that is a consequence of the rising productivity could be invested, paid out as profit, or could be used to increase wages. Prosperity growth is therefore mainly productivity growth. When the increase of productivity is possible in a certain sector, but difficult or impossible in another like the police, we face a problem: prosperity growth will not occur in the sector that is lagging behind, except when the price per unit is constantly raised. As a result, the costs of the policing will inflate quicker than the growth in the GDP.

Source: Reenan, 1999.

Further, for the police, the cost increase is not limited to the Baumol cost disease; the society does not wish maximum efficiency in law enforcement as it clashes with central societal and political values, for example, there can be no cost benefit analysis carried out in executing a legal decisions (Reenen, 1999). Then the compulsions of economics may not find application to policing when a set of central values define policing, such as, as little force as possible. In any given law and order situation, the police has to be equipped with appropriate arms and be in appropriate strength to ensure that minimum force is used to achieve the objective and this may not be the most cost-effective means. Another value is that technical policing cannot replace all the police work. For example, society wants a policeman and not a camera or another mechanical device in a street affected by crimes like snatching and eve-teasing. So, in that sense, there are cultural limitations to cost reduction within the police.

In the pursuit to look for the best possible service at the least possible price the core and culture strategy with meta-tools like strategic management and cross agency linkages will be discussed here.

Core strategy	Strategic management
Culture strategy	Cross agency linkages

Strategic management

The dynamics of police costing therefore would mean an impossible, ever-increasing demand on public funds by the police. However, in response to the growing fiscal stress the department has been trying to balance their budgets by making marginal adjustments in their operating procedures and expenditures, that is, they are following a policy of decrementalizm. Examples are: the use of vehicles for years after they have been condemned, putting of limit on the use of patrol, thinning out manpower on duties, and so on. Though such methods offer short-term solution, stretching resources over a period of time has resulted in compounding of the problems at hand for the department, such as:

1. *Human resource erosion*: There has been a decline in the skill level, health and commitment of the policemen due to stretched over deployment. This has led to decline in their responsiveness and performance.
2. *Overcentralization*: One of the immediate responses to cut expenditure has been to impose expenditure limits and centralized clearance of proposals above the fixed limits. In the long run, this kills initiative and builds in unnecessary delays and inefficiency.
3. *Allocation starving*: Some of the worst hit units are those that give benefits in the long run like the planning department or the training section. When they are worst affected by the cuts the effectiveness of the department in the long run is compromised.

Therefore, in place of the policy of decrementalizm, there is a need to develop a strategic perspective (Levine, 1985). Strategic management means having a clear understanding of what is the department's mission and core services are and to prioritize them to create sustainable long-term administrative arrangements to finance and deliver these services. The strategic management perspective encourages the officers in the police department to examine the linkages between police, other governmental and non-governmental departments as their focus of analysis and for developing law enforcement and crime prevention service delivery system.

Types of fiscal stress faced by the police department and some of the strategies that would work in coping with them are given in Table II.9.1

Table II.9.1 Types of Fiscal Stress and the Coping Strategies

Fiscal crunch (short duration low intensity): Stall payments to suppliers Expenditure freeze Defer maintenance	*Fiscal squeeze (long duration low intensity)*: Improve operations management Downscale logistics
Fiscal crisis (short duration high intensity): Defer equipment replacement Close peripheral programmes	*Fiscal crush (long duration high intensity)*: Reorient and shed functions; low level additions; spread of costs to other authorities, special police forces; spread of costs through 'self-help'; spread of costs by diffusion of tasks; on payment services; commercial utilization of land

Source: Levin, 1985.

Today, the police departments in India are facing the 'fiscal crush', long duration high intensity financial stress. Some of the ways to counter this problem strategically are:

1. *Reorient functions*: Traditional police management has been concerned with tactics, not strategy, and with 'how to do it' instead of what to do and why (Cizanckas and Hanna, 1977: 24). As a result, in the police department, there is a tendency to put too much emphasis on daily operations by maximizing patrol and investigations with not nearly enough concern devoted to defining the appropriate scope and levels of police services, that is, too much attention is devoted to tactics and the fine tuning of operations within the traditional framework of police management paying little attention to the question of grand strategy—mission, design, and service delivery options (Levine, 1985: 697). Over a period of time while some activities may be carried out efficiently their utility to public can be questioned.

One way of redesigning and aligning of policing activities is by identification of the basket of police functions that are most important to the people; that is the demand identification by holding public meetings directly with the people of the area and orienting police activities as per the requirements of the people. These activities are combined with the core/traditional policing activities so that the maximization of public satisfaction level is achieved, given the fixed resources.

Making use of the concepts of microeconomics in the field of consumer behaviour, we can try to maximize the satisfaction that police service can provide to people, given the limited budget allotted to the department. In Chart II.9.1, we see the demand graph of the requirements of people on the activities of the police department for a given yearly police budget. On the x-axis we have service-oriented activities to be undertaken by the police[2] and on the y-axis we have the traditional policing activities. Given the right mix of these two activities a 'market basket' is arrived at from public meetings and an assessment within the police department in consultation with officers. The maximizing market basket must satisfy two conditions: it must be located on the budget line and it must give the people the most preferred combination of services. These two conditions reduce the problem of maximizing people's satisfaction to one of picking an appropriate point on the budget line (Pindyck and Daniel, 2004). In Chart II.9.1, the original budget line L_1, with a given mix of core/traditional policing with very little service activities give the axis T_1 and S_1. Now, as we try to increase the service features in the police functions, sacrificing some of the traditional policing activities the new line of $T_2 S_2$ is arrived at, this line incorporates many of the activities such as de-addiction camps, training camps in schools, youth clubs, reception rooms in the police stations, etc. Corresponding to $T_2 S_2$, a new utility curve at U_2 is achieved. Further, if we augment the resource of the people to the police department through channelization of voluntary help, as a part of this scheme, the line shifts to $T_2 S_3$ giving a further higher utility curve U_3, as we see in Chart II.9.1. Here, since we are adding to the resources, a new budget line touching at x-axis at S_3 is achieved. However, the actual police budget from the government remains the same.

Thus with the right mix of core/traditional and service activities we get higher new utility curve U_3 which is providing the customers with higher satisfaction from the services offered by the police department with the same budget. This is what the department needs today; a reorientation of their activities to tune with the times and to the requirements of the people they serve, as after all the police exists for the society and the people.

[2] We express the hope that the future police station will not merely be a point of crime control and prevention, but will develop into a service centre (National Police Commission, 1977–81: para 61.19).

Chart II.9.1   The Demand Graph of the Requirements of People on the Activities of the Police

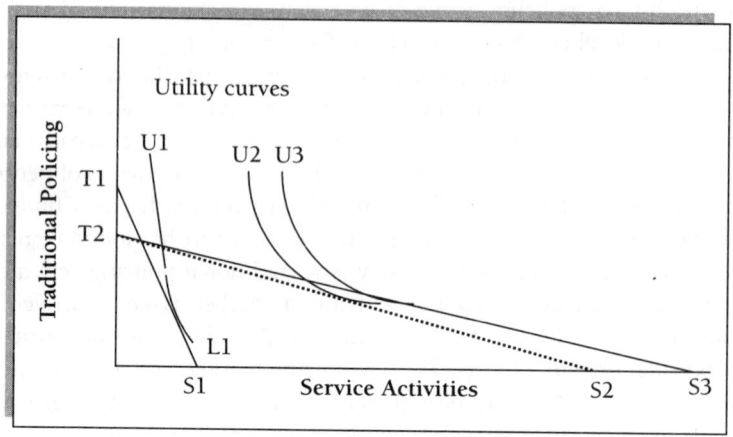

Source: Conceptualized by the author.

Other measures

Other useful adaptations and policy measures that could be undertaken by the police to tackle this problem of rising cost of policing could be (Reenen, 1999):

2. *Low-level additions*: In the police department there are varieties of jobs done by the trained police officers that may not require the skills of a policeman; we can very well do with a fully educated police officer who is supported by helpers—police assistants and wardens. Their education is lower, their tasks limited and their powers are less, and for some groups, equal to those of normal citizens. Their salary is, of course, lower and many are on temporary contracts. The total capacity is increased without affecting the position or the qualifications of the established profession. Some of the duties on which expensive trained manpower is deployed at present are: the reception duties, maintenance duties, telephone operators' duties, and so on. These duties could be handled by police assistants and wardens at cheaper rates and would avoid underutilization of specialized police officers (Box II.9.3). The Los Angeles Police Department made certain improvements in their records system and replaced many officers working indoors by well-trained civilian help. This served the double purpose of accomplishing those routine tasks by lower salary grades, plus

---

Box II.9.3   Police Community Support Officer in the UK Police

A Police Community Support Officer (PCSO) supports the work of the local police force and provides a visible and reassuring presence on the streets. It is a paid role, although they don't have the same powers as a regular officer. PCSOs particularly work to reassure the public and to tackle the social menace of antisocial behaviour.

Working under the direction of a police commander, they fight a range of crime and disorder problems, such as:

1. contributing to the regeneration of local communities,
2. increasing public safety,
3. dealing with truants, graffiti, abandoned vehicles, litter, missing persons enquiries,
4. confiscating alcohol being consumed in a public place,
5. helping to support victims, and
6. controlling crowds at major events.

Depending on the role, the PCSO may also be given some police powers, including the power to:

1. detain someone until a constable arrives,
2. direct traffic and remove vehicles, and
3. issue fixed penalty notices for antisocial behaviour.

Source: www.homeoffice.gov.uk.

releasing additional police officers for basic police work. During one year 108 police officers were transferred into the field in this manner (Parker, 1975: 44).

In the 1990s, while recruiting people to fight the war against terrorism, Punjab police realized that out of fear of terrorists people were not willing to join the police. The concept of recruitment of the Special Police Officers (SPO) and Home Guards (HG) with relaxed norms was introduced, and further, it was decided that recruitment of all the constables would be done from the SPOs. This gave actual fighters, like the victims of terror and their relatives, the chance to come into police with low pay scales and no further burden on the exchequer or resources (Interview K. P. S. Gill, 2007).

3. *Spread of costs to other authorities, special police forces*: A second development worth mentioning is the spread of costs over more institutions. In countries with state police systems, many municipalities take safety costs on their own account by paying an extra

slice out of their own budget. They pay for their local cops. This is, of course, not a cost reduction measure, but a cost redistribution measure. In a country like the USA, with its differentiated and fragmented police structure, the cost of policing is divided over thousands of local, county, state, federal and special budgets.

4. *Spread of costs through 'self-help':* The deficit can also be reduced in a different way. One could shift the work in part to the citizens. In countries like the USA, self-protection has always been a right, a right that can be executed by the legitimate use of firearms. In other parts of the world, this task has completely been claimed by the government. When citizens are made responsible for part of their safety, the demand on the police or the government may be reduced and part of the costs of security is in fact paid directly by the people. Fort Worth, Texas, in the US, the police department was grappling with unprecedented rise in crime and very vocal residents complaining about the crime situation. Police department initiated the scheme 'code blue' to work in close co-operation with city departments, communities, schools. A total of 44 new neighbourhood police officers were hired to implement non-traditional approach to policing: Church, schools, business organizations adopted officers in the neighbourhood to further this programme. The support in the community for the neighbour-hood officers was so high that community would go to the extent of asking for promotion or hike for the officers. The scheme also provided for network of 2,800 citizen volunteers to assist police and to act as their eyes and ears.

    The concept of formation of village defence committees by the citizens with the help of police is an integral part of police rules in India. In many countries, the inhabitants of neighbourhoods or villages have hired private security services which watch over the area next to, or instead of, the police or live in privately-guarded apartment buildings or compounds. Many companies have their own security guards and public business grounds are being watched by private security firms. In the USA, the number of private security guards is more than twice as high as the number of police officers.

5. *Spread of costs by diffusion of tasks:* These are not the times where policing functions in isolation, the issue of crime and disorder has a wider perspective today. Precisely for this reason the concept of collective responsibility of various departments and agencies in sharing the cost of programmes to combat these crimes becomes relevant. Thus, the 'old' police task is partially redefined and

converted into broader categories, and in this way can be distributed over more sectors of the government than in the past. The Department of Public Health takes a part of the responsibility and the costs of the drugs problem by defining drug addiction as a health problem. A second example is the concept of 'integral safety'. Through this broad policy concept, a large number of local officials get involved in crime and crime prevention problems. Policemen have to become the organizers of safety, not the producers, and their organizing role has to combine the efforts of a lot of local public and private institutions. Integral safety has started to take flight in the concept involves systematic organizations like housing associations, public parks, relief work institutions, social services, police and others in reducing crime. The function of diffusion here is that it creates the possibility of relying on funds, which carry a label other than police costs, and in this way, more resources become available.

6. *On payment services*: As of now, there is a tendency to look down upon the idea of charging from public as the police are a law enforcing organization, but the role of the police does not limit to law enforcing only. It has to do security duties, guard duties, crowd control and regulation duties also. These duties are done free of cost where it is a matter of common public concern or is arising out of the same. Increasingly the police are being called on to render services in the situations that may not be categorized in the public realm. They are doing duties in these areas but are not charging any amount as the private agencies do. There are certain areas of police activity such as 'passport verification', 'verification of domestic servant', 'security survey', and so on for which the beneficiaries should pay in some way or the other. To achieve this, it would be necessary to set up a mechanism which is uniform for the entire country and which is consistent with the laws and rules.[3] The Australian Federal Police (AFP) conducts some of their activities, such as criminal history checks, on a fee-paying basis. The current fee being USD 32.73 for each National Police Check application and USD 118.18 for a fingerprint and National Police Check application where fingerprints are to be taken and processed by the AFP (http://www.afp.gov.au/business/national_police_checks.html).

Another such area is the events security arrangements, like the one-day match of cricket. The cricket board is charging money

[3] Recommendations of the XXXIV All India Police Science Congress.

for the event and is making profit out of it, to be used by its officials to run their activities. In such event where the police are used heavily for arrangements with its manpower, vehicles and other resources, it would be prudent to charge for the policemen deployed on the basis of their daily salaries multiplied by the number of days of deployment. There are provisions in the police rules, which authorize the chief of police in the district to provide police force on payment at his discretion. Similarly, there are a large number of business establishments that would like protection on certain days at their premises or for transportation of cash, and so on. Such services can be provided on payment. For individual security there are demands from businessmen, this too can be done on payment with the monthly bill on the salaries of policemen charged to the concerned individual.[4]

7. *Retention of the revenue generated*: Police department generates revenue by way of fines and penalties, especially in the area of traffic regulation. As the traffic management in itself is capital intensive activity, it requires the capital for its engineering aspect. The funds generated from the fines could be deposited and used by police from a special purpose account for improvement in the traffic regulation. The Gujarat government, for example, has allowed the police to plough back its earnings, by way of fines to carry out projects. The collection in Ahemdabad itself amounted to Rs 4 crores in 2005. With this the officers felt that the projects long in pipeline will see the light of the day (*The Times of India*, 2007d). Another example has been the Punjab government's decision to allow the money earned from the scrap metal of ammunition to be used for the welfare of police officers.

8. *Commercial utilization of land*: Das-Gupta (2004a) suggests the following principle for selected government assets: 'Identification of under or unutilized government assets, including land and buildings, and improved utilization, with private sector participation in suitable cases, can reduce the direct cost of government services and also give rise to new sources of non-tax revenue.' Old *kotwalis* and some of the offices are built at prime locations. These spaces could be utilized by building multi-storied complexes that can house the present establishment in a more dignified manner and can also accommodate commercial establishments that can generate revenue for the department in terms of rents. Similarly,

---

[4] Actor Amitabh Bachchan wrote a letter to the police requesting for police security to his house for three days for his son's wedding. He was willing to pay whatever the cost came up to (*The Times of India*, 19 April 2007).

the police lines build more than 100 years ago house the stores and the reserve force for the district apart from providing training and other logistic facilities in the district. This land can also be used for commercial purposes such as marriage palace built at the premises could give good revenue as so much land inside the old city areas is scarce these days and parking paces that are needed for big functions can be easily provided in the police lines.

There is also huge demand for good schools with facilities for sports, swimming riding, shooting, and so on. Such schools can be run, on the police land in the police lines of the bigger districts, by the police. These can be open to public, with the administration given to a reputed management. The police can provide logistics, support which otherwise is not there in private schools. This will not only generate revenue for the police but also do service to the people of the city and would bridge a gap between the public and the police.

9. *Load-shedding*: 'Load-shedding' is 'a process...in which services are ceded to commercial or voluntary providers' (Johnston, 1992a). It involves the transfer of responsibility for service provision from the police to the private and voluntary sector (Box II.9.4). There has been a significant expansion of private policing, with the private security industry employing significant number of people and the trend is growing rapidly. In India too, the thinking has set in with government drafting a private detective bill, 2006, which would enable the government to select agencies to outsource jobs like issuing of summons, verification of passports and employment checking.[5]

Outsourcing

The issue of outsourcing is becoming increasingly important for the police, for those who see an increasing pluralization of policing; the ascendancy of outsourcing may represent a transitional stage between policing as a state monopoly and an increasingly competitive security market, where the public police will be but one among several players. For those who embrace a more state-centric model of policing, these

---

[5] Harminder Raj Singh, joint secretary, Ministry of Home Affairs says that while the core policing will still remain with the force, other jobs such as issuing of summons and passport verification can be handed over to private agencies (*Sunday Times of India*, 8 October 2006).

Box II.9.4   Other Groups in the Netherlands

The regular police officers receive support from two groups in the exercise of their duties, that is, the town watchers and volunteers.

Town watchers

Some 4,000 town watchers assist the Dutch police by patrolling in public places, thus enhancing safety and amenity. They carry out their duties on the basis of municipal safety and security programmes, whether for particular neighbourhoods or otherwise. They are often under the operational control of police officers. In general, their duties are confined to observation and supervision and they do not have powers of investigation. As they are in direct contact with the control room through their walkie-talkies, they can call in police assistance if necessary.

The presence of uniformed town watchers makes people feel safer and helps to prevent antisocial behaviour. They are one answer to demand of municipalities for a more visible policing presence on the streets. Moreover, they free up time for the police to concentrate on investigation offences and providing emergency assistance.

Volunteers

The Netherlands has around 2000 police volunteers. They make a major contribution to the provision of good policing, above all by helping out during busy periods. They have the same training as regular police officers and are used for the most part for work that would otherwise be carried out by a surveillance officer (that is, the lowest rank).

Police volunteers are generally used for police work proper as opposed to clerical work. They have investigative powers are entitled to use force. The manner in which volunteers are used differs from region to region. The force manager determines when volunteers are used, naturally in accordance with the national guidelines. Volunteers receive a small payment and their legal status is regulated separately.

Source: School of Police Leadership, 2006.

new developments will liberate the police from dependency on their own resources, provide them with greater freedom of choice, and enable them to realise economies and thereby achieve more with less (Ayling and Grabosky, 2006).

In the UK, towards the end of 1993, a Home Office review team, led by Ingrid Posen, was set up to 'examine the services provided by the police, to make recommendations about the most cost-effective way of delivering core policing services and to assess the scope for relinquishing ancillary tasks' (Home Office, 1995). It identified core and ancillary policing tasks and made 26 recommendations on changing the delivery of core policing tasks and relinquishing ancillary policing tasks to other agencies (such as local authorities and private contractors). An important effect of the Management Improvement Initiative in Australia have been identifying non-core activities and investigating 'outsourcing' of non-core activities. Services like laundering, catering, cleaning, publishing and maintenance of equipment, vehicles and buildings have been the subject of 'outsourcing' for decades. The outsourcing of more recent services like physical fitness testing, vaccination programmes, pathology testing and audits of financial systems are uncontroversial, but the purchasing of services that traditionally have been provided from police ranks is also growing. Many police organizations around the world outsource recruit training, some traffic functions, audiotape transcriptions (for example, of telephone interceptions), some forensic investigations and provision of prisoner custody and transportation services. In Scotland, a private firm is responsible for both prisoner transportation and the monitoring of electronically tagged adult and juvenile offenders (Jackson, 2005).

Consultants are frequently hired to carry out engineering works, develop and evaluate policing programmes, prepare budgets, plan accommodation strategies, conduct surveys of client satisfaction levels, implement organizational security and design and manage computer systems. Outsorcing can address a shortage of particular skills or equipment within a police organization. It is difficult for government agencies to employ top-quality experts in specialist areas like information technology and financial management because the government pay rates are low compared to those in the private sector. On the other hand, the police may have the skills in-house to provide a service but not have the resources (in terms of time and labour) to do so. The use of private security to guard police buildings is an example of this (Johnston, 1992b: 59). Such a strategy may also be cost effective (see Box II.9.5).

Apart from this, there are prospects of efficiency gains for police and outsourcing may result in higher quality service as the contractor may bring the skills necessary for the job not available, or readily available, from within police ranks, and a private sector mentality of flexibility in terms of employment arrangements and responsive service delivery. This is not to say that outsourcing always saves police organizations money. According to one commentator, outsourcing is most likely to produce savings 'where the required service can be easily specified and monitored' (Mulgan, 2001). In April 2005, the Boston Police Department

---

Box II.9.5   Outsourcing in the Police

The Australian Federal Police have entrusted the security of their headquarters to a private security firm (Ayling and Grabosky, 2006). London's Metropolitan Police has outsourced both the day-to-day operation and future development of its IT and radio communications networks. Outsourcing of cybercrime investigations has also been contemplated by Australian police forces (Police Commissioners' Conference Electronic Crime Steering Committee, 2001). The police in high-crime areas of Cape Town, South Africa, have chosen to use private armed response companies to protect their stations from attack and armed robbery while they carry on with basic job of policing the streets (Schönteich, 2004a: 12). In Scotland, the police have entrusted to a private firm, Reliance, prisoner court custody and transportation duties throughout Scotland and, more recently, 'non-core' escorting duties such as inter-prison transfers and transport to prisoners' hospital appointments in some parts of the country. Prison escort services are also outsourced in the Australian Capital Territory.

---

decided to outsource the forensics work previously conducted by its own fingerprint analysis unit. The private firm to whom the work was out-sourced found 109 fingerprints missed earlier by Boston detectives investigating crimes. Outsourcing the work was expensive, costing USD 30,000 per month, but clearly the benefits outweighed the costs (Ayling and Grabosky, 2006).

However, relying on outsourcing and procurement to supplement police resources can also be costly and may bring about risk. Because policing is a sensitive business, the costs and risks associated with these types of interactions between police and third parties are sometimes greater than they would be for other state agencies. Obvious financial costs, risks of over-dependency on a supplier, corruption and fraudulent practices, problems with quality of outsourced services, difficulties over accountability of contractors, police staff morale issues, threats to police legitimacy in the eyes of the public and inequities in the provision of police services—any one of these factors, if serious enough, can cause significant embarrassment to the police or to the government of the day.

Nevertheless outsourcing is here to stay and cannot be ignored; with-drawal of police from the market environment is not a realistic option any longer. There are some safeguards that can be put in place to reduce the risks involved, these include (Ayling and Grabosky, 2006):

1. It seems that decisions about outsourcing of police services are of considerable import for both the police and others because of their implications for the role of the police in society. However,

few opportunities currently exist for lower level police or the public to have an input into those final decisions, with police management tending to make such decisions behind closed doors. A degree of transparency in decision making in this area would ensure the airing of public interest considerations. Such a process could lessen the risk of internal resistance, as well as enhance the wider public legitimacy.

2. Contracts need to be properly negotiated, with precise specification of tasks to be undertaken or results to be achieved, and comprehensive provisions concerning monitoring, dispute resolution and termination. This would have obvious benefit in addressing the risks that legal and quality problems will arise.

3. In addition to monitoring systems for the contractor, police systems, in order to monitor the internal processes involved in reporting, need to be in place. A lack of such systems will increase the risks of collusion between staff and contractors.

4. Independent review works to mitigate risks that arise from the intimacy that commercial relationships often generate.

Reducing 'cost' for police service in India

- Practice strategic management in place of marginal adjustments in budget.
- Reorient and shed functions paying attention to mission, design and service delivery options.
- Low-level additions to police jobs like police assistants constables.
- Spread costs to other authorities for special police forces.
- Spread costs through 'self-help', voluntary work.
- Spread costs by diffusion of tasks to various agencies and departments.
- Provide on payment services.
- Retention some of the revenue generated.
- Commercially utilize prime land.
- Load-shedding to commercial or voluntary provides.
- Outsource some of the non-core activities.

Resources 10

'Place', in the marketing mix, includes the police activities that makes services available to the targetted customers. As an initial natural response to the issue of 'place', the following steps would help in improving police access and image:

1. The control room have to be well equipped and efficient to take any call and guide the policemen on duty to reach any spot where they are needed. The police helpline number—100, needs to be more publicized so that people are aware of this facility.

2. Care should be taken that the police stations and the police posts are kept neat and clean with proper white wash. There is not much money invoved, it is more a matter of will.

3. The police could also set up police help kiosks at busy and sensitive places. Such as, police helpdesks at airport, bus stands, railway stations and busy market places. In the market places, it may be named as 'police shop',[1] for a change and to catch attention. Wherever they are located, proper care should be taken that they are manned and equipped. Unmanned and ill-equipped kiosks/desks may create just the opposite impression.

4. The police should set up reception rooms, women helpline, child helpline and NRI helpline for the facility of citizens.

However, moving beyond improving the immediate physical accessibility there is a need to examine several practices and methods that finally

---

[1] The UK police has set up such police shops in the city centre of the towns which are the hub of activity. This is able to project the image of police as a service provider first and after that a law enforcer.

hampers the availability of resources and manpower resulting in eventual inaccessibility of the police. The reach of the department would also depend upon how mobilized is the force. Place would, therefore, also mean resources like locations, inventory, communication, transportation and logistics, with the police.[2]

The resource crunch and the lack of application of current management practices are the weakness of the department, while the technological advancements offer opportunities and means for providing better service to the people (Chart I.3.1). In police departments, innovations in working can lead to significant gains while there is considerable scope for innovation and resource leverage in the department. The strategies and the metatools to be employed for 'place' are shown here.

Core and culture strategy   Challenging the current practices resource leverage

---

Challenging the current practices

The scope for innovation and creativity cannot be over-emphasized in a department often faced with the stark reality of limited resources and yet expected to deliver results. A successful police administrator should have the ability to challenge the current practices in the department to increase effectiveness. Sometimes, a change in key policies can lead to reduction of requirement of resources.

1. Before 9/11, the Federal Bureau of Investigation (FBI), USA, realized that the two-step model of gathering evidence and prosecution was inadequate. Since 9/11, they also included analysis and sharing of information as a part of a four-stage process. They now gather information and share it with their domestic and international partners prior to taking action. Shifting focus from domestic to global and from law enforcement to security and law enforcement, the FBI today works as a more effective organization.

2. North Vietnam came up with the idea of building bridges just below the water level to avoid detection by the US airstrikes. More orthodox resource intensive solution would have meant deploying more troops to defend the bridges, construction of redundant bridges, more antiaircraft guns and more construction material (Hamel and Prahalad, 2002: 167–68).

---

[2] The Indian police in 2006 had 94,903 motor vehicles and 2,74,566 different types of wireless equipments to perform their duties efficiently (Government of India, 2006).

3. Set up in 2006, the Serious Organised Crime Agency (SOCA) of the UK adopted a novel approach to deal with the organized crime. It set its aim at reducing the social harm caused by organized crime, rather than just law enforcement. It focuses on the proceeds of crime realizing that organized crime is about money and profits; if you take the organized criminal's money away, freeze accounts and seize assets, it paralyses the entire chain of criminal activity. In keeping with this philosophy, the SOCA has established links with several organizations both law enforcement and non-law enforcement commercial organizations like the banks. Focusing on non-traditional methods is having a powerful disruptive effect.

4. Three times a year, the police in Germany (BKA) invites major banks, car and telecom companies, and other relevant parties not just to brief them on security measures, but to have a structured exchange of views, realizing the need to build network beyond law enforcement. One of the objectives is what the BKA can learn from them in terms of security. Also, to know from them what they expect from the police.

5. Terrorism in Punjab (Interview of K. P. S. Gill, 2007): The killing fields of Punjab, as they were called during the peak of terrorism in Punjab, were proving to be formidable for the jeeps and other vehicles at the command of security forces in the fight against the terrorists. A simple idea of introduction of bullet-proof tractors against the terrorists operating from the sugarcane fields, led to the police force gaining an upperhand and changed the complexion of future anti-terrorist operations altogether.

    The senior superintendent of police, Ludhiana, in 1992, demanded 100 vehicles and 10 men per vehicles to patrol the area divided into sectors. As there was an acute shortage of manpower for security and operational duties, it was decided to recruit large number of temporary SPOs, and they were given 15 days capsule courses and deployed at the routine static duties. The training manuals and the syllabi were also improvized. As a result the regular trained constables became available for the more important and critical anti-terrorist operations and for dominating the key identified roads in the nights.

    During the elections in early 1990s, there were 660 candidates for protection who were protected with 220 companies. It was observed that the protected people were killed; this was very demoralizing. It was ensured that this did not happen by providing separate vehicle to the security and the protected person. Each candidate was also provided a truck. Sometimes the truck also carried the bullet-proof *morchas* along for electioneering of the candidates.

   Many of the innovative measures on security, tactics and
strategies evolved during the battle of wits against terrorism in
Punjab were adopted by the centre, other states and agencies
(Sharma, 2006).

6. The use of 'bust buses' by the New York Police: Idle old buses
   were converted into arrest processing centres near the subways
   in New York. This led to reduction of processing time from 16
   hours to one hour (Kim and Mauborgne, 2003: 8). As a result, the
   availability of manpower to perform other key activities increased
   significantly.

7. For the Los Angeles police, the task of processing 100,000 common
   drunks per year through the jail system was using a dispropor-
   tionate share of police man-hours. Both experience and study made
   it obvious that a large proportion of these drunks were repeaters,
   sometimes ranging up to 40 arrests per year. In order to eliminate
   the time-consuming details of fingerprinting, photographing and
   preparing long typewritten record forms when processing repeaters into jail, police inaugurated a 'drunk-repeater' file, saving
   many thousands of man-hours which were once spent collecting
   arrest information already in police files (Parker, 1957: 43).

8. CompStat is based on the long-held values of maximizing every
   asset of the organization and each individual employee. All employees, regardless of their position, are encouraged and empowered (and evaluated on their ability) to think of new ways of
   doing business in order to achieve significant results. In today's
   environment of ever-shrinking resources, being able to apply the
   necessary resources to an identified problem area is crucial in
   successfully reducing crime. Historically, marked police vehicles
   have been randomly deployed in the belief that potential criminals would be deterred by seeing the police vehicles on patrol.
   CompStat provides information and intelligence to direct police
   resources to the exact problem area—be it a crime hotspot or
   a developing crime pattern. Without accurate information, the
   police response can only be based on the best instincts available
   and this meant scattering scarce resources (Schick, 2004).

9. Enabling the payment of traffic violations through the Internet,
   the Himachal Pradesh police not only ensured transparency and
   efficiency but also saved the tourists from undergoing undue
   harrassment in the payments.

10. The Andhra Pradesh (AP) police, with the strength of 80,000 police
    personnel, realized that imparting IT skills to all the employees
    in a time bound manner with the existing in-house training in-
    frastructure and facilities was next to impossible. To overcome

this problem, the AP police entered into an memorandum of understanding with the Technological University which has 300 engineering colleges affiliated to it, spread over in all the districts, for imparting training to all field police personnel. This acted as a force multiplier in enhancing IT skill levels of police personnel in AP and also forged a healthy relationship between the police, students and the academia.

11. 'Lok Samwad', an e-policing system was introduced in the Nagpur district in Maharashtra. Through the Bharat Sanchar Nigam Limited (BSNL) lines, web cameras, high speed scanners and network cards, the system connects district Superintendent of Police (SP) office with the police stations. Installed at the cost of Rs 5 lakhs, it allows the residents to interact online with SP. Besides hastening police action, the sytem has monetary benefits in terms of reduction of travelling expenditure for residents by Rs 2 crores annually and the police department will save almost Rs 2.5 crore annually by cutting down on personal visits and hand delivery of documents (*India Today*, 2006).

12. The district police often faces difficulties when offering services that take a significant amount of resources, but some police forces have found that collaboration in the form of Private–Public Partnership (PPP) can offer an attractive solution to the problem. The police has wide reach in the cities and in the remote areas. However, there is a need to upgrade the old and some times inadequate buildings. There have been examples of the same specially in the metropolitan towns and richer states like Punjab where people have come forward to augment the resources of police in building police posts and police stations. Businesses consider such collaboration as creating marketing alliances.

There is no other police force that harvests creative ideas better than the SPF. Innovation is the outcome of learning, and as noted in Peter Senge's book *The Fifth Discpline*: 'a small number of public organizations around the world embrace learning tools and principles in service of the same need for continual learning and adaptation. None have been more deligent in the effort than in Singapore Police Force' (Senge, 1990). The SPF has a systemic approach to develop, acquire, evaluate and implement innovative ideas through the SPF Innovation Model. The model supports innovations by structure, process and resources. The structure includes the SPF innovation panel, staff suggestion scheme portalite and innovation challenge bank that stores ideas generated from various sources. The process includes the staff suggestion scheme, the work improvement teams and the six-step design, and development and delivery process. The resources include the brainstorming fund, the trial fund and the enterprise challenge. Innovation is also a part of SPF's existing work process as the frontline patrol officers participate in the after-action reviews after their shifts of duty to share cases that they were handling during the shifts of duty and ideas for improvement. Ideas are also generated during in service classes. One of the important outcomes of such innovations is the formation of the Security Industry Regulatory Department in 2004, to manage the security industry better, resulting in streamlining of the industry and ensuring reliability and credibility. Rewards are given out to the teams at the annual Work Improvement Teams Convention and highly successful teams are given opportunity to patent their ideas. The innovation processes are reviewed at the monthly director service development and inspectorate forum (SPF Executive Summary, 2007).

Resource leverage

There is a significant gap between the department's aspirations and the resources, in management parlance this is termed as the 'stretch'. The stretch situation which the police departments face gives rise to the need for resource leverage. Resource leverage in the police department can be achieved by sufficiently concentrating, efficiently accumulating, creatively complementing, carefully conserving, and speedily recovering resources (Hamel and Prahalad, 2002: 175).

Concentrating resources

More effectively concentrating resources on key strategic goals. There can be lot that can be achieved with the resources that the department has by concentrating them at the places that are most in need and that has the biggest possible payoff. Few strategic goals at a time should be identified for the department rather than scattering the resources on too many goals at a time.

Government of India sanctioned reserve battalions to fight terrorism in Punjab. As a tactical move, the First Battalion was made into a commando battalion with the help of their own officers and this was very successful. Commando concept was carried forward and the subsequent four battalions were also converted into commando battalions. The strength of the police stations was increased so that they were able to meet the threat without reinforcements from outside. The weaponry was improved from the old 303s to AK-47 (seized/recovered) and the force then had weapons similar to those they were facing (Interview of K. P. S. Gill 2007).

The Delhi and Chandigarh police decided to introduce Global Positioning System (GPS) for their fleet of vehicles on the streets for quicker and effective police response to public. In Chandigarh, 30 Police Control Room (PCR) gypsies, official vehicles of all the SHOs and the traffic police interceptor will be fitted with the GPS receiver. The movement of all the GPS-fitted vehicles will be kept under track and the control room would know of their movement round the clock. The police officers maintain that this will help in utilizing the resources in a most effective way (*Times of Chandigarh*, 2007).

Accumulating resources

Police departments can more efficiently accumulate resources both by mining the resourses within the department and by borrowing the resouces from outside the department. It is not the cash that fuels the journey to the future, but the emotional and intellectual energy of every employee (Hamel and Prahalad, 2002: 139). The key asset of the police departments is their manpower; there is lot of knowledge and information stored to be exploited to the advantage of the department. Senior officers at the headquarters who were sitting in the offices and were only criticizing and clubbing at Chandigarh were asked to move out and were given the sub divisions to supervise for special operations and security arrangements for important events like the Republic Day during terrorism in Punjab (Interview of K. P. S. Gill 2007).

In the US cities, CompStat tactics encourage thinking outside the box and mandate that every resource, both internal and external, is considered when police respond to a problem. The tactics are designed to bring about permanent change and often this involves other agencies and organizations besides the police. For assessing resources of the partners, the arrogance inbuilt in the functioning of the police department needs to be replaced with humility.

Complementing resources

Complementing resources of one type with those of another to create higher-order value. This kind of resource leverage depends on the ability of the organization to blend different resources to multiply the value of each. There is an urgent need for connectivity of all the districts and the police stations through computers so that the data can be shared. Policing detection and prevention is all about information. So much of information stays only in police files and remains unshared that this kind of connectivity should be among the top priorities, not only for the department, but for the nation as a whole. If this disparate data was fully integrated and subjected to state-of-the-art analysis tools creating a seamless data grid that could be queried in real time, law enforcement agencies would be much more effective in both preventing crime and solving open cases. Such a project should be elevated to national priority mission. In the 11th Plan, the Government of India has allocated Rs 2000 crores for the computerization of the police forces across the country under the National eGovernance Plan. The Mission Mode Project, called the 'Crime and Criminal Tracking Network Systems', not only aims to automate all police functions from police station upwards but also provide for sharing of crime-related information amongst various stakeholders like jails, judiciary, forensic science laboratories, transport department, passport department, and so on.

In transportation, at present the department only procures a limited model of vehicles, whereas the market is full of different products for different uses. Even a cycle patrol can be more effective in certain conditions than a gypsy patrol. Similarly, a messenger can be sent on a moped rather than on an 'enfield' motorcycle, without any compromise on efficiency. Another form of resource complementation is the resource balancing. Presently, due to paucity of funds, more than 90 per cent of the police budget in many states is spent on salaries for the employees and only 10 per cent is spent on logistics and transportation. While the management research has established that for a force to be effective 30 per cent of the spending should be on logistics and transportation. By bringing about this balance in resources spending the resources effectiveness can be multiplied.

Conserving resources

Conserving resources wherever possible by recycling, co-opting and protecting. After the terrorism ended in Punjab the police units had a large stock of bullet-proofing sheets which were only occupying space in the stores and adding to the inventory. A decision was taken to use the sheets for building the temporary accomodation for the guards deployed at different locations and the problems of shortage of tents and extra bullet-proofing sheets were both solved. Sometimes it is possible to work collectively to create new process or standard. For example, in night patrolling, the large number of private security guards and *chowkidars* working in different localities can work collectively with police teams to supplement the manpower deployed for night surveillance and prevention duties. Very often once the resource is deployed, it is forgotten and consequently remains under-utilized for a long time. There is also a need to protect the resources from misuse by constant review of their usage and deployment. During terrorism in Punjab, the Light Machine Guns (LMGs) were lying unused in the central armoury and no one thought about them. It took a visit by the director general to the armoury to discover this and deploy them in the fight. Overnight, 300 LMGs were issued to different districts. These were then mounted on the gypsy cars and used extensively in encounters. They were also located at key exit roads and vulnerable points to act as a strong deterrent to attacks by terrorists (Interview of K. P. S. Gill 2007).

Recovering resources

Rapidly recovering resources by minimizing the time of its usage by expediting success: As an example, large number of police officers and vehicles deployed for prevention of snatching incidents can be provided relief by quick detection and apprehension of the gang indulging in the crime. In CompStat model (Box II. 12.1) everything the police department does—administrative, operational or investigative—is evaluated by the results achieved. Static operations that do not provide for successful results are immediately assessed for their value and changed to improve the overall operation of the department. In the year 2005, the Central Reserve Police Force (CRPF), the largest paramilitary force in India with a strength of about 2.5 million employees, introduced the 'SELO'—Service and Loyalty—intranet service connecting 84 offices in 51 locations in the country. With this the old traditions methods of messaging and communication were drastically altered and new workflows introduced to leverage information technology thus improving its operational and administrative effectiveness while simultaneously reducing its operational costs.

Procurement

Logistics, communication and transportation are very important for an organization like the police. The purchase of goods and services today is taking up increasing amounts of the time and energy of the police. The initial basic requirements of stationery, uniforms, weapons, furniture, buildings and modes of transport have been supplemented as police organizations have increased in size and complexity. Kitchen and bathroom fittings and equipment, specialized apparel (riot gear, ballistic vests, bomb suits, diving gear, and so on), photographic equipment, musical instruments and livestock (dogs and horses), together with associated food and equipment, must all be procured. Insurance, postal services, telephones, gas, electricity and rent have long been factored into the budget. Police organizations often require not only motor vehicles (cars, vans and motorcycles), but also aircrafts and marine launches. New forms of communication (radio communications and other information technology, both hardware and software), new intelligence gathering tools such as CCTV and new ways of investigating crime involving novel forms of scientific apparatus and computer programmes, have been adopted by the police. This increasing reliance on purchasing has also been driven by new techniques of policing in response to fresh challenges such as terrorism. Management principles and tools can be applied to different aspects in this area right from procurement to distribution to utilization and disposal (Box II.10.1).

Box II.10.1   E-Procurement

What is known as e-Procurement is becoming an increasingly popular means of acquisition in policing and across government agencies generally. This is 'the use of electronic methods in every stage of the purchasing process from identification of requirement through to payment, and potentially to contract management'. This use of internet-based technology to identify vendors and negotiate supply of goods comes in a variety of guises. Electronic procurement systems are designed to introduce more efficiency into the procurement process, but they may also have other purposes. Sometimes, governments are interested in 'leveling the playing field' for smaller companies competing against national or international firms and e-Procurement assists in this process by reducing costs for tenderers. Some police forces have begun to use electronic reverse auctions or e-Auctions, whereby vendors bid online (sometimes publicly) to supply goods such as stationery. In the UK, some forces are adopting e-Procurement under the auspices of the Police Electronic Procurement System (PEPS) initiative that aims to make available shared core e-procurement systems and collaborative solutions to all forces across England and Wales. There is also a government agency, or non-departmental public body (NDPB), called the Police Information Technology Organisation (PITO) which coordinates collective procurement arrangements for the UK police agencies, including establishing and administering contracts and agreements, coordinating tendering processes for high value purchases and giving advice and training on purchasing and legal issues.

Source: Ayling and Grabosy, 2006.

Resources' summary

- Systemic approach to develop, acquire, evaluate and implement innovative ideas in the department.
- Resource leverage:
  - Concentrate them at places where they are needed the most.
  - Mine them from within and borrow from outside.
  - Blend them to multiply the value of each.
  - Recycle, co-opt and protect them.
  - Minimize the usage time.
- e-Procurement for efficient and transparent procurements.

Effectiveness 11

As discussed in Part I, Chapter 2 in the section 'Characteristics of police service', the output that the department delivers to the public is not tangible; it is inseparable from the service provider, perishable and heterogeneous. The public measure their satisfaction based upon what they experience from personal contact, what they see and hear or from family and friends. The day-to-day contact between the policemen and the public is the focal point of public relations, as it is in these one-to-one contacts that the public support develops. Nothing affects people's perception of policing more than the quality of service they receive from individual officers, what happens to them on the streets, at police station enquiry desks and, crucially, the tone of the voice when the telephone is answered. Every look, every word, the very motion made by every man in the police department, every moment of the day, communicates the impression to the public and as such is public relations activity good or bad (Parker, 1957: 137). All this is earned the hard way, hour by hour of tedious work, backed by sincere devotion to duty. Therefore, for the police department, it is necessary that there is guarantee that each and every interaction—direct or indirect—is handled with consistent and constant quality. Three tendencies as regards public expectations could be extracted from various opinion polls conducted by the Belgian police (Bruggeman et al., 2007):

1. During contacts, on population's initiative: When people call the police, they expect quality service dealing with the reported

problem with professionalism, paying particular attention to that problem and providing information (concerning the manner in which the problem will be dealt with). Availability, accessibility and speediness are also important aspects.

2. In all cases, and therefore, of course when the police takes the initiative: People expect the police to be visibly present and accessible within the neighbourhood, to make contact and to remain in contact, and to adopt an active attitude towards (mainly local) problems.

3. As regards the policy: In terms of policy, the expectations are generally translated into enhanced attention for the efficient solving of all problems, priority being given to local (neighbourhood) problems encountered in the immediate daily environment.

However, for the Indian police, in the course of the visits to the states, the National Police Commission (1977) observed that there is a general reluctance of police to come to the aid of the people and there is indifference of the Station House Staff to complaints lodged. The commission found that people, who come with a complaint or any grievances, are either not heard promptly or are sometimes abused for coming and troubling the police. At other times, the nature of the complaint is belittled to avoid work (National Police Commission, 1977: para 50.4).

To bring about necessary transformation in the police, for providing the quality service, the consequence strategy would be the primary lever. The first step towards achieving quality would be the development of standards for the customer service in the police department, as discussed earlier. While creation of standards is one part, the more painstaking part is the implementation and maintaining of those standards. Therefore, to supplement the creation of customer service standards, the department should also provide for guarantees, complaint systems and means of redress. To ensure the proper monitoring accountability there would also be a need to create institutional arrangements to hold the police department accountable for meeting the quality. These institutions could be in the form of customer boards, councils or service agreements some of these are discussed here. The quality of service commitment is to ensure that victim, witnesses, suspects, and the general public—all clients should receive a high quality of service when dealing with the police (Box II.11.1).

Various components of an effective service quality assurance system for the police department would be service standards, quality guarantees, redress and complaint system (Osborne and Plastrik, 2000).

Box II.11.1   Quality of Service Initiative in the Police

The police service in England and Wales introduced its quality of service initiative in 1990. Forces ask local people for their views on police priorities for that area. A total of 39 police forces have already made public what they are doing to meet these community needs. Since 1995, members of the public have been able to nominate organizations for charter marks, making the links between service to the public and public recognition of good service even clearer. A total of 11 police forces have already been awarded charter marks for excellent service to the public.

In India, recently the Ludhiana district police and in 2004, the Delhi Police Licensing Branch, were awarded the ISO 9001: 2000 certificate for the Community Policing Resource Centre (CPRC), popularly known as the single window system (Punjab Newsline Network, 2006) and for establishing and maintaining a quality management system respectively. The Central Industrial Security Force (CISF) has received ISO certificates for 12 of its units and the prestigious Occupational Health and Safety Management Systems (OHSMS 18001: 1999) for its units at Nuclear Fuel Complex, Hyderabad. Developed by European countries, the OHSAS is an internationally accepted specification.

Source: The Economic Times, 2007f.

Service standards

The police department must set service standards for their organization that clearly define the quality and level of service they are committed to delivering to their customers. Customer quality assurance depends entirely on the service standards the organization sets. The standards that the police needs to set are both in the area of internal processes as well as the public interaction areas. Service standards relating to bigger issues like 'what percentage of the community rates police services as "good" or "excellent"'(see Chart II.7.2) and on routine matters like what would be the time for reaching the spot on call, time limit for clearing the applications relating to verifications, also need to be set.

For those who make contact, as per a study conducted by the UK police, 53 per cent of the overall satisfaction can be explained by just four factors (www.homeoffice.uk.gov):

1. Being taken seriously.
2. Being able to talk to someone who could deal with you quickly.
3. The police doing what they say they would do.
4. People that you dealt with being professional and efficient.

Ease of access to services, treatment by staff and the importance of the police keeping to the promises that have been given are consistent factors in determining overall satisfaction, but the research shows significant variation in the relative importance of service quality dimensions depending on the type of contact. This variation underlines the importance of being able to segment users by the method of making contact with the police and target service improvements accordingly. For different categories of public dealings, the outcome and response from the citizens can be a good starting point. Majority of interactions between the police and public are in the following areas:

1. Registering complaints.
2. FIRs lodged for various violations including economic offences.
3. Security requirements.
4. Requests for security for political, religious, sports or other functions.
5. Traffic regulation violations and services.
6. Provisions of certain services such as verification of passport, issue of armed licenses, permission for loud speakers, service verification, and so on.
7. Emergency service.
8. Checking points.

Each and every kind of contact is equally important as every contact is an opportunity for shaping favourable public opinion. It would be necessary to set up some guidelines/standards for handling the police–citizen interface such as on call, in the police station, on the street during patrolling or on traffic points and so on, by placing special emphasis on the drawing up Standard Operating Procedures (SPOs), training programmes and manuals.[1] The federal-funded COPS programme in the US produced more than 50 problem-oriented guides for the police covering a broad spectrum of crime problems from drug dealing to acquaintance rape to loud car stereos. The SPF frontline officers are guided by various guidelines and procedures during their work and these guidelines are available to all the officers through the SPF Intranet. In order to ensure that customers receive quality service, the Singapore Police Service Pledge was updated in 2004 (see Table II.11.1).

The majority of public contact in the cities today is made through indirect means such as a phone call or correspondence. The citizen's opinion is greatly influenced by these indirect contacts. Surveys done

[1] The police organization should through research and study, continually update the training and the operating procedures of the organization for effective role performance (National Police Commission, 1977–81: para 14.52).

Table II.11.1   Singapore Police Service Pledge

Service pledge, SPF	Target
Answer all '999' calls within 10 seconds	At least 90% of time
Arrive at non-urgent incidents within 30 minutes	At least 90% of time
Arrive at urgent incidents within 15 minutes	At least 87% of time
Attend to customers at police counters within 15 minutes	At least 75% of time
Respond to letters from the public within 5 working days	At least 90% of time
Update victims of crime within 7 days	At least 90% of time

Source: Singapore Police Force, 2007, Executive Summary.

world over reveal that the most common problem faced by the public sector customers is getting information or services over the telephone. In police departments too though the number 100 is well publicized, in many cities, the response is far from satisfactory and fails to instil confidence in the department. Therefore, each call, regardless of where received, must be handled according to certain guidelines/standards that guarantees that each and every call is handled with consistent and constant quality—with proper choice of words, of tone, attentiveness and follow-up to the matter at hand. Considering high-quality call handling central to good customer service and successful crime investigation, the UK police has set out to improve call handling, involving a review of current practices, development of national standards and a manual of best practice.

In the interaction with the public, the benchmarking standards set will have to be 100 per cent, that is, a zero-defect system. Anybody coming in contact with the policeman should have a positive experience, be it at the police station or outside. A 90 per cent success rate may also sound good here, but the amount of damage that the 10 per cent can do is all but known. It is the few bad incidents that catch the public attention and wipe out the good work done in 90 per cent of the cases. Various researches has indicated that satisfied people tell their stories of police contact to at least three other people, whereas dissatisfied individuals will tell, on average, 10 others about a negative experience with the police. However, as some mistakes are inevitable it is also important to have a good service recovery procedures, to undo any wrong done as quickly as possible.

Realizing the importance of standards the Dutch police has introduced the frames of reference for a number of primary work processes, such as the *Frame of Reference for Crisis and Conflict Management of 2002* and the standardization of educational programmes. The investments made by the service are critically monitored via the Dutch Quality Model (INK model) which was introduced in 1993. This quality management system uses self-evaluations, audits and peer control. It uncovers bottlenecks in the organization and in working methods and offers a basis for permanent improvement of organization. The Dutch police is clearly the pioneer among government bodies in the Netherlands in this regard. In the report *One Cycle Down—An Evaluation of Four Years of Quality Control* (2001) as written by the police inspectorate (which is part of the Ministry of the Interior and Kingdom Relations) the conclusion is drawn that the regional services, the KLPD and the Police Academy of the Netherlands have been energetic, ambitious and meticulous in introducing the Dutch Quality Model. The result is a police service that is more decisive, more efficient and more professional and that provides a higher quality standard than before the reorganization (Blok, 2004).

Finally, the standard must be meaningful to customers, must be something that the customer cares about and feels is most important to him/her. These standards must be measurable, should be constantly monitored to ensure their integrity and must be reviewed and updated to ensure that they are inline with the changing needs of customers. Care should also be taken to ensure that the standards set do not create very high expectations in customers, which the police cannot fulfil or live up to because after some hype this leads to loss of faith in the claims.

Quality guarantees, redress and complaint systems

Guarantees and redress are the two most important and powerful tools that make service standards meaningful to customers. The courts in India have recently begun compensating the victims of illegal detentions. The Mughal administration had a system of compensation for policing failure as accounted by an Italian traveller, Niccoloa Manucci. The *faujdars* had to supervise roads, and should any merchant or traveller be robbed in daylight, they were obliged to pay compensation.

The police department must set quality guarantees if they fails to meet the service standards. Guarantees should be specific, to the point and reasonable. For example, if the verification certificate is not delivered within a stipulated period, the police may decide to deliver the same to the given home address of the applicant. This will force the supervisory officers and police station staff to do whatever it takes to deliver what has been promised.

The police department must also formulate redress policies, which provide customers compensation (which may be financial or otherwise) when the police fails to meet its service standards. Redress policies are quite the same as guarantees, except that they offer an array of compensation options to customers. While guarantees offer money back or free redelivery of the service, redress policies can offer anything financial (refund, discount, voucher or other payment) or non-financial (an apology, an explanation, assurance that the same thing will not be repeated, and so on) as compensation. As the police department at present does not have any fund for compensations to be awarded, there will be a need to create a new fund for this purpose. Nevertheless, non-financial redress are as important and can be practiced right away. A letter of apology from the police department for delay in handling the application could be a good redress measure.

In the year 2006, a total of 62,822 complaints were reported in the country against police personnel, inquiries were instituted in as many as 16,228 cases (Government of India, 2006). Police departments already have variety of complaint systems in place which, however, have come under severe criticism time and again and have failed to build confidence of common man. Some points of criticism cannot be satisfactorily eliminated by the mere issue of instructions because they are linked with essential attitudes and approaches and the 'administrative culture' developed in the day to day working of the police (National Police Commission, 1977–81: para 10.12).

It is, therefore, necessary to have some institutionalized arrangements to counter these deficiencies and difficulties. Even the recently passed Supreme Court Order has included setting up of police complaints authorities with civilian members as one of the key directions. The desired complaint system should be such that it enables not only tracking and analyzing complaints, but also prompt responses and timely feedback to the department for improving its services. It should also hold the police accountable for the lack of service and exert constant pressure to improve service delivery. In the under-implementation of the Government of India, the Crime and Criminal Tracking Network and Systems police computerization project, the citizen interface module envisages online complaints filing and monitoring. Computerized system of complaints handling that is able to capture the number and the nature of the complaints and that can generate statistics and the trend to enable the police department to understand the customer requirements better can be very useful for the police.

This can possibly be achieved by re-engineering the complaint system of the police department. The complaints policy designed must include where, how and when people can complain, which complaints need to be handled by the frontline policemen and which would be handled by the higher levels of management. It should have a list of the various redress options and the number of days it will take to acknowledge, investigate and respond to a complaint. The procedure should be communicated to the customers and deadlines adhered to.

Cross-agency processes

Public policing today has become a part of a much larger security architecture, wherein policing is supplemented by other agencies such as regulators (commissions), business institutions (private security) and other agencies such as housing authorities, municipalities, schools and other social welfare agencies. Therefore, the traditional primarily internal approach of police ethnocentrism, both in activities and management, has to give way to a non-traditional, primarily external response. This would mean redefining the department's mission, plans, programmes and resources. The effectiveness of the department would depend upon the ability of the top officers to build networks that link service provision and delivery functions (see Chart II.11.1). Their role will then become more of arranger of inter-organizational networks from that of commander of a closed hierarchy that the police remain today.

Along with streamlining the operations within the department, the police has an even tougher challenge of streamlining the process with other agencies. This a new approach to work closely with partners to design and manage processes that extend beyond traditional departmental boundaries, will make the police leap from efficiency to super efficiency (Hammer, 2001). In the entire process of criminal justice system, various agencies involved are the police, judiciary, the prosecution department, the magistracy and the jail administration. Streamlining cross-agency processes is the next great frontier for reducing costs, enhancing quality and speeding operations. These agencies together have to start to see the entire process and manage it as it truly is: the chain of activities that are performed by different agencies. The coordination among these agencies is presently being done, at most of the districts, by the meetings between the chief of police, district magistrate and the district judge. However, what is required is collaboration, through a more rigorous and structured approach to streamlining cross-agency processes that would provide an effective criminal justice system to the citizen. This effectiveness will have direct fallout on the policing.

The Common Integrated Police Applications (CIPA), a Government on India Mission Mode Project that seeks to connect all the police

Chart II.11.1 Cross-agency Linkages of the Police Department

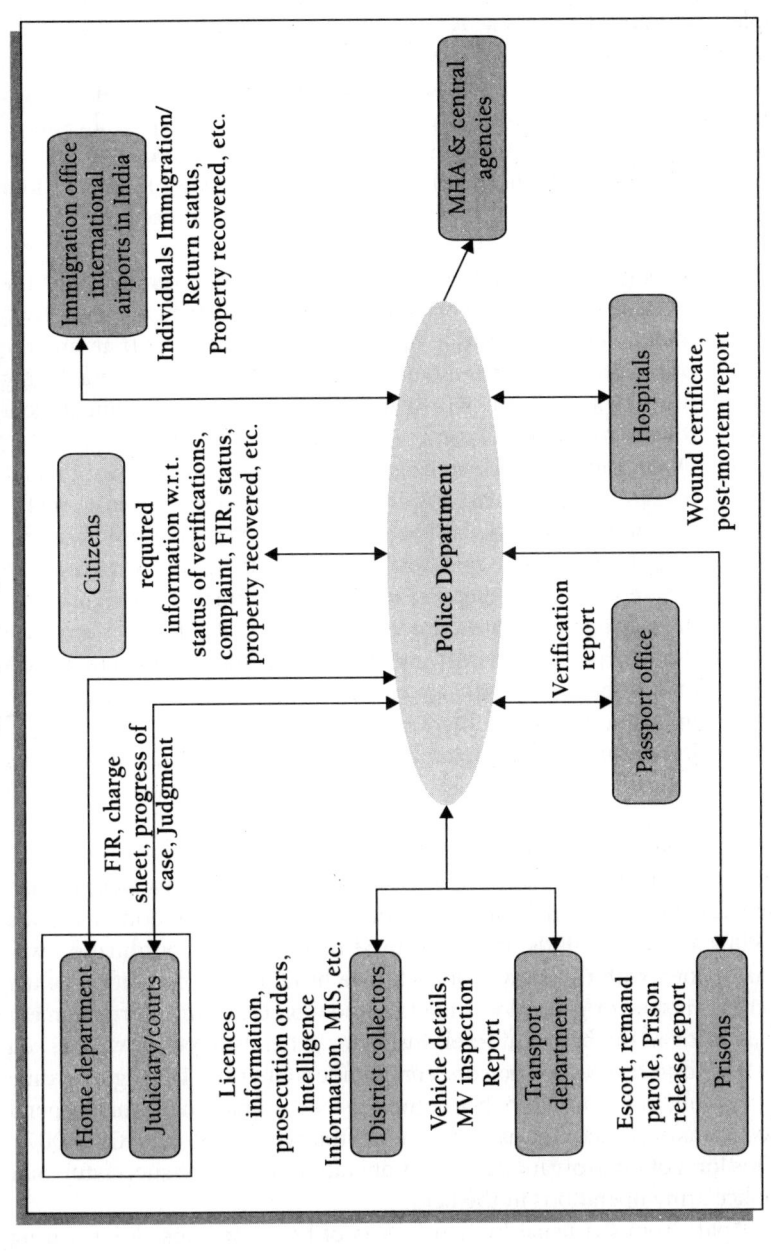

Source: e-Governance vision document, Punjab police, 2006.

stations and higher police offices in the country, would look at police processes not only to computerize them, but also to re-engineer them for effectiveness and efficiency. Among the scope of work undertaken in the project is to expand the linkages of police department to other sectors like courts, jails, etc. for efficiency and quick response. Similarly, the police has to interface with other departments like transport, hospitals, passport department, immigration department, and so on.

Michael Hammer, the re-engineering guru, suggests following four steps for (Hammer, 2001) streamlining cross-agency processes:

1. *Scoping*: The first step is to identify the processes that offer the greatest opportunity for improving the efficiency of the department. It could be putting *challans* in court, the court trials and the process of granting and denying bails, traffic *challans*, monitoring the activities of convicts or information related to criminals sent to jails and those released.

2. *Organizing*: Establish an executive steering committee with members from the partners agencies. It should define the roles, benefits and performance goals. The design team should also have members from different agencies; it should also have an expert in the existing process, a member who can recommend redesign.

3. *Redesigning*: Integrated process in a way that fulfils performance goals by putting the customer first. There should be no repetition of any activity and the activity should be done by someone best in position to do so, sharing a common database.

4. *Implementing*: The implementation should be quick and in phases and the communication between the agencies regular.

In the entire process of cross-agency streamlining, the most essential requirement is the collaborative mindset of the agencies involved. Punjab saw very heavy deployment of army for anti-terrorist operations in the late 1980s and early 1990s. It was ensured that excellent coordination was maintained with the army. For each core headquarter, one officer of the rank of inspector general was made a nodal officer. Similar arrangement was made at the battalion level. Inspector generals of police were asked to give due respect to the core commanders of army. During that time in Punjab, in the armed police complex, for the first time, Army General Joshi was accorded full parade honour (Interview of K. P. S. Gill 2007). This kind of inter-organizational co-operation was key to successful joint police army operations in the field.

Apart from the usual human factors of being nervous about tearing down the walls, resistance to concede a part of their fiefdom and resistance to change, there are several systemic impediments for this kind of collaboration to take place between different agencies involved in the criminal justice system. Some are involved out of their legal and constitutional position, others due to very nature of the duties performed by the agencies, where the procedures are essential and the costing is immaterial at many stages of the processes involved. The culture of mistrust and secrecy is inbuilt into the working of these agencies as information leakage has a potential of misuse to the advantage of the criminals. Despite these factors, even in the remaining stages, the scope to increase the efficiency and effectiveness is significant and should be considered as the next frontier of efficiency.

Accountability for results

Identification of public needs would have little meaning without customer empowerment, as discussed in Part II Chapter 6, which transfers the control to people. However, these strategies would only be fully effective with the support of consequence strategy of holding the police department accountable for meeting the responsibilities arising out of customer needs to be fulfilled through proactive policing strategies. As the new Police Acts in the states prepare to accord more autonomy to the police, proposed autonomy has to be accompanied by complementary accountability through performance measurement of the police department. There are different approaches to this issue adopted currently by different countries; on the one hand there is the CompStat (Box II.12.1) kind of measurement published weekly on website by the New York police department providing high degree of transparency and internal discipline. On the other hand is the rating on different performance areas (Table II.11.2) published by the Police Standards Unit of England and Wales based mostly on detailed public surveys.

Another recent example has been an assessment carried out by Altus Global Alliance of several police stations in different countries to judge their performance on community orientation, physical conditions, equal treatment, transparency and accountability, besides detention conditions. Rajasthan secured the first position scoring 85.3 per cent (*The Tribune*, 2006c). In India, Himachal Pradesh has taken a step in this direction by incorporating performance evaluation of police stations in the Police Act. A system currently is being developed whereby a number of parameters have been prescribed in the categories of policing efforts (30 per cent), policing results (40 per cent) and public satisfaction (30 per cent).

Table II.11.2   Performance Measurement in England

Performance Area	Delivery	Direction		
Reducing Crime	Fair	Stable*	POLICE AUTHORITY CHAIR Len Duvall	
Investigating Crime	Poor	Stable*	COMMISSIONER Sir Ian Blair	
Promoting Safety	Poor	Stable†	STAFF NUMBERS	
Providing Assistance	Good	Improved	Police Officers	31,073
Citizen Focus	Poor	Stable	Police Staff	13,561
Resource Use	Good	Improved	PCSOs	2,147
Local Policing	Good	Improved	Other Staff	629
			Special Constables	697
			Budget 2004/05	
			£2,343.3 million	

Source: www.altus.org.

Notes: * *Grades capped pending full compliance with national standard for crime recording.*
  † *Grade capped due to relatively low performance in a priority component.*

The police stations have been divided into three categories for this purpose depending upon the workload. Performance will be gauged in comparison to the Ideal Performance Index in a category.

The architecture of performance measurement has five linked components—policy outcomes, programme outcomes, outputs, processes and inputs. These five components are connected to each other like a production line: input creates process, which creates output, which determines strategy and programme outcomes, which impacts policy outcomes (Osborne and Plastrik, 2000: 249–51).

$$\text{Inputs} \rightarrow \text{Processes} \rightarrow \text{Output} \rightarrow$$
$$\text{Program Outcomes} \rightarrow \text{Policy Outcomes}$$

These components can be measured in the broadest possible terms by the quantity, efficiency, effectiveness, quality and cost effectiveness. As an example for the police department, the measure of policy outcome goals would be lower crime rates which can be measured in terms of effectiveness by the crime rate and cost effectiveness by dividing the crime rate by the cost. The measure of programme outcome goals would be the reduction in violent crime rate, the effectiveness can be measured by the violent crime rate and the cost effectiveness by dividing the violent crime rate by the cost. The outputs would be the arrests made measured in number for quantity, cost per arrest for efficiency, percentage of conviction for effectiveness and percentage of arrests thrown out by the courts as quality. The processes like investigations, arrests and registrations of FIRs can be measured in quantity by number of investigations, arrests and registrations. Effectiveness by percentage of convictions, arrests made in cases and cases sent to court. Quality can be measured by the error rate in registrations, that is, the cancellation of cases and acquittals.

The police department needs to develop efficiency (output) measures with linked effectiveness (outcome) measures to serve as the basic components of the new consequence model. In the year 2002, the Washington State Patrol (WSP) adopted an accountability-driven leadership model. As a part of the model the identification of core mission, elements in each bureau was critical to establishing the measures of efficiency that would be set and then linked to the measures of effectiveness desired. It also led to changes in administrative staffing.

The Field Operations Bureau in the US articulated four core traffic law enforcement efficiencies to guide the actions of road troopers: Driving Under Influence (DUI) of alcohol enforcement; aggressive driving enforcement; seat belt enforcement and dangerous speeding enforcement. The combination of these four efficiency measures are believed to be those most likely, taken together, to have the potential of altering driver behaviour and thereby preventing collisions. These four actions do not represent the only valued activities of the field force, but serve as a baseline and a link, to measure and report against the goal of reducing collisions, injuries and fatalities. The effectiveness is measured by district rates of property damage, fatality, injury, speed-related and DUI-related collisions. Just as with any law enforcement effort intended to alter behaviour, there must be a link to effectiveness (reduced collisions, injuries, fatalities, and so on) through the monitoring of efficiency (increased enforcement). With this kind of cause-effect link identified and measured the working of the policemen can get unambiguously directed towards the intended outcome for the department.

To make the police department accountable the Australian Government's Management Improvement Initiative (MII)[2] required the police to identify the 'classes' of its activities (which it has now called Key Result Areas) and the objectives and performance measures for these activities. The results of this process have been incorporated in the Victoria Police Force Business Plans from 1994–95 onwards.

In Poland, a revolutionary concept was introduced in the budget area in the year 1999. Till then, the budget came for the police forces throughout the country. Now, the district commanders get money from the heads of the districts in the form of 'goal donations'. The money is under the public's control and district commands are accountable for budget allocations to the heads of respective areas. The self-governing councils were vested with a significant input into police planning and operations. For example, the ability to influence and determine the number of lines available to a given police station, demand from the local chief of police to improve the level of service delivery, or to resolve a local conflict (Haberfeld et al., 2002).

Another example of building accountability into the system is the concept of partial performance-based financing, where police services are allocated part of their budget (say, 5 per cent) based on their achievements.

---

[2] *Management Improvement Initiative*: The Coalition Government in late 1992, was elected largely on the basis of promoting economic and government reforms. In keeping with their poll promises, the key instrument introduced was the Government's Management Improvement Initiative (MII). This was designed to ensure that the government departments and agencies have clearly defined objectives and performance measures that are incorporated in corporate and business plans. The state government then reviews these plans. The underlying principles of the MII are: a focus on clear responsibility and accountability for results; empowerment of consumers; minimalization of government bureaucracy; a preference for market mechanisms; professional and business like management of public agencies (Palmer, 1997).

Such accountability measures, presently absent in the governmental procedures, would have to be built into the governance arrangement, such
as the result-based management (Box II.11.2), for the police in India.

Box II.11.2 Result-based Management for the Netherlands Police

In the policy plan for the Dutch police, the policy targets are set out in the
form of results-based agreements in the Dutch Police National Framework
2003–06 and in regional covenants with the individual forces. The sum
total of the agreements in the individual covenants constitutes the national
agreement. The results are monitored and recorded at the central level for each
force. Where necessary, efforts are intensified to achieve the agreed results. A
system of performance-related pay for the forces is linked to the agreements.
One of the arrangements in the Dutch police national framework 2003–06
is that in 2006, the police forces should together refer 40,000 more cases in
total to the public prosecution service than in 2002. In addition, by 2006
there must be an increase of 180, 000 in the fines and fixed penalties imposed
by the police. The covenant also contains target results for the supervision
of aliens, improvement of police accessibility and availability, and the level
of public satisfaction about dealings with the police. Agreements have also
been made to reduce nationwide levels of sick leave among police personnel
to a maximum of 8 per cent, to improve police efficiency and to increase the
strength of the police force. The covenant also contains an undertaking by
government ministers to use their best endeavours to make whatever changes
are necessary to legislation.

Source: Police Department of the Netherlands, 2006.

At present the annual administration reports of the state police in India
are compiled on the basis of statistics and information collected from
the various levels in the organization to present the standard of policing
within the state based on the statistics, emanating from the police stations.
The annual administration reports generally projecting only a quantitative
assessment is submitted with a considerable time lag to the state government who after review present it to the assembly for discussion.

As a part of the policy, the government can arm the proposed state
security commissions with the power to hold the organization accountable for performance. The job of these commissions should include improving service quality and outcomes for customers, approving budgets,
commissioning customer surveys and focus groups, publishing performance scorecards and helping the police in writing service standards,
performance targets, guarantees and redress policies and customer
complaint systems. These may also have an independent cell to evaluate
police performance, both in quantitative and qualitative terms through
different means as discussed in citizen voice (5.2). This report can then be

also used to assess the achievements of the police with regard to the police plan on key indicators agreed and approved by the commission. This can be a powerful way of making police departments more accountable to their customers. As discussed later in the book (Chapter 13), to avoid conflicts and frustration, it is important to make very clear the role of these commissions and the power they will enjoy over the police departments.

'Effectiveness' for the Indian police

- Set customer service standards both the internal processes and for public interaction areas.
- Ensure quality guarantees.
- Re-engineer complaint systems.
- Formulate redress policies.
- Streamline cross agency processes.
- Accountability for performance of police department through:

  - Customer boards.
  - Councils.
  - Service agreement.

Response 12

Speed and responsiveness are very important to police service, as the nature of the job involves handling emergency situations on many occasions. The results from a comprehensive study conducted in the UK in 1995, with samples of citizens and the police, indicated that the most important police activity should be 'to respond immediately to emergencies', followed by 'detect and arrest offenders' and 'investigate crime' (Beck et al., 1999).

Only a well-energized, motivated and committed force, supported by up-to-date organizational structures and given the clear targets and standards to be met can offer the responsiveness that the police job demands. Radical changes in the organizational structure and procedures are called for to bring about requisite responsiveness and desired pace in the department. Some of the measures relating to processes like the service pledge, standards and those relating to organizational restructuring like the delayering, participative management and decentralization have already been discussed earlier. The role of leadership in this process of creating a sense of urgency or energy in the department is also very important.[1] Peter Vaill, the pioneer researcher in the field of 'high performing systems', says that the stellar outfits—whether Brownie troops or factories—all have a certain feel or 'asthetic motivation' or 'electricity in the air'. In Los Angeles Police Department, CompStat tactics also provide for a sense

---

[1] The role of leadership in motivating the police force and the motivators that may work today to energize the force are discussed earlier. See Chapter 2, 'motivating policemen'.

of urgency in responding to problems, every case or call for service is to be handled as if it were a big case and is thoroughly, rapidly, and systematically investigated (Schick, 2004). Besides internal scrutiny of the processes of the police, the role of suggestions from the citizen cannot be overemphasized in improving the pace and responsiveness of the department like police. If the police gets the feedback regularly and respond quickly there will be a large number of small, practical, inexpensive and implementable ideas coming to them—a win-win situation both for the police and the citizens.[2]

In addition to the measures that have been mentioned, the following table shows the mix of strategies and the corresponding metatools that would be useful for providing the desired 'pace' to police service in India.

Culture strategy	Co-operation and horizontal linkages
Core and culture strategy	Use of appropriate technology

Horizontal linkages and co-operation among wings

For the department to be quick to respond, while the virtues of delegating authority to frontline staff and empowering them to act without always waiting for the orders from above have been discussed, there is another 'half' of the delegation, growing in importance. That is the delegation to the frontline to act 'horizontally', to seek out fast connections with other functions, without checking 'up' (Peters, 1987: 457). The vertical movement of files and actionable information has to be cut down and the culture of communication across the functional groups promoted among the policemen and employees in the department.

Some ways of connecting policemen and employees horizontally could be to send the office superintendents and dealing hands in the offices to attend some of the crime meetings in the districts; attachments of wireless staff at the headquarters with police stations for few weeks and rewarding the good work done by the office staff in a monthly meeting of field officers.

There is also an important question of co-operation among the different wings of investigation, where sometimes the jealousy and bickering over publicity is very intense in the police department. The blame for this lies

---

[2] Some of the means to get to the customers were mentioned earlier under 'citizen voice', Chart II.7.1.

with the top management in the police which, out of political expediency or out of personal conditioning of mind, places a lot of importance on credit and notoriety. This kind of situation is witnessed especially when there are multiple wings working on an important or sensational case and the bitter rivalry within the department keeps the members from sharing any useful information—any bit of information is a closely held secret.[3] To check this practice the message that co-operative behaviour will be rewarded and the appreciation would depend upon taking responsibility for collective advancement as on making one's own numbers should go across the department. Systemic arrangements like those in the CompStat model (Box II.12.1) in the US can check this malady to an extent.

Box II.12.1   CompStat Model

CompStat, short for 'computer statistics' or 'comparison statistics', is a multi-faceted system for managing police operations with a proven track record in several major metropolitan police departments tracing its roots back to 1994 in the New York City Police Department (NYPD). Although there are many versions of CompStat, each is a system that identifies established and emerging crime trends for the efficient use of resource to target those trends. Crime statistics alone are not enough. CompStat requires law enforcement to think outside the box for solutions to issues, to question the status quo ensuring that policy, procedures, and tactics remain current. The four CompStat core principles are as follows:

Principle 1:   *timely, accurate intelligence*: Timely and accurate information and intelligence are absolutely essential in effectively responding to any problem or crisis. This need must be clearly stated when implementing a CompStat process and most likely it will require a major change in the way a department manages its information technology. Accurate crime data is needed daily, not months after the events.

Principle 2:   *effective tactics*: Traditional policing tactics are directed at apprehending the suspect. While criminal apprehension is an important part of CompStat, it does not stop there. It requires the police to give attention to the social and environmental situation that may be adding to or creating the problem.

(Box II.12.1 continued)

---

[3] Meerut police busted a gang of 35 people suspected to have killed about 250 people, including 50 policemen. The police believe that the gang exploited lack of inter district coordination between UP cops. They managed to repeatedly give slips to police despite striking as many as six times in a single day. See 'Gang behind 250 murders busted' (*The Times of India*, 2007f).

(Box II.12.1 continued)

Principle 3:	*rapid deployment:* For decades, police departments have been driven by calls for service and responded with limited resources in a reactive manner. With CompStat, the police department is now armed with vital information regarding emerging crime trends or patterns that allow for a proactive strategic police response. Once a tactical plan is developed it is necessary to organize and put into operation an assortment of personnel and resources.
Principle 4:	*relentless follow-up and assessment:* An essential element in any crucial operation is the need to critically assess past tactics and review what worked and what did not. One of the main differences between private enterprise and the public sector is the bottom line of positive returns. If a business implements an unsuccessful strategy or provides an unacceptable level of customer service, it is not long before it becomes a failed business. Much like a business, the bottom line with CompStat is results.

Source: Schick, 2004.

An important element of CompStat is the requirement that all units of the police department must work together. Traditionally, specialized units operated independently from other units and conducted police operations to achieve their own objectives. Under the old model, citywide specialized units have even worked in a station's area without the knowledge or support of the area commander or officers. In the CompStat model all units must be represented and held jointly responsible for the successes and failures. The benefit is that more creative and effective crime control measures are designed when all units develop and implement the strategy. The police can respond to problems using many forms, including traditional uniformed or plainclothes officer response as well as non-traditional stings and decoys. By breaking down the barriers among the operating units, a new spirit of cooperation and working together materializes and enables the rapid deployment of resources (Schick, 2004). The Washington State Patrol (WSP), US, has expanded the CompStat meeting format from its traditional focus on law enforcement to include other public safety-related fields and traditional management activities of any large organization (Box II.12.2). The WSP leadership team is better informed now about the entire mission of the patrol and how every unit must work in a collaborative fashion. The opportunity to turn sworn and professional staff into one unified force is critical. There can be a friction between sworn and professional staff, each side believing the other does not recognize or value their contribution. The weekly Strategic Advancement Forum (SAF) meeting gives each branch of the agency the opportunity to see that other branches' contributions are important and all personnel see the entire agency moving forward as a result. The WSP model also shows the leadership team that sworn and professional staffs are being held to the same standards of excellence and accountability, thereby demonstrating that every unit is critical to the success of the WSP. In the WSP's accountability-driven leadership model, it is common for bureau directors to commit immediately the resources under their control to solve a common problem. Gone are the days of endless correspondence, back and forth, between one organizational group and another, attempting to solve problems (Serpas, 2004).

Box II.12.2   The Washington State Patrol (WSP) Model

The WSP leadership model is designed to hold the agency's non-traditional policing functions, such as the state fire marshal's office, the state toxicologist's office and the missing child clearinghouse, to the same high standards. This more comprehensive approach to public safety and general management is meant to address problems that lay outside a narrow understanding of law enforcement, such as the failure of some facilities housing children and senior citizens to comply with fire safety codes; budgetary practices that historically result in overspending, inefficiencies, and under-achievement in such functions as accounting, fleet and property management, human resources, and information technology; and forensic laboratories' struggles to provide timely services to law enforcement and coroners state-wide while ensuring quality and correctness.

Source: Serpas, 2004.

In today's world of increasing globalization where the entire world is becoming one community, a traditionally localized activity like the policing also has to look beyond the physical jurisdiction, not just within the nation but outside the nation as well, similar co-operation has to extend among different forces within and outside the nation . Thus, the horizontal linkages with other police forces become equally important.

The attacks of 11 September 2001 had a variety of effects in Germany, in particular with regard to organizational aspects, police strategy and tactics as well as legislation. The basic aim of the measures taken was to counter the formation of networks identified on the terrorist side with a network comprised of security authorities in the sense of a nationally and internationally networked information exchange and action. In accordance with the federal structure of the Federal Republic of Germany, as a general rule, police matters fall under the jurisdiction of the 16 German states, each of which maintains its own police authorities. In addition to the state police authorities there are central police authorities such as the Bundeskriminalamt, which fall within the jurisdiction of the federation. The intelligence services are similarly structured. Structural deficits in the co-operation between the security authorities partly frustrated the necessary intensification of information collection, compilation and exchange as central factors for successful aversion of danger. With this in mind, the Joint Counter-Terrorism Centre was created in Germany[4] (Box II.12.3).

Box II.12.3   Joint Counter-Terrorism Centre of Germany

With the creation of the Joint Counter-Terrorism Centre in Berlin in December 2004, the co-operation between police authorities and various state and federal agencies responsible for security matters has been placed on a new basis. A total of 40 authorities are represented in the Joint Counter-Terrorism Centre—a novelty in Germany. Never before have so many authorities been brought together in a single place for daily co-operation. The most important objective of this co-operation is the timely recognition of possible threat scenarios in the field of terrorism/extremism by incorporating all available sources of information with a view to coordinating preventive and repressive measures. This joint centre ensures a smooth flow of information to all the agencies, expedites information exchange and consolidates available knowledge at the same time. Another significant advantage of the Joint Counter-Terrorism Centre is that it strengthens and concentrates analytic competence. Here, the most recent police and intelligence service information is exchanged, and initial assessments are drawn up as required. Furthermore, previous results of work are presented and, if necessary, further steps of work are agreed upon. In addition, threat and case assessments are carried out, operational information is exchanged and structural analyses are prepared.

Source: Stock, 2007.

Today, the small arms problem of Europe has a direct relation with its easy availability in Africa, the drugs landing in Spain affect the distribution in Amsterdam. The drug production in Afghanistan finds its route through India, the economic and the cybercrimes do not identify any national boundaries. In this scenario, for police international linkages and co-operation, it has become a need that cannot be ignored for long. The US has taken to organizing a large number of training programmes, especially, involving police officers from India, Pakistan, Malaysia and Indonesia, after 9/11 realizing the need to create a pool of police officers sensitized to international perspective, and those who can be a part of

---

[4] Contribution from Dr Jurgen Stock, vice president of the Bundeskriminalamt, Germany.

international coordinated efforts in the times of crisis. Police forces in the UK have encouraged exchange of police officers between India, Bangladesh and Pakistan, with a view to enhance their understanding of large population from these nations settled in the UK and tackle their crime problems by bridging the gap with these communities. The Dutch police has taken up the 'Pearl Fishing' project of creating a network of police officers across the nations of the world through a series of international conferences, to facilitate free exchange of ideas and co-operation. Europe has responded to the phenomena by establishing international priorities through the instrument of European Organised Crime Threat Assessment (OCTA), which though in a nascent stage can be very useful in establishing division of duties. Considering the importance of inter organizational networks after 9/11, the US has taken a lead in organizing a global network for data sharing and communication. The FBI, US, had the profound realization that they cannot prevent terrorist activities by keeping information to themselves (Box II.12.4).

Box II.12.4   'Global' Inter-organizational Communication and Data Sharing

One of the most important findings of the 9/11 commission report was the realization that information sharing between law enforcement agencies was seriously deficient. The report emphasized that the need-to-know culture of information protection needs to be replaced by a 'need-to-share' culture of integration (National Commission on Terrorist Attacks 2002). A very good example of interagency coordination is the Global—the efficient sharing of data among justice entities of the US, Canada and other nations. Global is a consortium of 32 local, state, federal, and international justice organizations that are working on sharing information using a common XML standard. Member organizations participate in it out of shared responsibility and a shared belief that, together, they can bring about positive change in inter-organizational communication and data sharing that will span the spectrum of law enforcement, judicial, correctional and related bodies. It released its first operational version of their XML Data Model (GJXDM) in February 2004.

Source: US Department of Justice, 2004.

Use of appropriate technology

Recently, the California police started using a mobile device capable of using wireless communication to match fingerprints from individuals encountered on patrol to a fingerprint database of 250,000 people arrested over the years. The system increases police effectiveness and saves the time to bring the suspect to the police station for identification. In San Diego, California, the police department implemented an Automated Field Reporting (AFR) and hired civilians to install and activate the system. The AFR allows the officers to complete reports in the field and electronically upload documents into an integrated central system. Resulting in quality, documentation, management and tracking. Officers get more time for community policing.

Technology has become a critical element both for committing and fighting the crime in the twenty-first century. The use of some modern transportation, communication, weapon or chemical related to crime, or advanced gadgets to execute the crime related to technology have become increasingly popular among the criminals. In response, the use of technologies in law enforcement is needed to combat the increasing technological sophistication of criminals. Earlier, with the criminals acquiring sophisticated weapons, once outgunned police agencies are now out-tech'd by a new breed of tech-savvy criminals. The police needs to be taking advantage of advances in technology rather than being on the receiving end of such advancements. In a scenario when the police assumes a more proactive role, policing will become more information led resulting in increasing information management for crime prevention as well as crime detection (Box II.12.5).

Box II.12.5   Information-driven Policing

The important emerging concept of Information-driven Policing (IDP) is being increasingly adopted by the police forces around the world due to the availability of a variety of data processing and transmitting devices, and their networking. It is expected that application of the concept will extend even further in the present information age.

The new information-driven strategy has the following characteristics:

1. IDP crosses the traditional boundaries such as physical distance, darkness and barriers (GPS, integrated information systems, ultraviolet light for night glasses, sensors that detect the presence of gas, explosives, weapons, drugs and nuclear materials through container walls or other packaging).
2. IDP transcends traditional time limits as the information is routinely stored, can be retrieved and is combined, analysed and communicated throughout the criminal justice system.
3. IDP is capital intensive rather than being labour intensive; it is more technology based, increasing the efficiency of the individual officers.

(Box II.12.5 continued)

(Box II.12.5 continued)

4. IDP is increasingly focused on the monitoring of groups of potential suspects rather than on individual suspects (e.g., systematic offenders, organized criminals and terrorists).

5. IDP is primarily aimed at prevention and is a more structural way of pointing out problems to and advising the administrators and other law enforcement organizations.

6. IDP establishes relationships between previously separate sources of information and lines of decision making.

Source: Hoofdcommissen, 2004.

New technologies in the police

Technologies used in law enforcement agencies have become increasingly complex as costs have declined and innovative ways of using the technologies have diffused among people. Computer-assisted forensics, biometrics, digital imaging, expert systems, training simulators and other surveillance approaches are now being used by the police departments routinely in the developed nations. Work is also underway to develop technology for police applications to recover latent fingerprints; Raman spectroscopy—to provide more sensitive drugs and explosives detectors (for example, roadside drug detection); cell type analysis—to determine the origin of cells (for example, hair, skin) and improved profiling—of illicit drugs to help identify their source (UK Home Office 2004–09: 9). Some of the new technological applications in policing are discussed (Nunn, 2001):

Biometrics

Biometrics use unique measurements of different components of the human body as a means of identification (International Association for Biometrics and the International Computer Security Association, 1998). Major biometric systems used in contemporary law enforcement include fingerprints, DNA testing, retinal scans and facial recognition, although several emerging technologies involving highly elaborate metrics are slowly taking hold. In order to adopt biometric approaches to surveillance, a substantial database management infrastructure must be present that contains images of fingerprints, retinal photographs, facial photographs, voice recordings and other templates to serve as measuring rods. In times to come, the combination of advances in video cameras and facial recognition software will elevate police surveillance during VIP security and at key entry points to another level of scanning and selecting individuals out of a crowd of people in real time. A recent development in the security systems is the arrival of the biometric gun. This 'Smart Gun' has a Dynamic Grip Recognition technology. The locking mechanism of the gun works with one owner. The technology consists of a handle outfitted with 32 pressure sensors that record unique holding pattern of the owner that unlocks in seconds on holding.

The use of DNA as a biometric identification device is hailed as one of the most powerful crime-fighting tools since the advent of latent finger-print technologies owing to its ability to convict the guilty and free the innocent. The UK leads the world in the application of DNA technology to the identification of criminals with the largest DNA database that represented 3.7 per cent of the population in 2003, the highest proportion among all the nations. A typical month has seen suspects identified for 15 murders, 31 rapes and 770 car crimes (UK Home Office Science and Technology Strategy, 2004–09: 9). The FBI in the US has developed the National DNA Index System (NDIS) that creates a more seamless means for interstate comparison and exchange of DNA profiles. The International Association of Chiefs of Police proposed a system in 1999 to sample DNA from all criminal suspects upon arrest; if charges were subsequently dropped or if the suspect was acquitted at trial, the sample would be destroyed (Dussault, 1999). A security company based in Wales, UK, has designed a spray with i-powder that marks the skin and clothes of intruders. The i-powder carries a uniquely-traceable DNA code that can be easily detected for several weeks as the spray cannot be easily removed from clothes or skin (http://www.redwebsecurity.com/pdfs/police_information_pack.pdf). The SPF has established its own DNA database of registered criminals. The SPF in collaboration with the National Technological University has also developed a mobile DNA analyser which can be used for on site analysis of samples.

In the field of fingerprinting, the traditional fingerprinting systems are merging with other biometric approaches. The Las Vegas Police Department combines fingerprint digitalization with digitized mug shots in a system called the Metro Automated Identification Network (MAIN). A kiosk-based biometric system that uses handprints to verify, identity and expedite flight processing for international travelers has been put in place by the US immigration and naturalization service in six North American airports, namely, LAX, Newark, Miami, Kennedy, Toronto and Vancouver (Paris, 1998).

Another form of biometric, the facial recognition systems are in use in embassies, ports of entry and in investigative venues in which crowds of people can be scanned for the presence of targeted suspects. The software of neural network systems used in this 'learn' to recognize patterns within very large databases by examining relationships among many variables and then identifying the particular patterns for which the network was programmed such as faces, credit card transactions, stock price adjustments or cardiac rhythms (Baatz, 1995; Stergiou and Siganos, 2000). In the US, private vendors are working with the agencies like the Office of Law Enforcement Technology Commercialization (a unit of the National Institute of Justice), Newham police and the Defense Advanced Research Projects Agency (DARPA) to develop more and more facial pattern systems. The project with DARPA is to perfect another facial recognition system called the Image Understanding for Force Protection, which is designed to pick faces from a crowd at distances up to 500 feet in an urban environment and to identify people who frequent the same site often as they might be planning a terrorist attack (Nunn, 2001).

The city of Tampa, Florida, began using Visionics' FaceIt system in the summer of 2006. The system can match recorded faces to thousands of facial images of criminal suspects and sex offenders stored in a database. FaceIt system is now in use as part of the video surveillance system in the Newham neighbourhood in London. The facial recognition systems are also being integrated with video surveillance systems to isolate strange or abnormal behaviour in a delimited spatial area. For example, an invention was patented in 1998 in which the video camera scrutinizes an area and if the software detects inconsistent patterns (for example, two persons rather than one taking money from an Automated Teller Machine—ATM), it alerts authorities. Another system used in London, called Cromatica, monitors subway stop activity to alert personnel to dangerous crowding, abnormal behavior, or even suicide attempts.

Locational monitoring

More popular approach in using the GPS is to track the location police cars or cars equipped with theft-prevention GPS sensors. However, the Iowa Division of Criminal Investigation thought of a more imaginative application by placing of mobile tracking devices on the cars of suspected burglars and then using satellite-based monitoring subsequently to connect the vehicles to the scenes of several burglaries. Similarly, in Spokane, Washington, the sheriff's office attached GPS sensors to a suspected a child murderer and over the next few days gathered data indicating that he visited two different grave sites. These data became part of the evidence used to charge him with murder. Another use of the GPS can be to monitor the location of individuals on parole or probation to determine whether those individuals are staying within a circumscribed space. A low-cost alternative to the GPS is the automatic Radio Frequency Identification (RFID) system which is finding widespread use in logistics operations. Like the barcodes, the RFID systems are made up of at least one reader/scanner and a tag mounted on the object that is to be identified. Tags are resistant to rain, dirt and light sources, therefore, correct object identification is assured even if it is scratched or painted over. Since no line-of-sight connection to the reader is necessary, tags can be completely integrated in the objects. The technology holds promise in preventing piracy and movement of authenticated material.

In parts of Washington D.C., gunshot detection system called Shot-Spotter allows the police to respond immediately within seconds of the shots fired. The system works on acoustics-based GPS equipment system that automatically picks up the location of the shot fired and notifies the police. A different type of monitoring system sniper positioning system (SniPos), suited for VIP security, identifies the location of gunshots by calculating the direction, elevation and distance to the source of a gunshot within two seconds after the detector receives the sound of the shot, using four microphones mounted in a small triangular pyramid, linked to a personal computer using a Windows interface. In Iraq, the US patrol vehicles are mounted with similar device called BOOMERANG that identifies the distance and direction of the shot fired within seconds.

In video surveillance, IP-Surveillance solutions with networked cameras and servers have emerged as an attractive alternative to the digital video recording. With the IP-Surveillance technology, the video server and network server represent the next level of improvement by connecting existing cameras to the network with a video server and then storing the images on the network server. Cameras can be viewed and controlled from any point on the network. Cisco's 3200 series 'mobile access router' sits in the trunk of a police vehicle. It allows the car to remain connected to IP networks, regardless of what types of wireless systems are delivering the signal. This 'always-on' network allows police officers in the field to access several types of data and information such as IP-based video surveillance, photos from crime databases and fingerprints obtained from other officers' scanners and from databases. With the wireless link, officers at the scene of a bank robbery, for example, can view live video surveillance footage from bank cameras.

Computer monitoring

Several technologies are capable of remote monitoring of information contained within computers. The use of these systems has grown in recent years as a response to the use of information technology in various criminal activities (Denning, 1999). One popular technology relies on the interception of electromagnetic radiation from computer monitors. These monitoring systems, known as the transient electromagnetic pulse emanation standard (TEMPEST) devices, are capable of intercepting data from a target computer at distances up to a kitometre or more, depending on the strength of the emissions and the TEMPEST device. There is another software system that uses a virus 'trojan horse' which is capable of recording keystrokes made by the user to capture personal computer inputs and outputs. Law enforcement personnel can attempt to convince suspected criminals to open e-mail messages that unleash a virus. This software technology, known as the Data Interception by Remote Terminal (DIRT), has been used to gather evidence from alleged child pornographers and hacker groups (Spring, 1999).

Imaging systems
Modern imaging technologies are used to document and examine crime scenes or to deconstruct and reconstruct photos from other still and video cameras. Imaging technologies are essentially machine systems designed to decode information embedded invisibly within an urban space or hidden behind physical barriers that might be actual walls and partitions or simply poorly resolved physical images in existing photographs or video imagery.

The Albuquerque Police Department began using a prototype system called heterodyning that uses fluorescent emissions that come from organic molecules to identify crime scene evidence that would otherwise be invisible to human sight, but does so under ambient light conditions (Robinson, 1997).

Thermography and digital photography are increasingly common in police agencies in the developed nations. Forward looking infrared (FLIR) radar enables users to see under conditions of darkness, based on the thermographic 'signature' of an entity, that is, the temperature of objects under surveillance focusing on the electromagnetic frequencies at which heat radiates from biological organisms or structures. Police agencies in the US use the FLIR to identify structures where unusual amounts of heat are being purged, arguing that they are possibly linked to drug labs or marijuana cultivation. Other criminal justice uses of thermal imaging include perimeter surveillance, vehicle pursuits, structure profiles, disturbed surfaces analysis, location of hidden compartments and hidden grave sites.

Information technology

The main uses the police makes of computers are for administration such as pay roll, employee e-mails, storing of minutes of meetings, maintaining personal records and performance analysis; storage and retrieval of information from databases on missing persons, wanted persons, stolen cars and convicted criminals; and operational control such as allocation of police resources, officers on the beat and cars, balanced scorecards, and so on, planning such as the scenario planning, conduction and analysis of surveys, and so on. The Metropolitan Police in the UK use 100 different databases to find information about an individual. These include databases held by traders in personal data, all government departments, doctors, banks, trade unions, security services and private detectives. The SPF uses computer-based trends, statistical, and cause and effect analysis for their planning. The SPF Knowledge Management Framework was established through the Knowledge Management Steering Committee for efficient sharing of information within and outside the organization.

For the Indian police, today, the constellation of clues and evidence related to criminal activity are often spread across disconnected databases and paper files in thousands of local, state and national agencies. In many cases criminals, who have been stopped by the police, are freed when local law enforcement data searches are unable to access information that is stored outside their own systems. Related to this is the increasing demand for cross-jurisdictional co-operation and information sharing as a requirement for tapping into fragmented databases and allowing jurisdictions to share crime data so that the jurisdictions do not get 'linkage blindness'—the inability to synthesize massive amounts of decentralized data (Rossmo, 2000). Considering the importance of timely availability of information for a knowledge-intensive organization like the police and to leverage the advances in information technology for taking policing in the country to the era of seamless data integration, the Government of India has rightly allocated funds to the tune of Rs 2000 crores in their 11th Plan for the police computerization project 'Common Integrated Police Applications' covering 14000 police stations and about 6000 higher offices in India.

Need for strategy on the use of technology in the police

The police service needs to be able to understand in depth the links between policing requirements and the technologies which exist and are emerging, to implement changes in the technology, operational requirements or legislation, without wasting resources by over-reacting to every possible development. Some of the key capabilities identified by the UK police that would impact the police performance the greatest, for science and technology application are:

1. Identifying and eliminating threats at public places in view of recent terrorist threats.
2. Effective use of intelligence gathering technology.
3. Inter-agency and intra-agency information exchange such as development of seamless and secure information processing across the criminal justice system.
4. Mobile data input and retrieval such as airwave as enabler for improved and secure data provision.
5. Maximising the value of evidence, such as video recordings and increased use of DNA evidence to convict the offenders.
6. Effective management of investigations including the use of intelligent systems to assist decision making.
7. Monitoring and surveillance.
8. Effective location and recovery of evidence.
9. Security of individuals and locations. (UK Home Office 2004–09: 7)

Then merely acquiring a new technology is not the answer, the technology needs to be absorbed, accepted and linked with other systems. For example, while currently we tend to find all the solutions to connectivity via the internet, TCP/IP network should not be the only way to access information; SMS over cellular networks has become an important method to access information in the entire developing world. Cellphones and (personal digital assistants) PDAs are already the most popular access devices many applications can run on phones to access information using cellular network which can be a cost effective way to the desired results. Similarly, we are obsessed with highly expensive security measures from outside threat to our systems even though it is well known that insiders are greater risk.

Untrained manpower, mismatching of resources and adoption of inappropriate technology in the police department becomes another problem. In fact, the success of any single machine system used in law enforcement may be a function of the presence and effectiveness of other independent technology systems. Grabbing video images of apparent lawbreakers is less valuable if there is not also in place a compendium of faces against which to compare the video still. Biometric measurements are less useful without an ancillary database of templates against which comparisons for identification can be made. In this sense, many law enforcement technology systems are sequential and highly dependent on other systems. The practicality of a technology in a particular category may depend on its linkage to other sequentially-linked categories.[5] Lastly, in the use of latest technology, there are impediments such as bureaucratic delays in clearance of projects and delay due to procedures in purchase decisions both of which results in the technology becoming obsolete by the time it is cleared for implementation.

The COPS programme in the US has played an instrumental role in supplying more than 3,000 policing agencies with technology to advance and support community policing efforts. Through the Making Officer Redeployment Effective (MORE) programme and other technology programmes, the COPS has provided over USD 1 billion to fund crime-fighting technologies. These technology grants and funding help improve police effectiveness and the flow of information among police, local government service providers and the citizens they serve. Undoubtedly, sophisticated technology is highly valued; some equipment clearly serves as a force multiplier, freeing up police officers' time. Such equipment increases efficiency by reducing costs. An example of a force multiplier is a dictation system. Officers can dictate in less than 10 minutes what takes more than 30 minutes to type on a laptop. Tapes can be entered by fast-typing clerical personnel, who are paid much less than police officers. Other equipment, however, increases operating costs because the equipment requires ongoing support. For example, laptops and mobile data terminals in cars allow officers to check licence plates expeditiously. Effectiveness increases, but efficiency decreases (costs go up) because such equipment requires support personnel. Therefore, in place of using grant funds to buy laptops at Rs 50,000 per laptop, they use PDAs at a unit cost of Rs 20,000, thereby also avoiding hiring additional support personnel may sometimes be a good idea.

However, at present, there is neither a system nor an agency to develop, evaluate or benchmark technologies appropriate for police in India. In Canada, the Canadian Police Research Centre has supported research and development relevant to the demands of law enforcement (Defence Research and Development Canada 2009). In the US, the responsibility of

[5] Unmanned aerial vehicles were deployed by the police in the difficult terrain of Chattisgarh to collect data on the movements of the Naxalites. However, given the expanse of the extremist-infested Bastar region and its heavy foliage the forces have to move on foot and the areas mapped by the UAV could be days march away. As of now the state has only one helicopter to support the follow up operations from the data collected by the UAVs which cover as much as 300 kms in a day. They have to be reinforced with adequate force multipliers like the helicopters. Deployment of unmanned aerial vehicles are of little help in counter insurgency operations given the serious manpower crunch and the lack of reinforcements like the helicopter to paradrop the force for expeditious action on the data collected by the UAVs (*The Economic Times*, 17 March 2007).

fulfilling the special technology needs for state and local law enforcement lies with the National Institute of Justice (NIJ), the criminal justice research arm of the US Department of Justice. NIJ's Office of Science and Technology fosters technology research and development. UK's Home Office Scientific Development Branch (HOSDB) provides advice and operational support for the Home Office and its partners on any issue relating to science and technology, creating new solutions where none exists (The Home Office Scientific Development Branch 2009). In such a scenario there is a pressing need to set up an Indian Police Technology Development Centre that can act as the National Nodal resource centre for all major technology applications in the Indian Police. In addition, such a centre would not only need adequate funds and logistic support from Government of India but would also need an overreaching strategy for the effective use of science and technology by police in India. Such a strategy that is ongoing and institutionalized can be developed by setting up of a strategy group which can also act as a board for the Indian police technology development centre (see Box II.12.6).

Box II.12.6   Police Science and Technology Strategy Group of the UK

The Police Science and Technology Strategy Group, created in July 2002, remains the main driver of the science and technology strategy in the UK. It includes representatives of the tripartite parties (Home Office, ACPO and APA) and other key stakeholders, key providers of science and technology, including the Forensic Science Service (FCS), the Police Information Technology Organisation (PITO) and the Home Office Police Scientific Development Branch (PSDB) along with staff associations and independent input from the Office of Science and Technology and the Royal Academy of Engineering.

The Group oversees the development and implementation of the police science and technology strategy and also provides the home secretary with authoritative advice on the strategic management of police science and technology.

The three key aims of the strategy are:

1. To establish priorities for current and future science and technology applications and research.
2. To co-ordinate the development and implementation of technology between users and suppliers to ensure a coherent and effective process.
3. To implement processes for future scanning to ensure that the police service can exploit new technology at the earliest opportunity and is prepared for new technology-based threats.

Source: UK Home Office Science and Technology Strategy, 2004–09: 3.

The developed strategy should be able to set up high-level priorities for research, improve co-ordination, partnerships with corporate and identify technology in view of current and future threats and opportunities. The strategy should also take into account the human and the social factors that are essential for effective use of science and technology by identifying the underlying social issues, for example, the use of video cameras at public places raises the issue of individual privacy. Similarly, the DNA databank being repository of sensitive personal information has given rise to debate on underlying ethical question of the manner of its management to protect the civil rights of those concerned.

Private–Public partnership (PPP/P³)

The International Association of Chiefs of Police (IACP) has been a strong proponent of partnerships between the police and private security. At a national policy summit PPP convened by the IACP and the COPS office in January 2004, in Arlington, Virginia, more than 140 executive-level participants from law enforcement and the private sector were brought together to examine the issue of PPP.

Technology is proving to be a useful means of linking the police and the private agencies with minimal costs and efforts for the benefit of everyone, and increasingly the police agencies are beginning to realize the same (Box II.12.7).

Box II.12.7   P³ Networks

The Nassau County Police Department implemented an internet-based Public–Private Partnership (P³) network allowing law enforcement agencies to leverage the vast resources of the private security industry, as well as community-based civic organizations, to significantly enhance public safety and homeland security. P³ network can help keep the private sector informed and connected to the local police department. Being connected implies not only the ability to receive information but also the ability to communicate back to the police. This type of information-sharing partnership enhances public safety not only by developing a more aware community, but also by increasing the level of community involvement through the process itself. The result is a form of twenty-first century community policing, wherein technology is used to aid in both community partnering and problem solving. By definition, a P³ network has a public component and a private component. On the public side of the network is law enforcement and non-law enforcement government agencies, while on the private side are security directors, chambers of commerce, neighbourhood watch groups and civic associations. The 'non-law enforcement' governmental agencies includes

(Box II.12.7 continued)

(*Box II.12.7 continued*)

officials from various departments such as fire services, health, highway, emergency management, public transportation and executive government, all of which are part of critical infrastructure. P^3 network can function as its own unit in a police department; ideally it should operate as part of an intelligence centre, where intelligence gathering and analysis as well as crime data analysis occur. Being embedded in the centralized intelligence function has great advantages relating to the expeditious flow of information. Incoming information can be quickly analysed and distributed to the appropriate recipients. Information and intelligence can be sanitized, if necessary, and shared with the appropriate individuals or groups with a few clicks of a mouse. The importance of being closely linked to the crime data analysis function becomes evident as statistics regarding the latest crime trends and patterns is shared with members of the network. Furthermore, the opportunity exists here to tailor crime prevention information to meet the specific need. Distributing these materials over the network will help communities protect themselves. This type of proactive approach to crime prevention not only enhances the effectiveness of the partnership but also yields positive results in reducing overall crime. The kind of information shared on the network is robbery and kidnapping notifications, missing person alerts, crime stoppers and wanted posters, major fire or explosion reports, major road closings, suspicious packages or circumstances, disruptions in public transportation, planned evacuation drills, weather advisories, identified crime patterns, crime prevention and training materials, and weekend events and parades.

Source: Simeone, 2006.

Further, as a part of partnership, the police can develop an Internet electronic bulletin board where vetted members with secure log-in privileges can post questions or messages, or respond to others on the network. Facilitating this type of cross-talk as a matter of everyday communication can have a significant effect in preventing crime. As an example, security personnel from the various retail stores in the jurisdiction can post information regarding shoplifters or school security personnel can discuss the latest signs of gang activity.

The technology is not only making it convenient to forge partnerships, but also making them the only option available to the police, in view of certain areas of sophisticated criminal activities. Here, the police can only benefit from the shared technological expertise with the private sector and catch up with the latest developments in the fields like the cybercrime, DNA fingerprinting[6] and transborder terrorism and financing of such activities (Box II.12.8).

[6] Science and Technology Strategy Group in the UK police has worked to identify the scope for leverage from commercially financed research and development (R&D) that would enhance police capabilities more quickly and more cost effectively. In this direction plans are afoot for DNA R&D funding by the pharmaceutical industry to police requirements.

Box II.12.8   Public–Private Sector Co-operation

At their meeting in Los Cabos, Mexico, in October 2002, the Asia Pacific Economic Council (APEC) leaders noted the threat of global terrorism and the importance of increasing the protection of global infrastructures and that global communications are only as secure as its weakest link, and collectively committed to: enact comprehensive cyber-security laws, on a par with existing international standards; identify or create national cyber-crime units and international high-technology assistance contact points and establish Computer Emergency Response Teams (CERTs) that exchange threat and vulnerability assessments and information. They also called for closer co-operation between law enforcement officials and businesses in the field of information security and fighting computer crime by endorsing the APEC cyber-security strategy. The elements of the strategy cover: legal developments; information sharing and co-operation; security and technical guidelines; public awareness; training and education; and wireless security. APEC's telecommunications and infrastructure working group has been most active in sponsoring projects to increase the ability of the APEC member economies to more effectively address cybercrime, including through greater inter-governmental and public–private sector co-operation.

Source: www.apectelwg.org/apecdata/telwg/28tel/estg/telwg28-ESTG-09.htm.

'Response': steps for the Indian police

- Develop horizontal linkages by empowering the frontline staff to seek out rather than looking up.
- Have good service recovery.
- Develop SOPs for routine processes.
- Encourage suggestions from the public.
- Set up Indian Police Technology Development Centre.
- Set up strategy group to identify high level priorities for research, improve co-ordination, partnerships with corporate and identify technology for implementation in the police.
- Create a sense of urgency.

Politics 13

The police chiefs, in a survey carried out in Michigan, US, listed the most discouraging and dissatisfying aspect of their job as being the frustration of working in the political environment and dealing with politicians (Benson, 2004). The scenario in India would reflect no different picture. The police officers do not trust the politicians considering them to be narrow interest seekers, constituency builders with little concern for rule of law, dishonest and irresponsible. On the other hand the politicians too have strong feelings about the police, whom they consider to be highhanded, self-seeking, pliable and corrupt. The common perception among politicians is that the media bashing of the police is bound to earn them some measure of appreciation from the public. There exists an atmosphere of general mistrust. In the literature of the police administration, there is very little attention given to the problems of the police administrator who encounters 'politics', as the word is commonly used in the derogatory sense and many police officials believe that a forthright discussion of the police and politics is somehow on the forbidden list of thoughts which must remain only in the verbal form (Wilson, 1972: 15).

Politics and police have become so inseparable in the Indian context, that it is difficult to imagine one without the other. Being responsive to the community, the legislators and the chief minister is part of the police chief's political reality because the chief works for them. Effective politics is about effective relationships. Chiefs who are not political do not last long and those who play political games have even shorter careers.[1] The influence of partisan politics on the police remains one of the greatest handicaps to effective police management. There is still an unacceptable amount of postings and transfers of police administrators on the basis of their political affiliations. Whenever the police is perceived as a tool in the hands of the politicians in power to meet their political ends, it does irreparable damage to the image of the police. The confidence of people in the institution is shaken. As Wilson writes:

> Ideally, any chief of police or executive head of the department should have enough independence, courage, and integrity to consider himself to be "bigger than the job". In other words, if he is asked by the Chief Minister or any politician to carry out an unethical order or if he is placed in an untenable position, the chief should be prepared to resign if he is unable to effect a change in the direction of events. Unfortunately, of course, the chief of police may not always have this strength. Moreover, because of the prestige inherent in the position of chief of police, there will doubtless be others to take his place who are more willing to accept compromise. In such a situation the chief of police should feel no hesitation about enlisting public support in his behalf. (Wilson, 1972: 25)

Day-to-day interference by politicians is a weakness of the department and misuse of the police by politicians a threat, while the constitution of new regulatory bodies is an opportunity presented to the department in the SWOT analysis (Chart I.3.2) and the core strategy is the recommended reinvention strategy (Table I.3.1). As discussed in the STP analysis, in dealing with the politicians and sovereigns the core strategy with a well-developed vision and the customer strategy by working in partnership, briefing and sharing, the credit can be the key to successful relationship. The control strategy of organizational empowerment with the setting up of police commissions and boards and the consequence strategy with setting up of police complaints authorities would be the levers for organizational transformation as given in the following table.

Core strategy	Vision for the department
Control and consequence strategy	Organizational empowerment—new regulatory mechanism
Customer and culture strategy	Police policy, working in partnership, briefing and sharing the credit

[1] With the Punjab government officially ordering the suspension of DGP S. S. Virk, a blue - eyed boy of the former CM Amarinder Singh. Now, ex-DGP's plans of getting himself transferred to one of the para-military forces on deputation has come a cropper. Virk was also considered to be a contender for the CISF top post (*The Times of India*, 2007c).

Managing difficult situations and police policy

In policing, the handling of politicians representing different sections of society forms an important part of the job. Yet very little is clearly laid down to guide an officer, much is left to the 'tactful' handling of the situation as it unfolds with no right or wrong answers. There are several other difficult situations that a police officer faces in the working and dealing with the politicians and the consummate handling of these situations can make or break all the efforts put in by the police. A police officer must not adopt so inexorable an attitude as to create enmities that will forever block the attainment of his/her purpose, provided there is no compromise with crime or corruption. Principles and objectives must be weighed on the scale of expediency, by the police officer, keeping the main objective in view, but yield a secondary objective when to remain obdurate threatens the success of the programme (Wilson, 1972: 24). Sometimes, matters of principle may take the form of stubbornness and a prestige issue. Such stance should be avoided and this can at times lead to irreparable damage and cascades into major crisis seriously affecting the reform efforts. In the words of Wilson:

> 'No' Is Sometimes the Wrong Answer. The police must not build up such a 'sales resistance' to outside influence as to be unable to consider worthwhile proposals. Constant guarding against pressures and frequent denial of requests tend to establish a behavior pattern that prompts the police to say 'no' when they might better say 'yes'. They must guard themselves against putting on such a thick, defensive armor that they cannot distinguish between influence and wise suggestions and advice. The police should not say 'no' until they have studied all the facts. (Wilson, 1972: 25)

However, there are times when there is no option to 'no', in such situations consistency in handling of issues can be an important armour for any police officer to shield him or her from any criticism that saying 'no' to a work that cannot be done may invite. In dealing with politicians of different sections, a clear strategic intent acts as a guiding light leading to consistency in dealing with the issues that are brought before the police by the politicians.

The skill of avoiding unnecessary issues is important for any police chief to learn. In the daily functioning of the police, there are a great number of influences that place the chief at some time or the other in opposition to influential persons in the community. As a consequence some enmity may be created. It is tempting to make an issue or to meet it squarely, merely as a show of force. Such temptation is better avoided as if the chief loses, he/she may be out of office while on winning nothing is gained beyond the making of an everlasting enmity. However, there are issue that clearly jeopardize the objectives of the department and the public good they should meet it squarely with all the force, for example, an issue involving compromise with crime and corruption cannot be dodged; it must always be faced squarely (Wilson, 1972: 25).

Many times the police has to respond to riot situations, community tensions, campus unrests, labour lockouts, bandhs and traders/farmers agitations. These emotionally-charged situations often bring the police executive in conflict with the political executive regarding the use of force, method of handling the situation, commitment of resources, community expectations and political compulsions. In dealing with such situations, it should be borne in mind that the police alone cannot dictate public policy and it would be wrong to assume that force would control dissidence. Sometimes single minded pursuit by the police agencies can lead to avoidable disasters of unforeseen magnitude. What appears to be a logical next step in run up to the planned operations to the officers of the law enforcement agencies may look unjustified from other stakeholders' perspective (Box II.13.1).

Box II.13.1   Waco and Ruby Ridge Siege

On 28 February 1993, the Bureau of Alcohol, Tobacco, Firearms and Explosives (ATF) raided the Branch Davidian ranch at Mount Carmel, a property located nine miles east-northeast of Waco, Texas. The initial raid resulted in the deaths of four agents and six Davidians. The subsequent 51-day siege by the FBI ended on 19 April when fire completely consumed the complex killing 79 people, including 21 children and the Davidian leader David Koresh that has come to be known as the Waco siege.

In the aftermath of the initial raid, the ATF drew heavy criticism for proceeding, despite being aware that the Davidians knew of the offensive and of the months-long surveillance of Mount Carmel. Some critics also continue to ask why the ATF agents turned down a direct invitation given months before the initial assault, in which Koresh spoke with the agents by phone and asked that they come and talk with him about their concerns. The Waco siege has been the subject of a number of documentary films.

Ruby Ridge refers to a violent confrontation and siege involving white separatist Randy Weaver, his family and Weaver's friend Kevin Harris, and federal agents from the United States Marshals Service and the FBI. The events took place in late August 1992 on the Weaver family property, located on a hillside between Caribou Ridge and Ruby Creek near Naples in northern Idaho.

The focal point of the Senate's criticism was the FBI's 'Hostage Rescue Team', which originally only operated in foreign countries, was overtly militaristic

(Box II.13.1 continued)

(*Box II.13.1 continued*)

and aggressive and was used in situations where there are no hostages to be rescued.

Both Waco and Ruby Ridge incidents are highly documented and analysed and have become important case studies in illustrating what the law enforcement and negotiating agencies should not do.

Source: http://www.wikipedia.com.

A problem-solving and policy-making approach by the co-ordinated efforts of civil administration, elected representatives, community leaders and police administrators is the appropriate response under these situations. In 2003, to tackle the growing public order problem of hooliganism during football matches, the Dutch police adopted a policy framework for combating it. The policy is based on the principle that each link in the chain should make a contribution to the solution based on its own responsibilities and duties. The parties concerned include the football clubs and the Royal Dutch Football Association, the police, the municipalities and the public prosecution service and at the national level, relevant government ministries. Supporters' organizations too have endorsed the policy framework and are cooperating with the authorities (Chan, 2004: 15).

In the aftermath of conflict, the police need to re-establish their relationship with local communities. The important message is that the police are increasingly becoming information managers, but they are relationship managers too. In dealing with the aftermath of police–community conflicts, such as riot situations or police shootings, there are several useful do's and don'ts[2] for a police administrator.

1. Do not publicly defend the police and their actions before the facts are known.
2. Do not provide the media with information before verification of the information.
3. Do not discredit those who are complaining about police behaviour.
4. Do not resist an independent inquiry.

But:

1. Start as soon as possible a dialogue with the key people.
2. Be open and show willingness to listen to complaints and learn.

[2] Professor Philip Stenning in pre-conference debate in the Pearl Fishing conference, Hague 2007.

3. Operate with independent team that has no stakes in the conflict.
4. Commit to full and open accountability.
5. Make clear to the police officers that they can expect fair treatment.

Police policy making should be an open process in which all the stakeholders work together to determine the priorities, philosophy and special concerns. Essentially, it is the public concerns that should decide the police policy. As in England, where the public is systematically given more influence on the choices the police makes. Their initiative of 'Signal Crime Perspective' provides for police priorities to be set methodically from the citizens' perspective. The Canadian police, with their policy document 'Sustainable Community Police Relations', focuses on improving trust between police and public. Integrating the methodical English process and the human Canadian approach can yield a successful proactive police policy (Police Academy of the Netherlands, 2006).

Regulatory bodies for the police

The Supreme Court in its Judgment number R. 639/06, dated 22 September 2006, directed the states to constitute for each state State Security Commission, Police Establishment Board, Police Complaints Authority and a central National Security Commission. Soli Sorabjee Committee's new Police Act draft and the Supreme Court Order number R. 639/06 passed recently aim at insulating the police administrators with inappropriate pressure, greater transparency in transfers and postings, and acknowledge that the police administrators have the authority and responsibility for the administration of the department while being accountable to the law and the people.

Role

The Metropolitan Police Authority of London plays the role of building trust, co-operation and understanding between the police and the community by encouraging the participation and assistance of the community. Functions discharged by the Metropolitan Police Authority are: setting the budget, issuing a policing plan, recruiting and appointing the senior ACPO ranks such as chief constables, deputy and assistant chief constables, employing all civilian staff, arranging for appeals from police officers who have been dismissed or reduced in rank, monitors performance of the force, publishes an annual report and ensures consultation takes place regarding local matters with the community. In a nutshell, the Authority provides two roles, first is the independent scrutiny and public accountability to the service, including close analysis and monitoring of the budget and performance. The other more supportive role is to work in partnership with the police service, to promote and speak for the service and provide a degree of strategic direction and oversight (www.homeofice.uk.gov).

The functions of the Victoria Police Board in Australia are to advise the minister and chief commissioner on improvements in administration, such as 'the structure, organization and management policies of the force' for the Victorian Police Board.[3] The Australian New South Wales Police is, 'charged with promoting efficient and effective policing, formulating policy and overseeing the appointment of commissioned officers [while] responsibility for operational command would remain with the Police Commissioner' (Palmer, 1997: 665–79).

Not only are there police boards and authorities, some countries have Civilian Review Boards that are external to the police consisting of citizens. These boards are charged with the mandate of reviewing the complaints and making recommendations as to disciplinary action. A key concern with instituting a civilian review board is how binding its recommendations are. Many countries also have an independent monitor/auditor to review the procedures in the police department and suggest the implementation of best practices.

The regulatory bodies for the police exist in different forms in the nations around the world performing variety of functions (Stevens and Yach, 1993) such as:

1. Setting overall priorities for policing.
2. Identifying particular policing needs of different sections of the community.
3. Police budget and expenditure.
4. The criteria for recruitment and training.
5. The appointment of senior police officers and civilians and levels of overall police establishment and strength.
6. The promotion of greater understanding by both communities and the police of the policing needs of the state.
7. Legislation that affects any aspect of policing.
8. The dissemination of information on crime, law, powers, rights and duties of police and public.
9. Police response to the problems relating to community.
10. Carrying out research work.

[3] Based on an article by Palmer (1997: 665–79).

11. Inquiry into police complaints and recommending disciplinary action.
12. Setting targets and measuring performance.

The regulatory body can play an important role to improve policing. However, care should be taken that the work of the board must be properly resourced so that recommendations can be based on research and surveys and have an effective secretariat to document and support its work (Stevens and Yach, 1993).

The bodies should also be given sufficient powers to enforce their decisions. If their decisions have no impact then the members lose interest in participation. However, it should also be seen that they are not allowed to step over the line into the day-to-day operations and functioning of the police department. They must let the leadership in the police develop and implement own action plans to carry out the strategies and show outcomes. At the same time, the commission should guard against the reluctance to determine the law enforcement and police service policy on the assumption that the police receive all necessary guidance in law enforcement from the courts, the prosecution and the law. This is not true, as most police operations are outside criminal justice process, and there are vast areas of police discretion with which the law, the courts and prosecutors are not concerned.

The effective and impartial functioning of such bodies would largely depend upon the manner in which the members of authority are selected, their functional autonomy, their self-sufficiency in terms of infrastructure and operating expenses (see Chart II.13.1).

Independence

The Korean police had been under the direct control of the Interior Ministry, which oversees various elections, including the presidential election. There had been no independent civilian oversight, which could check and prevent the politicization of the Korean police. Promotions of high-ranked officers have not been based on the performance of their duties, but were based on their relationship with the ruling parties and loyalty to the regimes. In addition to the lack of external control mechanism, the structure of the Korean police itself—a highly centralized and vertical para-military structure, from the top to the bottom, make it easier to be manipulated as a political tool by appointing and assigning politically-oriented officers in high ranks.

There was a long standing demand from the civilian organizations and even the police at various forums to have a mechanism that could insulate the police from political misuse. Finally, with the enactment of

Chart II.13.1   Role and Do's and Don'ts for the Police Commission

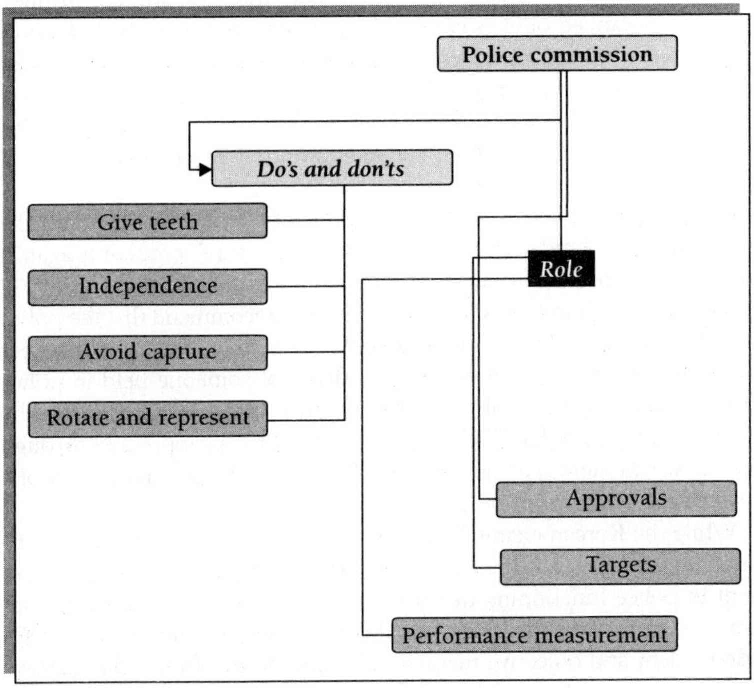

Source: Conceptualized by the author.

the Police Act in 1991, the National Police Board was created to ensure political neutrality and autonomy for the police. The current police, Korea National Police Agency (KNPA), was brought out of the direct control from the Ministry of Interior.

However, despite the enactment of the Police Act in 1991, it has not been effective in ensuring political neutrality of the KNPA. The reasons for the same are (Moon, 2004: 128–36):

1. Board belongs to the Minister of Interior as an advisory committee, thus significantly diminishing the political neutrality of the Korea Police Board itself.

    (i)   The board is only responsible for advising police policy such as budget, equipment, and personnel administration. It is not given actual power to supervise the operation of the police and thus becomes a perfunctory organization, making it useless for ensuring and increasing political neutrality and transparency of the KNPA.

    (ii) The National Police Board did not become a superior office, and is not vested with actual authority to administer the

KNPA in many areas, especially the appointment of high-ranked officers in top administrative positions, including the commissioner general. The commissioner general has been frequently changed at the will of the president. The average tenure has been around a year, thus significantly diminishing the political neutrality and autonomy of the police.

On the other hand, the Police Complaints Authority (PCA) in the UK is a publicly funded organization that makes sure complaints against the police are looked at fairly. The PCA supervises the investigation of the most serious complaints. It has the power to recommend that the police force begins disciplinary proceedings against the officer. It oversees investigations into cases involving the death of someone held in police custody, or incidents involving police firearms, the role that is played by the magistracy in India. The chairman of the PCA is appointed through open advertisement, just as it is done for the chief executive officer of a private sector enterprise.

While the Korean example highlights the fact that despite the constitution of regulatory mechanism for the police, there has been no improvement in police functioning due to lack of independence to these bodies there. Countries like the UK ensure that these bodies function in a totally independent and objective manner. The experiences from other nations provide important lessons for India, to ensure independence and effective functioning of the regulatory Security Commissions.

Selection of members

Selection of the members should be done carefully as the selected members need to think boldly, have a vision, focus on results and have the ability to think strategically. There should be some provision for training for them also. In addition, the membership of the authority should be reviewed periodically to see if it is representative of the community, so that they enjoy the confidence of all sections of the community and the police. Care must be taken to ensure that not a single interest group dominates the proceedings.

There should be a majority of members, especially in the district-level complaint authority, that should not hold any other office of profit and they should receive emoluments from the authority's budget. They should be fully accountable for the actions undertaken by the authority. This is essential as the district level police authorities would also have to do the job of inquiries into police complaints; it requires dedicated office bearers and staff with full accountability. The New York City Civilian Complaint Review Board (CCRB) is an independent and non-police mayoral agency. It is empowered to receive, investigate, hear, make findings and recommend action on complaints against the New York City police officers, which allege the use of excessive or unnecessary force, abuse of authority, discourtesy or the use of offensive language. Investigations are conducted in an impartial fashion by the board's investigative staff, which is composed entirely of civilian employees. Complaints may be made by any person whether or not that person is a victim of, or witness to, an incident. Dispositions by the board on complaints are forwarded to the police commissioner. As determined by the board, dispositions may be accompanied by recommendations regarding disciplinary measures. The Civilian Complaint Review Board has 13 members. Five members are designated, or nominated, by the New York City Council (one from each borough)[4], three by the police commissioner and five by the mayor. However, the mayor must appoint all members, even those designated by the city council or the police commissioner. No member of the board may have served previously in law enforcement (other than those designated by the police commissioner) and none may hold other public office or employment. Board members serve three-year terms and receive compensation on a per-diem basis.

While the regulatory body is meant to make the police accountable, it is also equally important that accountability mechanism for the members should be created. The authorities should be able to negotiate with the government concerning which policy or programme outcomes should be achieved on priority. When these goals are met, the members should be rewarded. When the goals are not met, the government should review the role of members from time to time.

The road ahead

While there is undoubtedly a need for such a mechanism as discussed, sufficient euphoria has been created by the Supreme Court order on setting up of such bodies in India. Among the police officers, media and public there are certain concerns that have to be kept in mind. Too much should not be expected too soon from the Security Commission and Complaints Authorities, as it takes time to produce results. Even the infrastructure and building, for such bodies to operate, would take several years.

No mechanism can be a panacea for all the ills in any department. In the event of setting up a proposed authority too, how much the police is able to keep itself aloof from the politicians in power is difficult to predict. Unless a strong will to resist the pressure from outside is exhibited by the

---

[4] Borough is something similar to a police district or a contiguous area with similarity in issues faced.

police officers themselves, no amount of outside support or legislation can ensure the police neutrality. There is always a possibility of mutually beneficial nexus being formed between some of the police officers and the politicians.[5] Then in various other logistics and service matters, the police would remain by and large dependent on the government and cannot ignore the ruling party in it's functioning. As Justice J.S. Verma, a former chief justice of India had observed:

> The monitoring by the Supreme Court in the Hawala case provided full autonomy to the CBI in the conduct of investigations by it, with the authority to prosecute all those found guilty by it. In spite of this freedom, the level of its performance can be gauged from the fact that charge sheets filed did not make a prima facie case to frame the charge in any case, and all the accused were discharged by the court. The impression is that the purpose of filing half-baked charge sheets was only to get rid of the monitoring by the Supreme Court led by me.

Another concern would be the post-appointment conduct of the members of these authorities. There is a danger that these members may start misusing their authorities and these authorities slowly may act as another power centre.

The police till now were completely dependent upon the politicians in power and the interference in the department had reached even to routine administrative matters. In order to provide greater autonomy to the police accompanied by greater accountability to the people for their performance and ethical conduct, a beginning has been made by the establishment of state security commissions and police boards.

Along with ensuring the political neutrality and autonomy of the police, by reforming the institutional system of the Indian police, it is important that the police themselves make sincere efforts to present themselves as a democratic police force. The structural changes for ensuring political neutrality may help the Indian police to be reborn as a democratic police organization, but they cannot guarantee that it will happen unless the police themselves show genuine determination to reform it (Bayley, 2001).

Reforms and politics

Any process of reforms or changes is bound to disturb the existing order and will invite uproar form those whose interests are threatened, while

---

[5] 175 crore mega project sanctioned in the name of an IPS officer's family (*The Times of India*, 2007a).

those who stand benefited may support in a mild manner. Something that Machiavelli wrote 500 years ago is so very relevant today:

> It must be remembered that there is nothing more difficult to plan, more doubtful of success nor more dangerous to manage than the creation of a new system. For the initiator has the enimity of all who profit by the preservation of the old institution and merely lukewarm defenders in those who would gain by the new one. (http:// www.quitedb.com/squotes/3895)

A police chief dealing with the politicians on a regular basis has to have the courage to take on the special interests in the march to reinvent the police and serve the common man. Osborne and Plastrik have a useful list of tips for winning the political war (Osborne and Plastrik, 2000: 290–96):

1. In bringing about necessary reforms the people and the policy elite need to be convinced with the help of data that the current system does not work. In the US, the federal government acted as a facilitator in promoting policing reforms, by enlisting universities and the corporate sector in evaluating existing police practices and exploring innovations. Projects taken up studied police departments spread in different parts of the country, an additional benefit was that this process created a constituency of opinion makers that extended beyond just the law enforcement community or government. These influential groups also assumed the role of an informed and involved force in the police reform process something which is generally missing in matters relating to police.

2. The interest groups that tend to lose from the reforms tend to get quickly and aggressively organized, it is the beneficiaries that need to be brought together. The police officer should take pains to organize these constituencies that benefit so that the counter balance is always ready at hand. There could be series of seminars and debate forums organized where the support groups from the public have the chance to voice their support. The debate should be so structured that it poses the general interest against the special interests. Taking onboard stakeholders, like business and community groups, will be helpful and building consensus among the employees in the police department will be of some help too. Here, a classical case is New York Police Chief Bratton's approach to the opposition of his zero-tolerance policy by courts on the ground that such a policy would lead to large number of cases and clogging in the courts. Through a series of press conferences and

articles and at every interview opportunity, Bratton put the issue on the front and centre of public debate with a clear message: if courts do not help crack down on quality of life crimes, the city's crime rate would not improve. Bratton could also win the support of the city mayor. The courts had to relent and the police chief could push his policy through (Kim and Mauborgne, 2003: 11).

3. Sometimes the interest groups are just fearful of change and in such a situation lack of communication can make them further apprehensive. Having open channels for dialogue is very important and the human side to it should not be ignored.

4. The opportunity to seize the moral ground to portray the reforms in the right perspective as many interest groups would like to paint the reforms as elitist and anti-vulnerable and poor sections of the society.

5. Out of passion for reforms sometimes the police officers discuss in detail the process with the people and media. This can be counter productive as it may be of little interest to people who would be more concerned about the results—to win political battles, sell results and not the process. Once results start coming they should be measured and documented to be presented at different forums. The police chief should develop his programme and his departmental and community support by doing the easiest things first. Nothing succeeds like success, and as he succeeds with the less difficult, the more difficult becomes easier to accomplish.

6. The police chief should test public reaction for his programmes before undertaking them and not initiate action for which the community has not been prepared. Undertaking premature action that may cost him his job is not an intelligent approach to the task of providing the community with the best possible police service, on the other hand, failing to take suitable action because of probable opposition and unpleasantness is cowardly (Wilson, 1972: 25). A high order of intelligence and judgment is needed to make such important administrative decisions. Perhaps using opinion polls to prove the support to the programme can be another useful tool as the politicians care to a great measure about the poll. Whenever interest groups oppose any programme with wide public support, this can prove to a useful tool.

7. More often than not the reform process may become politicized if one party supports it. The other party as a matter of natural course would oppose them. In such situation, there is a real danger that the issue may be lost in the inter-party politics. Therefore, a police officer should develop champions for the cause in both the parties.

8. While dealing with the opponents it is advisable to follow the conventional wisdom and not to take too many opponents at the same time.

9. Avoid election times for the reform process as during this time any process initiated can be easily halted by the politicians looking for easy ways to appease different constituencies.

10. Once the process of reform has been initiated with some success, it is advisable to stay rolling and be on the offensive. There is no wisdom in resting before the process is complete and while you are winning. For the opponents it is difficult to shoot the moving target compared to the static one. Under the circumstances the best strategy to adopt in order to bring about changes in the department is to define the objectives clearly and go ahead full speed, giving little time for the opposing interests to regroup.

11. Lastly, do not compromise on the fundamentals to the interest groups; a compromised ineffective reform is no better than no reform. If it does not serve the public it may boomerang at a latter date and would jeopardize the future initiatives too. In such situations, in place of pushing the reformatory measures, it is better to wait for the right time. The world cannot be reformed nor a police department reorganized in a day; an act, directed toward either of these ends, that might fail today may be acceptable tomorrow.

'Politics': steps for the Indian police

- Develop foresight for the future and a vision for the department.
- Translate the vision in terms that holds interest for politicians.
- Maintain consistency in handling the issues.
- Avoid stance in which matters of principle may take the form of stubbornness and a prestige issue.
- Avoid unnecessary issues by weighing principles and objective on the scale of expediency.
- Any process of change or reform is bound to invite uproar from interest groups; use thumb rules that can help in winning the political war.
- Along with reforms in the institutional system, police themselves should make efforts to present themselves as a democratic and independent force.
- Police policy making should be open and integrated process involving all the stakeholders to determine the priorities, philosophy and special concerns.

Promotion 14

I n the words of one of the most respected Chief of Los Angeles Police, William H. Parker:

> Public relation is not an organizational position, or a subdivision, or something you consciously do. It is a state of affairs. It is relationship between the public and some identifiable group. As such it is not something you can either accept or reject. It is in continual existence. The only choice an administrator has is whether the state of affairs, this relationship is to be good or bad. (Parker 1975)

Public relations is not performance reporting that improves the image of an agency. It is not a pacifier of dissident, active community groups and it is not a coverup for bad police practices. As a concept it means that a well managed organization should inform its clients, influence them to support its programmes and practices and measure response and acceptance (Cizanckas and Hanna, 1977: 224–25). Once the police develops plans, programmes and new services, they must communicate these initiatives to their constituents. The police department can have many services, but if no one knows about them, they waste resources.[1]

---

[1] Non-registry of complaints by the police remains the biggest grievance of common citizen to be tackled by the top officers. Keen to provide the facility of registration of complaints the director general of police of Himachal Pradesh undertook a progressive and commendable step of offering online registration through the internet for all the 88 police stations, since January 1, 2007. However, till February 13, 2007 not a single complaint was received. 'It is probably lack of awareness about the facility extended to public which has resulted in not even single complaint on the internet,' said a senior officer (*The Tribune*, 2007a).

The ultimate aim of a PR programme should be to give better service to people. Moreover, the respect and public support to the police depends upon the wider public knowledge of both police policy and practice. Communication constitutes a vital link between the police and the community and it can develop a positive relationship between the two entities. Public support is critical in any public endeavour and more so with policing, which is highly public centric. In such a situation it is very important that both the citizens and policemen understand the problems and responsibilities of each other. Public relations therefore becomes a controlling factor in all police efforts (Kooken, 1957: vii). Public relations, the single most important mass-promotions tool that significantly can impact the department's image, has the ability to create favourable publicity, build on the department's image and prevent or handle rumours and incorrect information. Proactive steps by the department's leadership are necessary to make the public aware of the department's good work and to improve the department's image in the community. Failure to take advantage of the available resources and opportunities to tell the department's story will leave it to others (such as the makers of television shows and movies and the writers of newspaper headlines) to shape public perceptions of the department and its personnel, and these perceptions may not be accurate. News media may be the primary source for citizens' perceptions of police legitimacy (Surette, 1998). When the former New York Police Commissioner William Bratton was sworn in as chief of police for the Los Angeles Police Department in October 2002, he faced a wide variety of problems inside the department and in the community. Quickly he assessed that the department was at odds with the community it served. To win back the city's trust, Chief Bratton and the department put systems into place to create an organization where information and changes occurring in the department would be freely shared with the community and media (Schick, 2004).

Dark days of terrorism witnessed curfew-like situation at nights in the towns and roads of the border districts in Punjab. The police were patrolling and laying ambush, but it was a secret and people did not know, so the police presence in the night was not visible. To instil confidence in the minds of people 'Operation Night Domination' was conceived. A meeting of all the officers was called at Mohali to demonstrate the concept of night domination; many then were sceptical, only few were convinced. Yet it worked and the police took advantage of TV media. About 100 journalists travelled at night with the police to see and show to the world that police are out and dominating in the nights. Then latter, to prove to people that normalcy has returned dances and bhangras were organized even in the worst affected towns and were widely covered by the media (Interview of K. P. S. Gill 2007).

Police–Media relations

What we witness today is news explosion on the television screens with a variety of channels—local, state and national—beaming news non-stop and on the print media with newspapers devoting special pages to local news in their editions. News relating to crime and police finds special favour with plenty of space available with the media for reporting. In such a situation, the importance of the media cannot be underestimated. The media can be both a help and a hindrance to police work. It can effectively assist ongoing investigations by publicizing wanted suspects and by supporting new policing initiatives. For example, the Omaha police, US, wanted to have very visible successes to build confidence in law enforcement. Among other issues, they decided to focus on traffic safety. The police chief met with media representatives that included not just reporters, but also assignment editors invited for lunch and explained the new initiative. They were also taken to interstate overpasses to explain how laser technology would detect speeders. The media played up the story, using videos to show how the laser technology worked and how the department was changing driving behaviours. The results followed with average speed decreasing by 11 miles per hour, 25,000 speeding tickets issued in the first month and accidents declined by 79 per cent. On the other hand, media can also skew public perception about security in the area with lopsided reporting and sensationalization. Police organizations need to appreciate that the media are a double-edged sword and develop strategies to manage media effectively.

Among all the relationships which a police officer must establish, one of the most important is his contact with the reporters of news media. Therefore, law enforcement agencies must have an excellent working relationship with the local media. Positive media stories are free marketing ads about the department. The question remains, though, whether routine crime reports generally portray police positively or negatively. However, news media usually focus on failed attempts by the police to control crime and neglect to cover positive crime control efforts (Garber, 1980). In the words of Lawrence (2000: 31), '...news media help to create and sustain the legitimacy of police, but they also sometimes subject police to critical scrutiny that erodes police legitimacy.'

Local newspapers and radio and television stations can carry news of department activities and services, as well as provide editorial comments to influence public opinion of the department. However, it should also be kept in mind that most mass-media outlets are in the entertainment business, and not information business, to demonstrate higher market share they need to entertain the readers or viewers. They focus on stroies that grab attention. Therefore, it is important to present the data about the achievements in an interesting manner. Robert Mark, commissioner of London in the 1970s, employed the matrimonial metaphor to describe the relationship between the police and the press, calling it 'an enduring, if not ecstatically happy marriage' in which both partners 'help each other in difficulties, tolerate each other's faults and try to promote each other's interests without too much disregard of our own' (Mark, 1971).

The more trusting a relationship the department has with reporters, the better it will be able to work with them during times of crisis. However, policemen have 'an almost unconscious but natural bent towards reticence and secrecy in all matters', explicable in terms of their professional socialization, experience of newspapers' superficiality and distortion and the obligations and responsibilities of security, the privacy of victims and the need for unprejudiced legal proceedings (Chibnal, 1975). This gives the relationship between the press and the police an unfavourable starting note. Therefore, it would serve the cause to appoint one media-savvy officer as the media officer, who can act as nodal point for media interface in the districts/units. For the police headquaters in this media age, it would pay dividends if the police departments set up a information/media cell at the headquaters both for internal and external dissemination of information in a professional manner (Box II.14.1). This cell may have two sections, media relations and force information. As the names suggest, the former would deal with external media while the latter would be responsible for internal communication.

Box II.14.1   Police and Media Strategy

The Strathclyde police in the UK, with its head office in Glasgow, set up one such unit in 1994 to begin the process of professionalizing the forces of media realtions. The unit is headed by a superintendent of police while the senior media relations officer has a staff of eight media relations officer under her. The majority of these are civilians with media expertize while the police officers are seconded for a period of six months to the unit. The benefits are evident as the media professionals understand the requirements and constraints of various media and the police officers provide inputs on police procedures, issues of law and practices. With this once traditional 'off the record' media briefing disappeared and was replaced with organized one point briefng of media. This also reduced the media's need to develop sources within the department to pull of scoops. For the Strathclyde police, this exercise was not just about integrating the media into operational strategies and enhancing coporate image, but an adaptation to the demands of changing society.

Source: Boyle, 1999.

Media policy

It is also important that the police department has a well defined media policy to be followed by all the districts uniformly. Such a policy would not only provide for norms and procedures to be followed, but would also remove the haze between the media and the police as either side would be clear of the practices, what to expect and what is expected. At the time of development of the media policy, it is important to seek the views and suggestions from the media and there must be full understanding of the standards that the editorial and reporting staff are expected to follow. Policy should be such that it can be practically followed both by the police and the press. While the co-operation of the fourth estate is important, the primary job of the police is to investigate and apprehend the criminals. Many a times there is a conflict between the immediate objectives of the police and the press at the scene of crime, assistance of the media must be kept in balance with the police tasks. Final agreement on media policy should be written and copies be issued to the representatives of media and the personnel of the police department.[2]

Enlisting the support of the media for a noble cause by selling police to the media can be a very important strategy. The police chief is justified in taking the press into his confidence and discussing his proposed plans with them in order to ensure their understanding and approval and to gain their assistance in informing and further winning the support of others to meet the opposition to the reform plan. The police officer should not just wait for the media to come but take a step forward in briefing the media about the initiatives backed with data. Media loves dramatized stories and not just plain data. Therefore, it is useful to provide the media with some real-life stories of changed lives and the effects of new measures on the common man. Excellent handling of the media was done by Bratton in his efforts to handle minor quality of life crimes. The courts appealed to the city's legislators, appealing them to exempt them from handling such cases on the plea that it would clog the system and entail significant costs. Bratton placed his case before the press particularly the *New York Times*; as a result of this savvy politicking the legislation was not enacted (Kim and Mauborgne, 2003: 11).

When police officers have contact with the media, it helps if they are: prepared, honest and use straight answers; prepared also to listen to what is being said; avoid using unfriendly police slang, chewing gum, or

---

[2] For guidance in releasing information to the news media, also see the model policy on police–media relations published by the IACP National Model Policy Center.

playing with pen; show emotions (it shows you are a normal human being) and maintain a general atmosphere of cordiality; keep inner balance, quietness and stay cool; react immediately if the reporter is giving wrong interpretation about statements made; are careful with long formulated questions; don't give them bad news step by step (play fair and be confident). In the US, the Omaha police department, for instance, trains its officers to think and talk in sound bytes, saying nothing longer than seven seconds.

Marketing outlets

News outlets are not the only means to market police agency there could be other ways by which the police can stretch their marketing efforts. The police officers should use many different local outlets to market the agency to the community. The police can also engage the following outlets with little or no strain on their resources:

1. Publishing newsletters, magazines and producing TV programmes by the department and contributing to newspapers and journals to share the information with people. This can take the message from the police to a large number of people who otherwise are not in touch with the police. In Holland, the National Crime Intelligence Service (Dienst Nationale Researche Informatie, NRI) is responsible for production of the weekly TV crime watch programme 'Opsporing Verzocht'.
2. Service club meetings and events: Every social organization, like the Rotary Club and the Lions Club, in their monthly meetings, look for speakers from different walks of life. The police can use these occasions to share information with lots of new people.
3. Organizing sports and cultural events by the police earns the department both the goodwill and positive publicity. They also offer the police officers to interact with public in a different way. In the year 1994, Batala police district in Punjab embarked on the mission to organize a series of village games to revive sports in rural areas of one of the most terrorist affected areas of Punjab, after seeing the end of terrorism from the district. Not only did it engage the susceptible youth in a constructive activity waning them away from any further influence of the terrorism, the efforts also showed police in different positive role (*The Times of India*, 1994). Similarly, the cultural teams and police bands not only win the hearts of people, but also at provide free publicity to the department.

4. Partners with others: The police can partner with complementary services to create co-operative advertising campaign. For the drive against drugs, the campaign can be created with the health department, for traffic awareness the highway authority can be roped in, similarly many non-profit organizations work for the common cause and campaign very enthusiastically. Most services provided by the police departments are intangible. When possible, the department should look for ways to leave a tangible product behind. For example, officers can leave brochures, patches, rulers, frisbees, stuffed animals and other departmental memorabilia with citizens. Such an exercise can be undertaken in partnership with private organizations of proven credentials.

5. Internet sites: In today's technological society, the Internet should play an important part in any marketing plan. A department's website can offer services reaching large groups or providing for one-on-one contact. Some possible uses of a website include: sharing department information, crime statistics and safety tips; providing opportunities for citizen feedback; adding a silent witness programme and using e-mail as a vehicle for communication with the public. Video clips from a department's website can serve as an easy way to have community members see and hear what it has to offer. The Internet is an economical and valuable tool for reaching out to the community and beyond. Other useful information on the Internet can be grievances redress system and forms and procedures. However, very often it is seen that after launching the websites, the euphoria in the department dies and there is no updating of the information on the site. It not only makes an adverse news in the media, people also stop referring to the site and the opportunity is also lost, that than needs great deal of time and efforts to recover. The Scottsdale police in the US has a city cable programme, a quarterly magazine, and a website. Crime information is posted monthly on the website, enabling citizens to know what crimes occurred in their neighbourhood. The police says that the public has enthusiastically responded to his agency's website.

6. Business/inter-organizational communication networks (also see Box II.11.2): Baltimore County in the US also has a telephone number by which citizens can get crime statistics for their area. If a specific crime problem is occurring in a neighbourhood, the phone system automatically calls homes with listed numbers in the area to alert them to the trend. Similarly, SMS text messages to alert individuals in the neighbourhood to transmit safety alerts can be used.

7. Another useful media strategy can be partnership with the local radio by setting up a hotline to which people can phone with information and problems in the area. The public response to non-police hotlines is much higher than for the police control room phones.

'Promotion': steps for the Indian police

- Make public relations the central controlling factor.
- Outline media policy of the department.
- Create information unit and appoint nodal officer for the media.
- Develop trust and appreciation of each other's needs with reporters.
- Provide positive stories to the media.
- Present achievements in an interesting way.
- Effectively use different marketing outlets.

Megadigm Shift for the Indian Police

15

Today, we are in times when we are accepting the principle that the police derive their power from the public and must be held accountable to them by the recently constituted regulatory bodies in the form of police boards, complaints authorities and state security commissions. These bodies, in times to come, would decide what has to be done, but the police would have freedom to decide how this is to be achieved, giving police considerable professional autonomy. The police are no longer to derive their authority solely from their relationship with the competent authority and work in vertical orientation, but also from the competencies that they develop in the course of their direct contact with the people they serve, which means also working in horizontal orientation. The new mechanism would allow police to put in practice their views developed by being close to public, on the best way to improve safety. However, it also places an increased responsibility on the shoulders of the police administrators towards the people. This can be shouldered by a professionalized force enjoying the trust and confidence of the public. Gradually, the police are to become so dependent on public that in time to come it would seem inconceivable that in the past police could overlook it. Working with empowered communities will remain the bedrock of emerging policing. However, only an empowered department can have empowered employees and can empower the community, this can be seen as a tripartite empowerment cycle (Chart II.15.1).

Many police administrators, not long ago, believed that public relations activity for the police is a criminal waste of time and funds. They were given to the attitude that they are not salesmen and are paid to be

Chart II.15.1   Empowerment Cycle

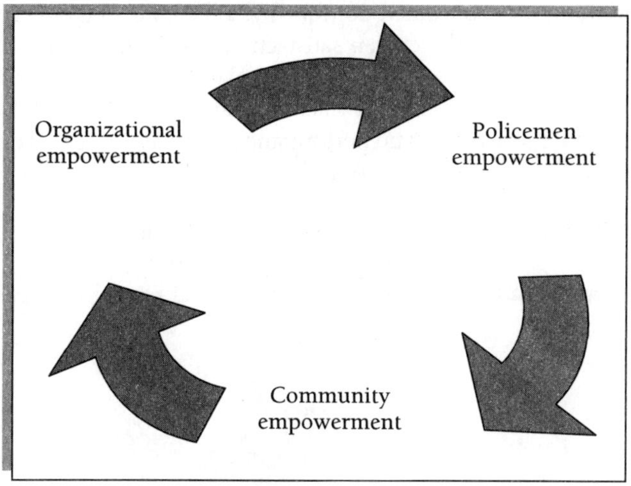

Organizational
empowerment

Policemen
empowerment

Community
empowerment

Source: Conceptualized by the author.

policemen who are out to do pure and simple police work—no frills, no explanation and no information. It is not that police departments till now have not accepted the need for good public relations, some cells were created, observations were made in the conferences and some lectures delivered in the training institutes. Yet, it did not quite worked out the way it was expected for the police. In the field, familiar positions of 'they' and 'us' remained for the police in relation to the public. This led many to rationalize that the police work is an underprivileged, persecuted and peculiarly distinct class of endeavour to which the basic rules of organizational management and socio-psychology do not apply (Parker, 1957). With this backdrop, marketing the police would appear to be an impractical exercise to undertake, even to the diehard optimists and pro-changers among the police administrators. Yet, the opposite may be true, and an effort to market the police—by putting the customer at the centre of police planning and activity—may provide answers to many of the problems police is facing today.

Marketing is not just the publicity and the spin, it is the management process to identify and satisfy customer requirements profitably. How is it relevant to policing? We can quite easily substitute the word citizen for customers, and replace the word profitability with service, greater reassurance and with safer society. Communicating these core messages is central to marketing the police. Being marketing orientated requires a well-developed and deeply-rooted corporate philosophy that guides every part of the organization in all of its activities, and is not just a question of floating some marketing initiatives; it has to actually reflect on everything that policemen do (Mawby, 2002). For the police department, ultimately it is the citizen satisfaction that is the key to sustained and true marketing. The total formulated plan for the police can be seen by making use of the citizen satisfaction chain (Chart II.15.2) that links service firm's effectiveness and performance with employee and customer satisfaction (Kotler and Armstrong, 2006).

**Chart II.15.2   Service–Citizen Satisfaction Chain
for the Police Department**

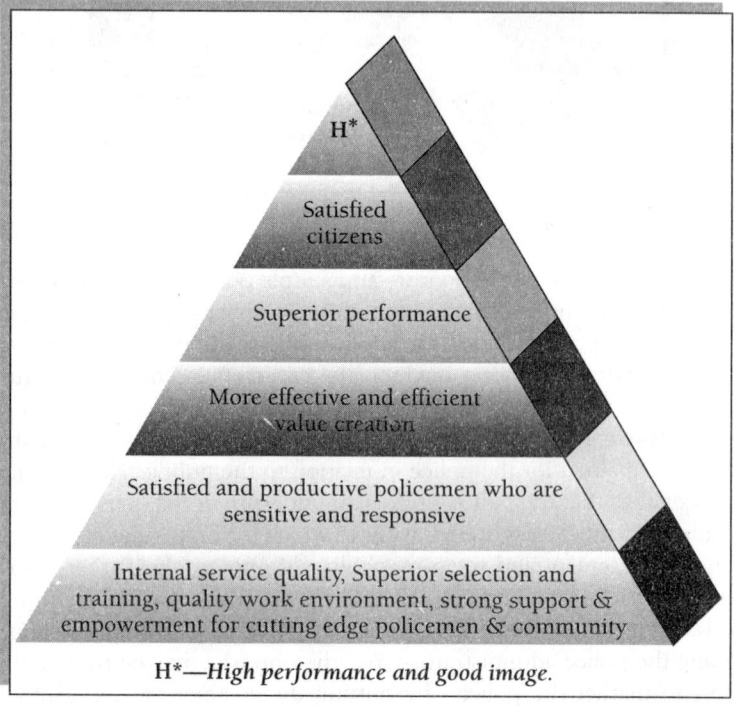

H*
Satisfied citizens
Superior performance
More effective and efficient value creation
Satisfied and productive policemen who are sensitive and responsive
Internal service quality, Superior selection and training, quality work environment, strong support & empowerment for cutting edge policemen & community
H*—High performance and good image.

Source: Conceptualized by the author.

The poor image that the police have today can be attributed to a formidable mix of organizational weaknesses, such as the lack of professionalism, skills, apathy, inefficiency, brutality, corruption and inequity. There is a tendency in the police to favour the powerful, and to take recourse to extra-legal measures for crime control and maintenance of public order. The police force today is ill-equipped and untrained to understand and far less equipped to respond to the challenges posed by the changing profiles of crime and criminals. The police force lacks the right orientation and functions through an organizational command structure that is more suited to the armed forces. These are the maladies that cripple the functioning of the force and with such an array of problems, no outfit can deliver the desired service. In addition to these existing problems, new emerging trends of crime and terrorism, social upheaval, the rising aspiration of large number of unemployed youth and easy access to means of transport and sophisticated communication to the criminals pose threat to the department.

We are, however, to take cognizance of the conditions or the environment under which the force operates—public apathy, outdated police rules, poor pay, housing and working conditions and long hours of work with no weekly holidays. We also have to take into account the sorry state of our criminal justice system and interference by the bureaucratic and political class. Thus making the job of police more difficult as the criminals have no fear of law and there is no deterrence to commit crime.

On the positive side, the police department has large outreach, day-to-day contact with community, rich history and traditions, monopoly, powerful organization supported by the law of the land, highly educated and capable leadership, huge organizing capability and vast experience in handling crisis situations and natural calamities. It is also the time for the police department to look forward to and take advantage of the opportunities offered by the situation in the country today, like increased awareness in people for the need of police reforms and the happenings around the world like the ascendancy of the markets, emergence of new public management, liberalization and globalization.

At present, the department is working in the matrix block of mediocre performance and low image. The objective of the marketing plan developed is to take police department to high performance and good public image. For this the police departments would have to position themselves as agencies in service of people and get out of the colonial mindset of being an oppressive tool of the political masters. Basic paradigm shift required in the approach of the organization is to treat the citizens of the country as customers.

While today, there is pressing need of *reinventing* the police department, tomorrow, there will be no choice. For the police department this would mean a transformation from being a traditional militaristic bureaucracy to a *new age entrepreneurial department*. This can be achieved by the application of the customer strategy, strongly supported by culture, control, consequences and core reinvention strategies targeting different segments—the internal customers; community and the citizens; politicians, media, judiciary and policy elites and the compliers.

Internal customers are the policemen and employees in the department and are the most important players in the reinvention efforts. Only an empowered officer on the street can be truly responsive, capable, committed and motivated to meet the demands on policing today. The police departments with their rigid militaristic structure and hierarchy place a premium on compliance and hardly encourage initiative and self-management. Participatory management with just an improvement in upward and downward communication, by introduction of linking pin structure in the department, would be of considerable assistance to top officers in a department and would lead to greater organization commitment and job satisfaction among the lower level police officers. Other steps required for empowering the policemen are eliminating layers of middle-level officers that perform the same function and shift of control from top-level officers at the headquarters to the districts and from districts further to the police stations in field, while strengthening the inter-linkages between them. The best suggestions for the organizational development come from the frontline staff; therefore, the suggestions from the field officers need to find a place in the organizational decision making in an institutionalized manner. Empowerment would also mean loss of some old forms of controls; in that situation, the way to check malpractices would be full information, consequence for performance and prosecution for illegal activity. A well-designed and well-communicated appraisal system helps achieve organizational objectives and motivates employee performance. The appraisal system needs to be used as an aid for organization and employee development rather than merely used as a tool for disciplining the employees. Police department needs a system that provides for means to measure performance rather than personal traits as the existing system reflects heavily.

The culture of improving service quality, preventing crime and building strong relations with the community would have to be developed, through the implementation of culture strategy, as a part of internal marketing to make the plan successful. The policemen would deliver to the public what they 'receive' from the department. If there is openness and fairness within the department, there is transparency and justice in the rewards, punishments, postings, transfers and promotions, the policemen will carry a high sense of justice and equity. In turn this is what they will deliver to the citizens who come in contact with them. The unethical conduct and use of extrajudicial methods by the policemen can lead to short term gains, but do considerable damage to the image of police department. The police department needs to reinforce code of ethics and set up a monitoring and control mechanism in the department to develop culture consistent with values and ethics. Fostering workplace spirituality in the police department can not only promote ethical behaviour and integrity, but can also lead to sustained motivation, commitment and satisfaction of the policemen. To support new culture in the department, training the policemen would be of utmost importance, along with the mock drills, surprise checks and inspections. The basic approach to police training should highlight self-directed learning, which is aligned to field working and also leads to wholesome development of the trainees. Creation of national and international centres of knowledge and excellence and their networking for joint learning initiatives would be the required for updating skills and for reaping the benefits of pooled knowledge source.

Empowerment without any sense of direction can lead to anarchy. While the employees want the freedom of empowerment, they as much need the sense of direction which can only be provided by the senior officers from the top, by creating a strategic intent of the department. The strategic intent should not only be emotionally compelling, but it should also be personalized for every policeman, which means that they should understand the linkage between his or her job and the attainment of the organizational goal. The precise nature of these challenges will be determined by the police department's strategic architecture. Vision once created, the leadership in the police then has to become the biggest living example of this vision through their actions, emphasizing the vision time and again to the frontline policemen. Authentic servant leadership, practising management by walking around to be in touch with the public and the policemen both, empathizing with the poorest and the remotest section of the society can act as the centre of gravity in developing culture of integrity and would be ideally suited to provide direction to the policemen to produce extraordinary results and deeds.

The police must understand the make-up of their communities, as well as the needs and expectations that citizens have of their police services. Once the needs of the customer is identified, the policing activities should be oriented towards meeting these needs. Having identified the needs and tailored the policing activities to meet these needs, the issue of implementation with sustainability is very important. The CRM framework ensures that the insights garnered from its customer interactions are translated into customer requirements.

While the enforcement duties have strict laws and procedures defining the police role and leave little discretion on the part of the police to follow, it is an equally important aspect of crime prevention that has a lot of scope for innovation. While the department needs to cater to the needs of the communities they serve, the community in itself can be the best ally for the police. It is being appreciated, though implemented incrementally, that in order to give better service, the police has to address the problems confronting the society with their help.

Identification of public needs would have to be supplemented with customer empowerment which transfers the control to people. From employee empowerment, the next step forward is the community empowerment, complimented with police department's accountability for results. This can be achieved through community policing, governance bodies, collaborative planning, partnerships, community-based compliance and result-based management. Community policing has come to occupy centre stage in policing strategies around the world, however, there are several impediments in implementing this approach to policing. A close examination of the strategies adopted by some of the developed nations, practicing community policing over the years, point towards useful methods to firmly root community policing in India. For community policing, funds are a necessary vehicle, but the most important aspect is the conviction and belief in community policing, in the minds of policemen on the street, who can work both as policemen and community officers at the same time.

Listening to community is central to the police, yet, an important organizations like the Indian police departments cannot be satisfied just by following the customers. They have to go beyond and lead the citizens, to where our society and nation needs to go; to seize the opporunity to 'shape the future'. The foresight required to shape the future will come from this kind of empathy, and more than anything else, it will come from the will to make a difference to the lives of the people.

An important yet neglected area for the policemen is the skills of quality police–citizen interaction. This is where the interactive marketing is important for the police department. In fact, both internal as well as the interactive marketing should prepare the ground for the external marketing. Police department must set service standards for their organization that clearly define the quality and level of service they are committed to delivering to their customers. Each and every kind of contact is equally important as every contact is an opportunity for shaping favourable public opinion. The standards that the police need to set are both in the area of internal processes as well as the public interaction areas. In order to improve the quality service from the police, while establishing standards, it is equally important and more painstaking to maintain them. Quality of service commitment is to ensure that victim, witnesses, suspects and the general public—all clients should receive a high quality of service when dealing with the police. To supplement the creation of customer service standards the department should also provide for guarantees, complaint systems and means of redress and create institutionalized arrangements to hold the police department accountable for meeting the quality.

The speed and responsiveness are critical to police service as the job involves responding to emergencies and attending to the distressed on many occasions. Ease of access to services, treatment by staff and keeping the promises that have been given are consistent factors in determining overall satisfaction of the public. It is also essential to have a good service recovery, to undo any wrong done as quickly as possible. Developing horizontal linkages within different units of the department, developing standard operating procedures for the routine policing activities, encouraging suggestions from the public and effectively using the technological advancements, while creating a sense of urgency in the staff can bring the desired pace in the services that police offers. Streamlining cross-agency processes is the next great frontier for reducing costs, enhancing quality and speeding operations involving various agencies like the judiciary, prosecution department, magistracy, army and jail administration.

The government suffers from the resource crunch and is unable to provide requisite funds to the police to carry out its functions as per the demands of the day. There is a marked pattern in which the police have been coping with the fiscal constraints; by and large they have resorted to responding by making marginal adjustments in their operating procedures and expenditures. On long term, this has led to human resource erosion, over-centralization, allocation shifts and decision paralysis affecting the efficiency of the police functioning. Under the present scenario, the police have to be prepared to live with long term resource scarcity, while protecting their department's capacity to fulfil its core mission. Therefore, the department needs to respond to the situation by strategic management in place of decremental responses. Some of the measures that can reduce the cost of policing are: reorient and shed functions; low-level additions; spreading costs to other authorities, through 'self help' and diffusion of tasks; providing some of the services on payment; retention of some of the revenue generated; commercial utilization of surplus prime land and outsourcing non-core activities.

Logistics and transportation are very important aspects for an organization like the police. Management principles and tools can be applied to procurement, distribution, utilization and disposal of material resources with the police. The stretch situation which the police departments give rise to the need for resource leverage. Resource leverage in the police department can be achieved by sufficiently concentrating, efficiently accumulating, creatively complementing, carefully conserving and speedily recovering resources. Here the scope for innovation cannot be over-emphasized as the department often face the discomfort of limited resources. Challenging the current practices can enhance effectiveness of the department and sometimes a change in key policies can lead to the reduction of requirement of resources. Therefore, a successful police administrator should have a keen eye for opportunities offered through such reviews, that can lead to resource leverage and efficiency gains for the department. Police departments in India today require a systemic approach to develop, acquire, evaluate and implement innovative ideas and work improvement methods, through a model that supports innovations by structure, process and resources.

Technology has become a critical element both for committing and fighting the crime. In days to come, policing will become more information-led resulting in increasing information management for crime prevention as well as crime detection. The police need to be taking advantage of advances in technology rather than being on the receiving end of such advancements by understanding in depth the links between policing requirements and the technologies which exist and are emerging. For this, an overreaching strategy for the use of science and technology in the police for exploiting the opportunities for effective policing needs to be developed. Such institutionalized and ongoing strategy on the use of technology in the police can be developed by setting up of strategy groups at the centre and the states.

Once the police develops plans, programmes and new services, they must communicate these initiatives to their constituents to earn a good image, trust and confidence of people. This can not only lead to improved image and performance but also more information from people, leading to further significant improvement in performance for the department. Moreover, the police department can have many services, but if no one knows about them, they waste resources. Public relations, the single most important mass-promotions tool that significantly can impact the department's image, has the ability to create favourable publicity, build on the department's image, and prevent or handle rumors and incorrect information. A well-defined media policy, a nodal officer to interface with media, interesting presentation of information and effective use of different marketing outlets can help police in achieving this.

Politicians are the most influential stakeholders and it is imperative to keep them on right side in the initiative to reinvent the police, build a positive image for the department and deliver quality service to the customers. However, whenever the police are perceived as a tool in the hands of the politicians in power to meet their political ends, it does irreparable damage to the image of the police. The confidence of people in the institution is shaken. In order to navigate in the political sea, it is necessary for the police to have a foresight for the future and a vision for the department. This vision should also be translated in terms that hold interest for politicians too. The politicians should also be involved in the reinvention activities so that they understand and also share a part of the credit of the good work done. A well-developed vision, working in partnership, briefing and sharing the credit can be the key to successful relationship between the police and politicians. Police policy making should be an open process in which all the stakeholders work together to determine the priorities, philosophy and special concerns.

Setting up of regulatory mechanism, state security commissions, police boards and authorities for transparency, greater accountability to the public and autonomy and insulation from political interference in functioning herald a new beginning towards organizational empowerment for the police. While these are to ensure the political neutrality and autonomy of the police by reforming the institutional system of the Indian police, the police administrators have the responsibility of providing inspiring leadership to improve the quality of service and to solve community problems of concern to police. Also, it is important that the police themselves make sincere efforts and present themselves as a democratic police force, as the structural changes for ensuring political neutrality cannot guarantee that it will happen, unless the police themselves show genuine determination to reform it.

The world today is undergoing changes at an unimaginable pace in which the exisiting institutions are constantly engaged in reassessing and reorienting their roles, activities and goals. The days when policing was a localized low-key affair are gone, in an increasingly globalized world the requirement that police will be facing is that of empowerment, partnerships, learning, standardization, ethics, transparency, accountability, diversity and urgency. Not surprisingly, the police departments in India governed by old rules and procedures find themselves out of sync with the times. One of the main contributions of modern marketing has been to help organizations see the importance of shift from being product centred to becoming market and customer centred (Kotler). The police in India have to acknowledge and accept this shift and embrace unique configuration of several reinforcing strategies, in order to present itself as a premier organization in *beat* with the new emerging world dynamics.

Marketing the police in India would mean its reinvention which would require numerous collective shifts that together create a *megadigm shift*[1] as shown in Table II.15.1.

In more general terms, this would mean: developing the human resources by giving employees a sense of meaning, control and purpose; adhering to highest standards of professional policing and being more

---

[1] Megadigm—a set of changes so deep and profound that they fundamentally alter the way we accept things and our world view (Belgard and Rayner, 2004).

Table II.15.1   'Megadigm shift' for Reinventing the Police

Traditional bureaucractic		Entrepreneurial department
Colonial mindset	....	Customer centric
Individual driven	....	New managerialism
Top-down	....	Employee empowerment
Centralized	....	Participatory management
Autocratic leadership	....	Servant leadership
Strict hierarcal structure	....	Linking pin structure
Lack of clarity of purpose, vision and goal		Strategic intent and architecture
Appraisal as a disciplining tool	....	Appraisal for employee development
Poor service quality	....	Customer service standards
Accountable to political bosses	....	Accountable to law and people
Decremental response	....	Strategic management
Resource crunch	....	Resource leverage
Police ethnocentrism	....	Inter-organizational networks
Culture of mistrust and negativism	....	Positive organizational behaviour
Traditional pedagogical method	....	Andragogy, self-directed learning
Unethical conduct	....	Workplace spirituality
Set domain of functioning	....	Shaping the future

Source: Conceptualized by the author.

flexible and adaptable in their functioning; developing and maintaining complete support and co-operation of public by empowering citizens; encouraging complete co-operation within and with other departments; elevating the standing of the police profession in the public mind by delivering and maintaining high-quality services; strengthening public coinfidence in the police department by being sensitive to the needs of their customers and maintaing high ethical standards; recognizing police work as an opportunity to render worthwhile service to the society; up-grading skills and technology and creating structures, procedures and culture in the department to support and enable effecienct and effective functioning.

The question will not be how urgently the police is able to react, but how quickly the police is able to generate changes within the organization, exhibiting flexibilty and adaptability, led by a vision and with realistic continuous small steps towards evolution rather than big revolutionary reforms, to reach to the required *megadigm shift*. This would, in true sense, be the marketing of the police in India.

References

Additional Director General of Police, Punjab. 2006. *e-Governance Vision Document*. Director General of Punjab Police, Chandigarh.

AFP. 2007. Speaking Notes of AFP Commissioner Mick Keelty, APM, Peals in Policing Conference, Monday, 11 June.

Alarid, Leanne Fiftal and Hsiao-Ming Wang. 1997. 'Japanese Management and Policing in the Context of Japanese Culture', *An International Journal of Police Strategies & Management*, 20(4): 600–608.

All India Police Science (AIPS) Congress. 2006. Recommendations of the 37th AIPS Congress.

———. 2008. Resolution passed by XXXV All India Police Science (AIPS) Congress. Available online at www.bprd.gov.in, accessed on 16 December 2008.

Alpert, G. and R. Dunham. 1988. *Policing Multi-Ethnic Neighborhoods*. Westport, CT: Greenwood Press.

Amin, Shahid. 1995. *Event, Metaphor, Memory: Chauri Chaura, 1922–1992*. Berkeley: University of California Press.

Anderson, John. 1995. 'Beyond Public Relations: Community Policing in Canada', *Royal Canadian Mounted Police Gazette*, 57(3): 18–21.

Ayden, A. 1996. 'The Future of Policing in Turkey: Current and Proposed Organizational Changes in Public Policing', *Police Studies*, 19(4).

Ayling, Julie and Peter Grabosky. 2006. 'When Police Go Shopping', *Policing: An International Journal of Police Strategies & Management*, 29(4): 665–90.

Baatz, E.A. 1995. 'Making Brain Waves', *CIO Magazine*.

Bandura, A. 1997. *Self-efficacy: The Exercise of Control*. New York: Freeman.

———. 1986. *Social Foundations of Thought and Action*. Englewood Cliffs, NJ: Prentice-Hall.

Bayley, D.H. 1976. *Forces of Order: Policing Modern Japan*. Berkeley. CA: University of California Press.

———. 1985. *Patterns of Policing: A Comparative International Analysis*. New Brunswick, NJ: Rutgers University Press.

———. 1994. *Police for the Future*. New York: Oxford University Press.

———. 2001. *Democratizing the Police Abroad: What to Do and How to Do It*. Washington, DC: National Institute of Justice. J 28.24/3:P76/2.

Bayley, D.H. and C.D. Shearing. 2001. *The New Structure of Policing: Description, Conceptualization and Research Agenda*, US National Institute of Justice, research report.

Beams, J. 1961. *Memoirs of a Bengal Civilian*. London: Chatto and Windus.

Beck, K., N. Boni and J. Packer. 1999. 'The Use of Public Attitude Surveys: What Can They Tell Police Managers?', *Policing: An International Journal of Police Strategies & Management*, 22(2): 191–216.

Becker, C.A. 1980. 'Semantic Context Effects in Visual Word Recognition: An Analysis of Semantic Strategies', *Memory and Cognition*, 2(6): 493–512.

Belgard, W.P. and R.R. Rayner. 2004. 'The Megadigm: Confronting the Six Shifts of Change', *Shaping the Future*, American Management Association.

Bennet, R.G. 2005. 'Innovations in Policing: New Focus in Aurora: Crime, Quality of Life, and Traffic', *The Police Chief*, 72(1).

Benson, B.L. 2004. 'View from the Top: The Frustrations of Police Chiefs, and How to Solve Them', *The Police Chief*, 71(8): 92–94.

Berlow, A. 1999. 'The Wrong Man', *The Atlantic Monthly*, November, Available online at: http://www.theatlantic.com.

Bernardin, H.J. and R.W. Beatty. 1984. *Performance Appraisal: Assessing Human Behavior at Work*. Boston, MA: Kent.

Birzer, M. 1996. 'Police Supervisors in the 21st Century', *FBI Law Enforcement Bulletin*, 65(6): 5–11.

Blok, Chan. 2004. *Policing in the Netherlands*, Police Department, Ministry of the Interior and Kingdom Relations.

Boice, Deborah F. and Brian H. Kleiner. 1997. 'Designing Effective Performance Appraisal Systems', *Work Study*, 46(6): 197–201.

Boyle, R. 1999. 'Spotlight Strathcilde: Police and Media Strategies', *Corporate Communications: An International Journal*, 4(2): 93–97.

Brand, R.F. and K. Peak. 1995. 'Assessing Police Training Curricula: "Consumer Reports"', *The Justice Professional*, 9(1): 45–58.

British Library, Oriental and India Office Collection (O.I.O.C.). 1904. *Curzon Collection*, MS. Eur. F111/281, India Office, Judicial No. 6, Broderick to Curzon, 4 March 1904.

———. *Robins Collection*, MS. Eur. R178, Robins interview, 2:1.

Broeck, Tom Van den. 2002. 'Keeping Up Appearances? A Community's Perpective on Community Policing and the Local Governance of Crime', *An International Journal of Police Strategies & Management*, 25(1): 169–89.

Brogden. 2005. 'Horses for Courses and Thin Blue Lines: Community Policing in Transitional Society', *Police Quarterly*, 8(1): 64–98.

Bruggeman, Willy, Jean-Marie Van Branteghem and Dirk Van Nuffel (eds). 2007. *Toward an Excellent Police Function*. Document of Belgium Police Department.

Brunetto, Y. 2001. 'Mediating Change for Public-Sector Professionals', *The International Journal of Public Sector Management*, 14(6): 465–81.

Bureau of Police Research and Development. 2008. Presentation. Thirty-eighth All India Police Science Congress, Jaipur, June.

Cable, V. 1994. *The World's New Fissures*. London: Demos.

Campion, David A. 2003. 'Authority, Accountability and Representation: The United Provinces Police and the Dilemmas of the Colonial Policeman in British India, 1902–39', *Historical Research*, 76(192): 217.

Cardy, R.L. and G.H. Dobbins. 1994. *Performance Appraisal: Alternative Perspectives*. Cincinnati: South-Western.

Champy, J. 1995. *Reengineering Management: The Mandate for New Leadership*. New York: Harper Business.

Charan, R. and N. Tichy. 1989. 'Speed, Simplicity, Self Confidence: An Interview with Jack Welch'. *Harvard Business Review*.

Charrier, K. 2004. 'Strategic Management in Policing: The Role of the Strategic Manager', *The Police Chief*, 71(6).

Chibnall, S. 1975. 'The Metropolitan Police and the News Media', *The British Police*.

China Law Association Editorial Board. 1991. *Law Yearbook of China*. China Law Press.

Choudhary, Rohit. 2007. *Understanding Volunteers in a Successful Spiritual Non-Profit Organization*. PGPPM dissertation, Indian Institute of Management, Bangalore.

Chwialkowski, Paul. 1998. 'Japanese Policing—An American Invention', *An International Journal of Police Strategies & Management*, 21(4): 720–31.

Cizanckas, V. and D. Hanna. 1977. *Modern Police Management and Organization*. Englewood Cliffs, NJ.: Prentice–Hall, Inc.

Clairmont, D. 1991. 'Community-based Policing: Implementation and Impact', *Canadian Journal of Criminology*, 33: 469–84.

Clarke, Curtis A. 1990. *Police Challenge 2000: A Vision of the Policing in Canada*. Ottawa: Solicitor General of Canada.

———. 2002. 'Between a Rock and a Hard Place RMCP Organizational Change', *An International Journal of Police Strategies & Management*, 25(1): 14–31.

Clarke, R.V. 1992. *Situational Crime Prevention: Successful Case Studies*. New York: Harrow and Heaton Publishers.

Claver, E., J. Llopis, J. Gasco, H. Molina and F. Conca. 1999. 'Public Administration: From Bureaucratic Culture to Citizen-Oriented Culture', *International Journal of Public Sector Management*, 12(5): 456–64.

Cleveland, G. and G. Saville. 2007. *Police PBL Blueprint for the 21st Century*. Wichita: Office of Cops, US Department of Justice and Regional Community Policing Institute. Available online at www.pspbl.com/pdf/PolicePBLBook2007.pdf, accessed on 16 December 2008.

Cope, S., F. Leishman and P. Starie. 1997. 'Globalisation, New Public Management and the Enabling State Futures of Police Management', *International Journal of Public Sector Management*, 10(6): 444–60.

Covey, Stephen. 1992. *Principle Centered Leadership*. New York: Simon and Schuster.

Crank, J. 2003. 'An Institutional Theory of Police: A Review of the State of the Art', *An International Journal of Police Strategies & Management*, 26(2): 186–207.

Crank, J. and R. Langworthy. 1992. 'An Institutional Perspective of Policing', *Journal of Criminal Law and Criminology*, 83: 338–63.

Crank, John P. and Michael A. Caldero. 2000. *Police Ethics, The Corruption of Noble Cause*. Cincinnati: Anderson Publishing Company.

Creech, B. 1994, *The Five Pillars of TQM: How to Make Total Quality Work for You*. New York: Dutton.

Crowe, T. 2000. *Crime Prevention through Environment Design: Application of Architectural Design and Space Management Concepts* (2nd edition). National Crime Prevention Institute, Boston: Butterworth-Heineman.

Curry, J.C. 1977. *The Indian Police*. New Delhi: Manuel Publications.

Daleidan, J.R. 2006. 'A Clumsy Dance: The Political Economy of American Police and Policing', *An International Journal of Police Strategies & Management*, 29(4): 602–24.

Dantzker, G., A.J. Lurigio, S. Hartnett, S. Houmes, S. Davidsdottir and K. Donovan. 1995. 'Preparing Police Officers for Community Policing: An Evaluation of Training for Chicago's Alternative Policing Strategy', *Police Studies*, 18(1): 51–53.

Das-Gupta, Arindam. 2004. *Suggestions for an Action Plan for Karnataka's Non-tax Revenues for 2004–05*. Report prepared for the World Bank and Government of Karnataka.

Davids, C. and L. Hancock. 1998. 'Policing, Accountability, and Citizenship in the Market State', *The Australian and New Zealand Journal of Criminology*. 31(1): 38–68.

Deccan Herald. 2006. 'Mission Impossible?', *Deccan Herald, Sunday Herald*, 18 June. Available online at http://www.deccanherald.com.

DeCenzo, David A. and Stephen P. Robbins. 1998. *Human Resource Management*. New York: John Wiley and Sons.

Defence Research and Development Canada. 2009. Available online at www.cssdrdc-rddc.gc.ca/cprc/index-eng.asp, accessed on 7 February 2009.

Dehler, Gordon E. and M. Ann Welsh. 1994. 'Spirituality and Organizational Transformation, Implications for the New Management Paradigm', *Journal of Managerial Psychology*, 9(6): 17–26.

Denning, D. 1999. *Information Warfare and Security*. Reading, MA: Addison-Wesley.

Dhillon, K.S. 1998. *Defenders of the Establishment*. Shimla: Indian Institute of Advanced Study.

Dixon, J., A. Kouzmin and N. Korac-Kakabadse. 1998. 'Managerialism—Something Old, Something Borrowed, Little New: Economic Prescription Versus Effective Organisational Change in Public Agencies', *International Journal of Public Sector Management*, 11(2/3): 1–19.

Donohue, John J. and Steven D. Levitt. 2000. 'The Impact of Legalized Abortion on Crime', *Theory and Society*, 29(4): 427–31.

Dunham, Alpert G. and R. Dunham. 1988. *Policing Urban America*. Prospects Heights, IL: Wareland Press.

Dussault, R. 1999. 'Police Chiefs Propose DNA Database', *Government Technology*, 12(13): 12.

Ebbe, E.O.N. (ed.). 1996. *Comparative and International Justice Systems*. Boston, MA: Butterworth-Heinemann.

Edwards, M.R. 1990. 'An Alternative to Traditional Appraisal Systems', *Supervisory Management*, 36(6): 3.

Feltes, Thomas. 2002. 'Community-Oriented Policing in Germany Training and Education', *An International Journal of Police Strategies & Management*, 25(1): 48–59.

Fridel, L. 2004. 'The Results of Three National Surveys on Community Policing', in L. Fridell (ed.), *Community Policing: Past, Present, and Future*, pp. 39–58. Washington, DC: Police Executive Research Forum.

Garber, Doris Appel. 1980. *Crime News and the Public*. New York: Praeger.

Gentel, W.D. and D.G. Hanna. 1971. *A Guide to Primary Police Management Concepts*. Springfield, Illinois, USA: Charles C Thomas.

Gill, K.P.S. 2007. Interview taken by author. Jalandhar, June 2007.

Gilliard, S.W. and J.C. Laglon. 1998. 'Creating Performance Management Systems that Promote Perception of Fairness', in J.W. Smither (ed.), *Performance Appraisal: State of the Art in Practice*, pp. 209–43. San Francisco: Jossey-Bass.

Gimshi, D. 1995. Report and Six Months Planning—Implementation of Community Policing in Israel National Police-Phase B, Community Policing Unit, Israel National Police, Jerusalem.

Goldstein, H. 1990. *Problem Oriented Policing*. New York: McGraw-Hill Publishing Co.

Goleman, D. 1998. 'What Makes a Leader?', *Harvard Business Review*, November–December.

Government of India. 2006. *Crime in India 2006*. New Delhi: National Crime Records Bureau Publication.

Greenleaf, Robert. 1977. *Servant Leadership: A Journey Into the Nature of Legitimate Power and Greatness*. New York: Paulist Press.

Grove, A. 1998. *Only the Paranoid Survive*. UK: Profile Business.

Gull, G.A. 2004. 'The Transmutation of the Organization: Towards a More Spiritual Workplace', *Journal of Management Inquiry*, 13(2): 128–29.

Haberfeld, M., P. Walancik and A.M. Uydess . 2002. 'Teamwork—Not Making the Dream Work', *An International Journal of Police Strategies & Management*, 25(1): 147–68.

Hamel, G. and C.K. Prahalad. 2002. *Competing for the Future*. Bombay: TATA McGraw-Hill Ed.

Hammer, M. 2001. 'The Superefficient Company', *Harvard Business Review*, 77(6), October: 108–18.

Hammer, M. and J. Champy. 1993. *Reengineering the Corporation*. New York: Harper Business.

Harman, Wills. 1982. 'Changing Belief System', SRI International VALS, Report number 33, Menlo Park, California.

Hebenton, B. and T. Thomas. 1995. *Policing Europe*. Basingstoke: Macmillan.

Heffs, E. and J. Marshal. 2004. 'Authentic Leadership, Qualities Defined', *Financial Executive*. July/August.

Henderson, R.I. 1984. *Performance Appraisal* (2nd edition). Reston, VA: Reston Pubishing Company.

Herzberg, Frederick. 1987. 'One More Time: How Do You Motivate Employees?', *Harvard Business Review*, 65(5): 109–20.

Hindustan Times. 2007a. 'Citi Fears Maoists May Scare off Investors', *Hindustan Times*, Chandigarh, 22 January.

———. 2007b. 'Need to Replace the Archaic', *Hindustan Times*, Chandigarh, 22 January.

Hollins, S.T. 1954. *No Ten Commandments: A Life in the Indian Police.* London: Hutchinson and Co.

Holmberg, Lars. 2002. 'Personalized Policing Results from a Series of Experiments with Proximity Policing in Denmark', *An International Journal of Police Strategies & Management*, 25(1): 32–47.

Home Office. 1995. *Review of Police Core and Ancillary Tasks*, Report by Posen. London: HMSO.

Home Office Scientific Development Board (HOSDB). 2009. Available online at http://scienceandresearch.homeoffice.gov.uk/hosdb, accessed on 7 February 2009.

Hong Kong Police. 2007. Hong Cong Police Presentation at the Symposium conducted by the Independent Commission Against Corruption (ICAC), Hong Kong. Available online at http://www.icac.org.hk/symposium/2003/Presentation/Day1, accessed on 12 September 2007.

Hood, C. 1991. 'A Public Management for all Seasons?', *Public Administration*, 69(1): 3–19.

Hoofdcommisen, Rand Van. 2004. 'Projectgroep Foreensische Opsporing', in *Police in Evolution* (2006). Hague: Netherlands Police Institute.

Hoogewoning, F.C. 2006. *The Police in Evolution: Vision on Policing.* The Hague: Dutch Police Institute.

Hunter, R.D. 1990. 'Three Models of Policing', *Police Studies*, 13(3): 118–24.

India Today. 2006. 'The Long Arms of the Law', *India Today*, New Delhi, 27 November.

Indian Police Commission. 1903. 'Report of the Indian Police Commission, 1902–03. Simla: Indian Police Commission. Available online at www.bprd.gov, accessed on 16 December 2008.

International Association of Biometrics and International Computer Security Association. 1998. *Glossary of Biometric Terms.* Available online at http://www.afb.org.uk/docs/glossary.htm, accessed on 12 October 2005.

Interview of Wilson. 1997. Available online at http://www.onpatrol.com/wilsonint.html.

Ivkovic, Sanja and Kutnjak. 2003. 'Police (Mis)Behavior: A Cross-Cultural Study of Corruption Seriousness', *Policing: An International Journal of Police Strategies & Management*, 283: 546–66.

Jackson, K.T. 1999. 'Spirituality as a Foundation for Freedom and Creative Imagination in International Business Ethics', *Journal of Business Ethics*, 19(1), March: 61–70.

Jackson, R. 2005. 'Reliance Wins Longer Deal to Monitor Tagged Criminals', *The Scotsman*, 11.

Jacocks, A.M. and M.D. Bowman. 2006. 'Developing and Sustaining a Culture of Integrity', *The Police Chief*, 73(4): 16–22.

Jalan, Bimal. 2005. *The Future of India.* New Delhi: Penguin Books India.

Jepperson, R. and J. Meyer. 1991. 'The Public Order and Construction of Formal Organizations', in W. Powell and P. DiMaggio (eds), *The New Institutionalism in Organizational Analysis.* Chicago, IL: University of Chicago Press.

Johnston, L. 1992a. 'British Policing in the Nineties: Free Market and Strong State', *International Criminal Justice Review*, 2: 1–18.

Johnston, L. 1992b. *The Rebirth of Private Policing*. London: Routledge.

Joycelyn, M. Pollock. 2004. *Ethics in Crime and Justice*. CA: West/Wadsworth.

Kamarck, Elaine C. 2004. *Government Innovation around the World*, KSG Working Paper No. RW, 26 February 2004. An Institute for Democratic Governance and Innovation, Harvard University.

Kandula, Ramesh. 2007. 'Terrorism Most Dangerous Threat, says Manmohan', *The Tribune*, Chandigarh, 27 October.

Kane, J.S., H.J. Bernardin and M. Wiatrowski. 1995. 'Performance Appraisal', in N. Brewer and C. Wilson (eds), *Psychology and Policing*, pp. 257–89. Hillsdale, NJ: Lawrence Erlbaum Associates.

Kansas Law Enforcement Training. 1998.

Kaplan, R.S. and D.P. Norton. 1992. 'The Balanced Scorecard: Measures that Drive Performance', *Harvard Business Review*, January–February 71–80.

Kealty, Mick (Australian Federal Police Commissioner). 2007. Speaking Notes, Pearl in Policing Conference, Hague, 11 June 2007.

Kelling, G. and M. Moore. 1998. 'From Political Reform to Community: The Evolving Strategy of Police', in J. Greene and P. Mastrofski (eds), *Community Policing: Rhetoric or Reality?*, pp. 1–26. New York: Praeger.

Kelling, G.L. 1999. *'Broken Windows' and Police Discretion*. Washington, DC: US Department of Justice.

Kim, W. Chan and R. Mauborgne. 2003. 'Tipping Point Leadership', *Harvard Business Review*, April.

Kleinig, John. 2005. 'Ticking Bombs and Torture Warrants', *Res Publica*, Centre for Applied Philosophy and Public Ethics. The University of Melbourne, 14(1): 614–27.

Knowles, M.S. 1990. *The Adult Learner*. Houston: Gulf Publishing.

Kooken, Don L. 1957. *Ethics in Police Service*. Illinois, USA: Charles C. Thomas Publisher Springfield.

Koshy, K. 1992. *Punjab Police Rules, 1934*. Rohtak: Bright Law House.

Kotler, Philip and Gary Armstrong. 2006. *Principles of Marketing*. India: Prentice-Hall of India Pvt. Ltd.

Kotter, J.P. 2001. 'What Leaders Really do', *Harvard Business Review*, 79(12).

Kozlowski, S., R. Chao and R. Morrison. 1998. 'Games Raters Play: Politics, Strategies and Impression Management in Performance Appraisal', in J. Smither (ed.), *Performance Appraisal: State of the Art in Practice*. San Francisco, CA: Jossey-Bass Publishers.

Kumar, Promod. 1999 'Community Policing in India: Findings of Citizen's Survey'. Available online at www.idcindia.org, accessed on 16 October 2005.

Latham, G.P. 1986. 'Job Performance and Appraisal, *International Review of Industrial and Organizational Psychology*. Chichester: Wiley.

Lawrence, R. 2000. *The Politics of Force*. Berkeley, CA: University of California Press.

Lee, Charles. 1989. 'Poor Performance Appraisals Do More Harm Than Good', *Personnel Journal*, 91.

Leiber, R.B. 1998. 'The Search for Spirit in the Workplace', *Training*, 30(6): 21–27.

Leishman, F.S. Cope and P. Starie. 1996. 'Reinventing and Restructuring: Towards a "New Policing Order"', in F. Leishman, B. Loveday and S.P. Savage (eds), *Core Issues in Policing*. Harlow: Longman.

Levine, C.H. 1985. 'Police Management in the 1980's: From Decrementalism to Strategic Thinking', *Police Administration Review*. Vol. 45 (Special Issue: Law and Public Affairs): 691–700.

Levinson, Harry. 2003. 'Management by Whose Objectives?', *Harvard Business Review*, 81(1).

Likert, R. 1961. *New Patterns of Management*. New York: McGraw-Hill.

Lilley, D. and S. Hinduja. 2006. 'Officer Evaluation in Community Policing Context', *An International Journal of Police Strategies & Management*, 29(1): 19–37.

Lloyd, T. 1990. *The Nice Company*. London: Bloomsbury.

Loader, I. 1999. 'Consumer Culture and the Commodification of Policing and Security', *Sociology*, 33(2): 373–92.

Lowenberg, G. and K.A. Conrad. 1998. *Current Perspectives in Industrial/Organizational Psychology*. Boston, MA: Allyn and Bacon.

Luthans, F. 2002a. 'The Need for and Meaning of Positive Organizational Behavior', *Journal of Organizational Behavior*, 23(6): 695–706.

———. 2002b. 'Positive Organizational Behavior: Developing and Managing Psychological Strengths for Performance Improvement', *Academy of Management Executive*, 16(1): 57–75.

———. 2002c. 'Positive Psychology Approach to OB', in F. Luthans (ed.), *Organizational Behavior* (9th edition), pp. 286–322. New York: McGraw-Hill/ Irwin.

Luthans, F. and C. Youssef. 2004. 'Investing in People for Competitive Advantage', *Organizational Dynamics*, 33(2): 143–60.

Malimath Committee. 2003. *Report of the Malimath Committee on Reforms of the Criminal Justice System*. Submitted to Ministry of Home Affairs, Government of India, New Delhi.

Management Accounting. 1994. 'On the Budgetary Beat', *Management Accounting: Magazine for Chartered Management Accountants*, 00251682, February 1994, 72(2).

Mark, R. 1971. *Address to the Institute of Journalists*. London.

Markowich, M. Micheal. 1994. 'Response: We Can Make Performance Appraisals Work', *Compensation and Benefits Review*, 26(3): 25–29.

Mastrofski, S. 1998. 'Police Organization Structure', in J.-P. Brodeur (ed.), *How to Recognize Good Policing. Problems and Issue*, pp. 161–92. Thousand Oaks, CA: Sage Publications.

Mastrofski, S. and C. Uchida. 1996. 'Transforming the Police', in B. Hancock and P. Sharp (eds), *Public Policy: Crime and Criminal Justice*. Prentice-Hall.

Mastrofsky, S.D. and R.R. Ritti. 1996. 'Police Training and the Effects of Organizations on Drunken Driving Enforcement', *Justice Quarterly*, 13(2).

Mawby, Rob C. 2002. 'Marketing the Police—From a Force to a Service. By: Worthington, Steve', *Journal of Marketing Management*, 18(9/10): 857–76.

Mayhall, P.D., T. Barker and R.D. Hunter. 1995. *Police Community Relations and the Administration of Justice*. Upper Saddle River: Prentice-Hall.

Mclaughlin, E. and K. Murji. 1997. 'Public Policework and the Managerialist Paradox', in P. Francis, P. Davies and V. Jupp (eds), *Policing Futures: The*

Police, Law Enforcement and the Twenty-First Century. Houndmills: Macmillan Press Limited.

Medalone, Laura M. and Joseph Cecile. 2001. 'Patrolling Neighborhoods for Prevention', Spring, 16(2).

Meyer, H.H. 1991. 'A Solution to the Performance Appraisal Feedback Enigma', *Academy of Management Executive*, 5(1): 68–76.

Meyer, J. and B. Rowan. 1977. 'Institutionalized Organizations: Formal Structure as Myth and Ceremony', *American Journal of Sociology*, 83(2): 340–63.

Mills, Anne. 2003. 'Ethical Decision Making and Policing—The Challenge for Police Leadership', *Journal of Financial Crime*, 10(4): 331.

Mohrman Jr., A. and S. Mohrman. 1995. 'Performance Management is "Running the Business!"', *Compensation & Benefits Review*, 27(4): 69–76.

Moon, B. 2004. 'The Politicization of Police in South Korea: A Critical Review', *An International Journal of Police Strategies & Management*, 27(1): 128–36.

Morse, Gardiner. 2003. 'Why We Misread Motives', *Harvard Business Review*, 81(1): 18.

Moyer, Don. 2005. 'Different Strokes', *Harvard Business Review*, 83(11): 172.

Mulgan, R. 2001. 'Accountability the Key to Successful Outsourcing', *The Canberra Times*, 20 January.

Murphy, K.R. and J.N. Cleveland. 1991. *Performance Appraisal: An Organizational Perspective*. Needham Heights, MA: Allyn and Bacon.

———. 1995. *Understanding Performance Appraisal*. Thousand Oaks, CA: Sage Publications.

Napa Valley Academy. Available online at www.nvccjtc.org/nvcinstructionalskills. html, accessed on 1 September 2006.

Nash, M. 1998. 'Managing Risk—Achieving Protection? The Police and Probation Agendas', *The International Journal of Public Sector Management*, 11(4): 252–61.

National Commission on Terrorist Attacks upon the United States. 2002. Report submitted to the President of the United States. Available online at http://www.9-11commissionggov/report/911Report.pdf, accessed on 16 December 2008.

National Institute of Justice. 'A National Assessment of Police Chiefs' Experience in the Budgetary Process', supported by Grant #97-LB-VX-KOOB, Office of Science and Technology, National Institute of Justice, Office of Justice Programs, U.S. Department of Justice to the Police Executive Research Forum.

National Police Commission. 1979–81. Reports 1–8. New Delhi: Government of India Press. Available online at www.bprd.gov, accessed on 16 December 2008.

Neck, C.P. and J.F. Milliman. 1994. 'Thought Self Leadership: Finding Spiritual Fulfillment in Organizational Life', *Journal of Managerial Psychology*, 9(6): 9–16.

Netherlands Police Institute. 2006. *Police in Evolution*. Hague: Netherlands Police Institute.

Nicholson, Nigel. 2003. 'How to Motivate Your Problem People', *Harvard Business Review*, 81(1).

Nunn, Samuel. 2001. 'Cities, Space and the New World of Urban Law Enforcement Technologies', *Journal of Urban Affairs*, 23(3–4): 259–78.

Oettmeier, T. and M. Wycoff. 1997. *Personnel Performance Evaluation in the Community Policing Context*. Washington, DC: US Department of Justice.

Offical Airline Guide. 2007. 'Airlines Offer Record Number of Seats in July', 10 July. Available online at www.oag.com/oagcorporate/pressreleases/07, accessed on 16 December 2008.

Oliver, Willard M. 2000. *Community Policing: Classical Readings*. Upper Saddle River: Prentice-Hall.

Operational Policing Review. 1990. Joint Committee, Police Federation, Surbiton, Surrey.

Oppal Commission. 1994. *Policing in British Columbia*. British Columbia.

Osborne, D. and P. Plastrik. 1996. *Banishing Bureaucracy: The Five Strategies for Reinventing Government*. New York: Plume Book.

———. 2000. *The Reinventor's Fieldbook: Tools for Transforming Your Government*. San Fransisco: Jossey-Bass Inc.

Osborne, D. and T. Gaebler. 1992. 'Reinventing Government: How the Entrepreneurial Spirit is Transforming the Public Sector from the Schoolhouse to the State House', *City Hall to Pentagon*. Reading, MA: Addison-Wesley.

Pakes, Francis. 2007. *Pearls in Policing: The Discussion Continues*. The Netherlands: School of Police Leadership, Police Academy of the Netherlands.

Palmer, Darren. 1997. 'Reforming Police Management: The Introduction of a Police Board in Victoria', *An International Journal of Police Strategies & Management*, 20(4): 665–79.

Palmiotto, M.J., M.L. Birzer and N.P. Unnithan. 2000. 'Training in Community-Policing: A Suggested Curriculum', *Policing: An International Journal of Police Strategies & Management*, 23(1): 8–21.

Paris, T. 1998. 'US Takes Immigration in Hand', *Wired News*. Available online at http://www.wired.com/news, accessed on May 2000.

Parker, W.H. 1975. *Parker on Police*. Illinois, USA: Charles C Thomas Publisher.

Patton, Chris. 1999. *A New Beginning: Policing in Northern Ireland: The Report of the Independent Commission on Policing for Northern Ireland*. Available online at http://www.nio.gov.uk/a new beginning in policing in northern Ireland.pdf.

Peters, T.J. and R.H. Jr. Waterman. 1982. *In Search of Excellence*. New York: Harper Row.

Peters, Tom. 1987. *Thriving on Chaos*. New York: Pan Books.

Pindyck, Robert S. and Daniel L. Rubinfield. 2004. *'Consumer Behaviour' Microeconomics*. London: Prentice-Hall of India Pvt. Ltd.

Plummer, Larry C. 1995. 'In Pursuit of Honest Leadership', *FBI Law Enforcement Bulletin*, 00145688, 64(4): 16–18.

Police and Criminal Evidence Act (PACE). 1984. Available online at www. Police. homeoffice.gov.uk/operational-policing/powers-pace-codes, accessed on 16 December 2008.

Police Academy of the Netherlands. 2006. 'Public Concerns Determine Police Policy', in *Working Differently in New Times*. Warnseld: School of Leadership of the Police Academy of the Netherlands.

Police Department of the Netherlands. 2004. *Policing in the Netherlands*. Hague: Netherlands Police Institute.

Politie. 2006. *Anders werken in nieuwe tijden*. The Netherlands: Police Academy of the Netherlands.

Pratt, H. 1991. 'Principles of Effective Performance Management', *Records Management Quarterly*, 25(1): 28–32.

Punch, Maurice Vijer, Kees van der and Olga Zoomer. 2002. 'Dutch "COP" Developing Community Policing in The Netherlands', *An International Journal of Police Strategies & Management*, 25(1): 60–79.

Raleigh, Christopher, Keith Biddla, Celia Male and Stella Neema. 2000. *Uganda Police Project Evaluation*, Evaluation Report EV 591, London, London Department of International Development.

Rauch, J. 2000. 'Police Reform and South Africa's Transition', Paper presented at the South African Institute for the International Affairs Conference. Available online at www.csvr.org.za/papers/papsaiia.htm, accessed on 16 October 2006.

Reenen, P. van. 1999. 'The "Unpayable Police"', *An International Journal of Police Strategies & Management*, 22(2): 133–52.

Reiner, R. 1985. *The Politics of the Police*. Hemel Hempstead: Avebury.

———. 1992. 'Policing a Postmodern Society', *The Modern Law Review*, 55(6): 761–72.

———. 1995. 'Community Policing in England and Wales', in J.P. Brodeur (ed.), *Comparisons in Policing: An International Perspective*. Avebury, Aldershot.

———. 2000. *The Politics of the Police* (3rd edition). Oxford: Oxford University Press.

Reiter, M.S. 1999. 'Empowerment Policing', *FBI Law Enforcement Bulletin*, 68 (February): 7–11.

Robinson, G. 1997. 'LCD Viewing System Makes Evidence Shine', *Electronic Engineering Times*, 979: 38–43.

Rogers, Robert W. 1995. 'The Psychological Contract of Trust', *Executive Development*, 8(2): 15–19.

Rosenbaum, D.S. and A. Lurigio. 1994. 'An Inside Look at Community Policing Reforms: Definitions, Organisational Changes, and Evaluation Findings', *Crime and Deliquency*, 40: 354–70.

Rossmo, D.K. 2000. *Geographic Profiling*. Boca Raton, FL: CRC Press.

Royal Commission on Criminal Procedure. 1981. *Report of the Royal Commission on Criminal Procedure*. London: Royal Commission on Criminal Procedure.

Rubinstein, J. 1973. *City Police*. New York: Farrar, Strauss and Ciroux.

Sahl, Robert J. 1990. 'Design Effective Performance Appraisals', *Personnel Journal*, 69(10): 53–60.

Salzmann, J.C. 1997. 'Thriving during Organizational Change. The Role of Metaphors for Change. Optimism and Pessimism, and Attributional Style', Dissertation Abstracts International: Section B 58[5-B], 2734.

Sardar Vallabhbhai Patel National Police Academy. Available online at www.svpnpa.gov.in, accessed on 12.09.2007.

Sarkar, Prabhas C. 2005. *Indian Evidence Act, 1872*. New Delhi: Orient Law House.

Scarman, Lord. 1981. *The Scarman Report: The Brixton Disorders*. London: HMSO.

Schein, E. 1993. 'On Dialogue, Culture, and Organisational Learning', *Organisational Dynamics*, 22(2): 40–51.

Schick, W. 2004. 'CompStat in the Los Angeles Police Department', *The Police Chief*, 71(1).

Schönteich, M. 2004. 'Introduction', in M. Schönteich, A. Minnaar, D. Mistry and K.C. Goyer (eds), *Private Muscle: Outsourcing the Provision of Criminal Justice Services*, Institute for Security Studies, Tshwane, Monograph No. 93.

School of Police Leadership. 2006. *Policing the Netherland*. Warnseld: Police Academy of the Netherlands.

Schulman, P. 1999. 'Applying Learned Optimism to Increase Sales Productivity', *Journal of Personal Selling and Sales Management*, 19: 31–37.

Schumpeter, J. 1942. *Capitalism, Socialism and Democracy*. New York: Harper and Raw.

Scimeca, J. 2004. 'Low Cost Innovations: Police-Community Partnership Program', *The Police Chief*, 71(9): 73–77.

Scott, R. and J. Meyer. 1983. 'The Organization of Societal Sectors', in J. Meyer and R. Scott (eds), *Organizational Environments: Ritual and Rationality*, pp. 129–55. Newbury Park, CA: Sage Publications.

Scrivner, E.M. 1995. 'Community Policing: New Roles for Police Psychology', in M.I. Kurke and E.M. Scrivner (eds), *Police Psychology Into the 21st Century*, pp. 419–33. Hillsdale, NJ: Earlbaum.

Sen, Shankar. 2008. 'Changing Police Mindset: Murder of an Encounter Specialist', *The Sunday Tribune*, New Delhi, 13 April.

Senge, Peter M. 1990. *The Fifth Discipline*. New York: Doubleday.

Serpas, R. 2004. 'Beyond CompStat: Accountability-Driven Leadership', *The Police Chief*, 71(1).

Sharma, O.P. 2006. 7th Convocation address by O.P. Sharma, Former DGP, Punjab and Former Governer Nagaland, Punjab Police Academy, 1 December 2006.

Shaw, M. 1994. 'Point of Order: Policing the Compromise', *South African Review*. Johannesburg: Ravan Press.

Shaw, T. 1992. 'The Evolution of Police Training', *FBI Law Enforcement Bulletin*, 61(1): 3.

Shearing, C. 1992. 'Reflections on Police Management Practices', Discussion Paper 6, Royal Canadian Police External Review Committee, Ottawa.

———. 2001a. 'Punishment and the Changing Face of Governance', *Punishment and Society*, 32: 203–20.

———. 2001b. *The Guardian*, 14 November.

Shen, Jie. 2004. 'International Performance Appraisals', *International Journal of Management*, 25(6): 547–63.

Sheptycki, J.W.E. 1995. 'Transnational Policing and the Makings of a Postmodern State', *British Journal of Criminology*, 35(4): 613–35.

Simone, M.J. 2006. 'The Power of Public Private Partnership P3 Networks in Policing', *The Police Chief*, 73(5).

Singapore Police Commissioner. 2007. Singapore Police Commissioner's presentation, Hague, June 2007.

Singapore Police Force (SPF). 2007. *Singapore Quality Award with Special Commendation Winner, Executive Summary*. Singapore: Singapore Police Force.

Skogan, W. 1990. *Disorder and Decline: Crime and the Spiral of Decay in American Cities*. New York: The Free Press.

Skogan, Wesley G. 2004. *Community Policing (Can It Work)*. Belmont, CA: Wadsworth.

Skolnick, J.H. and D.H. Bayley. 1986. *The New Blue Line: Police Innovation in Six American Cities*. New York: The Free Press.

Smither, J.W. 1998. 'Lessons Learned: Research Implications for Performance Appraisal and Management Practice', in J.W. Smither (ed.), *Performance Appraisal: State of the Art in Practice*, pp. 537–47. San Francisco, CA: Jossey-Bass.

Smyth, Jim. 2002. 'Community Policing and the Reform of the Royal Ulster Constabulary', *International Journal of Police Strategies & Management*, 25(1): 110–24.

Sower, C. 1957. *Community Involvement*. Glencoe, IL: Free Press.

Spears, Larry. C (ed.). 1995. *Reflections on Leadership*. New York: John Wiley and Sons.

Spellman, W. and J.E. Eck. 1989. 'Sitting Ducks, Ravenous Wolves, and Helping Hands: New Approaches to Urban Policing', *Public Affairs*: 1–9.

Spink, N.B. Wells and M. Meche. 1999. 'Appraising the Appraisals: Computerized Performance Appraisal Systems', *Career development international*, 4(2): 94–100.

Spring, T. 1999. 'Getting DIRT on the Bad Guys', *PC World Online*. Available online at http://www2.pcworld.com, accessed on May 2000.

Stevens, P. and Dianna M. Yach. 1993. 'The Police Board Terms of Reference, Role and Method of Operation', *South African Defence Review*, 9.

Stergiou, C. and D. Siganos. 2000. 'Neural Networks', *Artificial Neural Networks*, Pacific Northwest National Laboratory (PNNL), operated by Battelle Memorial Institute for the US Department of Energy (DOE), Contract DE-AC06-76RLO 1830. Available online at http://www.emsl.pnl.gov:2080/proj/neuron/neural, accessed on May 2000.

Stock, Jürgen. 2007. Presentation at the Pearl Fishing Conference. Hague, June 2007.

Sunday Times of India. 2006. 'Police Jobs may soon be Outsourced', *Sunday Times of India*, 8 October, New Delhi.

Supreme Court order No. R. 639/06. Dt. 22 September 2006.

Surette, R. 1998. *Media, Crime, and Criminal Justice: Images and Realities*. Belmont, CA: Wadsworth.

Swank, C.J. and J.A. Conser. 1983. *The Police Personnel System*. New York: John Wiley & Sons.

Terrill, R. 1992. *World Criminal Justice Systems: A Survey*. Cincinnati, OH: Anderson Publishing Co.

The Economic Times. 2000. 'Court Grants Relief to 'Fake' Pathribal Encounter Accused', *The Economic Times*, 16 September.

———. 2007a. 'Punjab Yet to House Cyber Crime Cell', *The Economic Times*, New Delhi, 2 January.

———. 2007b. 'UAV's Useless with no Man to Process Data', *The Economic Times*, 17 March.

———. 2007c. 'Banks Alert to Online Fraud, to Defeat Phishers', *The Economic Times*, New Delhi, 7 April.

The Economic Times. 2007d. 'Airlines Clash against Menace of Frauds', *The Economic Times*, New Delhi, 21 October.

——. 2007e. 'Naxal-hit States Not So Keen to Beef up Police', *The Economic Times*, New Delhi, 5 December.

——. 2007f. 'CISF to Seek ISO Certification to Cover Vital Nuclear installations', *The Economic Times*, New Delhi, 4 March.

——. 2008. 'Malware Spreads in Nanoseconds', *The Economic Times*, New Delhi, 19 January.

The Economist. 2006. 'The Long Arms of the Law', *The Economist*, London, 29 June.

The Guardian. 24 October 1995.

The Times of India. 1994. 'Batala Police Change Their Hue', *The Times of India*, New Delhi, December.

——. 2006a. 'Cops, Politicians are Hand in Glove', *The Times of India*, Chandigarh, 10 July.

——. 2006b. '87 Meerut Massacre: Trial from Today', *The Times of India*, 14 July. Available online at http://timesofindia.indiatimes.com/articleshow/1754369. cms, accessed on 16 July 2006.

——. 2006c. 'Cops Cook up a Rape Case', *The Times of India*, Chandigarh, 5 August.

——. 2006d. 'Policemen, Defend Thyself', *The Times of India*, Chandigarh, 6 August.

——. 2006e. 'Gujrat Cops Can Hold on to the Fines', *The Times of India*, New Delhi, 9 October.

——. 2007a. 'Another Virk in CM's Battalion', *The Times of India*, Chandigarh, 25 January.

——. 2007b. 'RTI Outs Netas Transfer Bids', *The Times of India*, Chandigarh, 10 March.

——. 2007c. 'Virk Suspended, IGP R P Singh in Trouble', *The Times of India*, 6 April.

——. 2007d. 'Bachchans Pay Cops Rs 1 Lakh', *The Times of India*, Chandigarh, 19 April.

——. 2007e. 'States Reluctant to Implement Reforms', *The Times of India*, Chandigarh, 12 November.

——. 2007f. 'Gang Behind 250 Murders Busted', *The Times of India*, Chandigarh, 30 March.

The Tribune. 2006a. 'Police Force Needs Revamping', *The Tribune*, Chandigarh, 13 September.

——. 2006b. 'Maya Case Should Go On, says SC', *The Tribune*, Chandigarh, 28 November.

——. 2006c. 'City Police Simply the Best', *The Tribune*, Chandigarh, 7 December.

——. 2007a. 'No Takers for Online Police Complaints', *The Tribune*, Chandigarh, 13 February.

——. 2007b. 'Punjab Dithers on Reforms', *The Tribune*, Chandigarh, 12 April.

——. 2007c. 'Khalra Murder: Life Term for 4 Cops' and 'CP Shootout: ACP Rathi, Nine Cops Convicted', *The Tribune*, Chandigarh, 17 October.

The Tribune. 2007d. 'Licensed to Kill—Police Thinks It is the Law', *The Tribune*, Chandigarh, 18 October.

———. 2007e. Editorial 'Police in Dock', *The Tribune*, Chandigarh, 22 November.

TIME. 2006. 'Q&A Felipe Calderon. Mexico's President-Elect Tells TIME about Plans for Economic Reform', 168(21).

Times of Chandigarh. 2007. 'Hi-Tech Help for UT Police', *Times of Chandigarh*, Chandigarh, 8 March.

Trojanowicz, R. and B. Bucqeroux. 1994. *Community Policing: How to Get Started.* Cincinnati, OH: Anderson Printing.

Trojanowicz, R., V.E. Kappeler, L. K.Gaines, R. Sluder and B. Bucqueroux. 1998. *Community Policing: A Contemporary Perspective* (2nd edition). Cincinnati, OH: Anderson Publishing Co.

United Kingdom Home Office. 2004. *UK Home Office Science and Technology Strategy.* Available online at http:/www.homeoffice.gov.uk/documents/Police ST_S2_part11.pdf, accessed on 16 December 2008.

United Nations. 1999. 'Community Based Policing', ITSS handout, Internatinal Police Task Force (IPTF) headquarters, Sarajevo.

Union Public Service Commission (UPSC). 2006–2007. *Annual Reports.* New Delhi: UPSC.

United States Department of Justice. 2004. *Global Justice Information Sharing Initiative.* Available online at http://it.ojp.gov/topic.jsp?topic_id=8, accessed on 16 December 2008.

Vinzant, J. and L. Crothers. 1994. 'Street-Level Leadership: The Role of Patrol Officers in Community Policing', *Criminal Justice Review*, 19: 189–211.

Walker, S. 1992. *The Police in America: An Introduction* (2nd edition). New York: McGraw-Hill.

Weisburd, David, Orit Shaler and Menachem Amir. 2002. 'Community Policing in Israel: Resistance and Change', *An International Journal of Police Strategies & Management*, 25(1): 80–109.

Westermann, T. 1991. *Crime and Justice in Two Societies—Japan and the United States.* Pacific Grove, CA: Brooks/Cole Publishing Company.

Whisenand, P. and G. Rush. 1998. *Supervising Police Personnel: The Fifteen Responsibilities* (3rd edition). Upper Sadle River, NJ: Prentice-Hall.

Wilson, J.Q. 1968. *Varieties of Police Behavior: The Management of Law and Order in Eight Communities.* Cambridge, MA: Harvard University Press.

Wilson, J.Q. and George Kelling. 1982. 'Broken Windows', *Atlantic Monthly*. Available online at www.theattantic.com/politics/crime/windows.htm, accessed on 27 December 2005.

Wilson, O.W. 1972. *Police Administration.* New York: McGraw-Hill Book Company.

World Bank. 1997. *World Development Report.* New Delhi: Oxford University Press.

Wuestewald, Todd and Brigitte Steinheider. 2006. 'Shared Leadership: Can Empowerment Work in Police Organizations?', *The Police Chief*, 73(1).

Ma, Yue. 1997. 'The Police Law 1995: Organization, Functions, Powers and Accountability of the Chinese police', *An International Journal of Police Strategies & Management*, 20(1): 113–35.

Zhao, Z., N.P. Lovrich and Q. Thurman. 1999. 'The Status of Community Policing in American Cities: Facilitators and Impediments Revisited', *Policing: An International Journal of Police Strategies & Management*, 22(1): 74–92.

Websites

http:/www.altus.org. Date of access 16 December 2008.

www.apectelwg.org/apecdata/telwg/28tel/estg/telwg28-ESTG-09.htm. Date of access 12 October 2007.

www.artofliving.org. Date of access 16 December 2008.

http:/www.bprd.gov.in. Date of access 13 December 2007.

www.bscol.com: Presentation on 'Non-traditional Scorecards in the Public Sector'. Date of access 16 December 2008.

http://www.quitedb.com/squotes/3895. *Nicholo Machiavelli Quotes and Biography*. Date of access 16 December 2008.

www.homeoffice.gov.uk. Date of access 16 December 2008.

www.sapsjournalonline.gov.za. Date of access 16 December 2008.

www.svpnpa.gov.in. Date of access 12 September 2007.

http:/www.wikipedia.com. Date of access 29 December 2007.

http://specials.homeoffice.gov.uk/Good-practice/national-intelligence-model/. Date of access 16 December 2008.

http:/www.icac.org.hk/symposium/2003/Presentation/Day1. Date of access 12 September 2007.

http:/www.onpatrol.com/wilsonint.html. Date of access 16 December 2008.

http:/www.usdoj.gov/cops/. Date of access 16 December 2008.

http:/www.icac.org.hk/symposium/2003/Presentation/Day1.Date of access 12 September 2007.

http:/www.afp.gov.au/business/national_police_checks.html. Date of access 16 November 2007.

http:/www.police.homeoffice.gov.uk/publications/connectivity-policing/police_serving_community.pdf.

http:/www.police.homoffice.gov.uk/publications/community-policing/police_serving_community.pdf.

http:/www.mpa.gov.uk/about/default.htm. Date of access 16 December 2008.

http:/www.tribuneindia.com/2006/20061027/main1.htm. Date of access 29 October 2006.

http:/www.bscol.com. Presentation on 'Non-traditional Scorecards in the Public Sector'. Date of access 25 June 2006.

http:/www.sapsjournalonline.gov.za. Date of access 25 July 2007.

http:/www.hr.guide.come/data/209.htm. Date of access 16 December 2008.

http://www.oracle.com/applications/peoplesoft/hcm/ent/module/eperformance.html. Date of access 16 December 2008.

http:/www.redwebsecurity.com/pdfs/police_information_pack.pdf. Date of access 16 December 2008.

http:/www.popcenter.org/about/?p=triangle. Date of access 25 December 2008.

About the Author

An engineering graduate from Indian Institute of Technology (IIT), Roorkee, Rohit Choudhary holds a post graduate degree in management and public policy from Indian Institute of Management (IIM) Bangalore and Maxwell School of the Syracuse University, New York, USA.

Currently, he is an Inspector General of Police in the state of Punjab, India. He has been the police chief of three districts and Deputy Inspector General of two ranges of Punjab. He is a highly decorated police officer with the President's Medal for Gallantry, Police Medal for Gallantry, UN Peace Medal and Police Medal for Meritorious Service.